Environmentally Su Primary Care

This practical guide for primary care provides a context-specific introduction to the sustainability challenges associated with good healthcare delivery and provides easy-to-implement yet impactful actions that can be taken to reduce and mitigate the impact of primary care on the living world while also looking at the impact of the changing planet on healthcare that people will encounter.

The chapters address the following key questions: What is the issue? What can I do/what can my practice do? How do my actions help patients, practice, and planet? Included throughout are case studies, vignettes, and anecdotes of previous successful interventions, while a checklist of the most impactful actions for others to follow, as supported by the current evidence base, provides a convenient summary. References and additional resource recommendations give directions for further guidance. The book looks at the four pillars of primary care – dentistry, General Practice, optometry, and pharmacy – and includes international contributions.

Providing invaluable direction to turn good intentions into meaningful action, this book will be invaluable to health professionals and practice managers across all primary care disciplines and to students preparing to enter practice in those fields. It will also be of interest to integrated care system administrators and to health policymakers.

Environmentally Sustainable Primary Care

Good for the planet, good for practices, good for patients

Edited by
Matt Sawyer and Mike Tomson

CRC Press
Taylor & Francis Group
Boca Raton New York London

CRC Press is an imprint of the
Taylor & Francis Group, an **informa** business

Designed cover image: Jo Koster

First edition published 2025
by CRC Press
2385 NW Executive Center Drive, Suite 320, Boca Raton FL 33431

and by CRC Press
4 Park Square, Milton Park, Abingdon, Oxon, OX14 4RN

CRC Press is an imprint of Taylor & Francis Group, LLC

© 2025 selection and editorial matter, Matthew Sawyer and Michael Tomson; individual chapters, the contributors

Library of Congress Cataloging-in-Publication Data
Names: Sawyer, Matthew, editor. | Tomson, Michael, editor.
Title: Environmentally sustainable primary care : good for the planet, good
for practices, good for patients / edited by Matthew Sawyer and Michael Tomson.
Identifiers: LCCN 2024017754 | ISBN 9781032793580 (hardback) |
ISBN 9781032793573 (paperback) | ISBN 9781003491583 (ebook)
Subjects: MESH: Primary Health Care | Conservation of Natural Resources
Classification: LCC RA427.9 | NLM W 84.61 | DDC 362.1--dc23/eng/20240807
LC record available at https://lccn.loc.gov/2024017754

ISBN: 978-1-032-79358-0 (hbk)
ISBN: 978-1-032-79357-3 (pbk)
ISBN: 978-1-003-49158-3 (ebk)

DOI: 10.1201/9781003491583

Typeset in Bembo
by SPi Technologies India Pvt Ltd (Straive)

Contents

Contributors

Dr Veena Aggarwal is a final year GP Registrar in London. She did a one-year sustainability fellowship in 2021–2022. Alongside GP training, Veena chairs the Greener Practice Trainee Forum, Greener Practice South London, and is part of the clinical leadership team advising the Royal College of GPs on sustainability.

Tony Avery OBE, is a GP in Nottingham, Professor of Primary Healthcare at the University of Nottingham and National Clinical Director for Prescribing for NHS England. In the latter role he provides clinical leadership for a range of initiatives aimed at reducing overprescribing and reduction in medicines waste in England.

Manda Brookman is a third-sector facilitator with a background in network-building, behavioural/cultural shift, social justice, and climate/ecological engagement. She has developed international networks in the fields of development, justice, and climate breakdown. She currently works in Cornwall and the South West across multiple sectors with a focus on the health system.

Spencer Casey is a Partner at Probus GP Surgery and Probus Surgical Centre and a Director of Cornwall Medical Group. Previously, he studied Law at Kingston University and played rugby for London Irish and Saracens. He has worked for the NHS for several years and brings a wealth of senior managerial experience to the business.

Antonia Chitty PhD MA BSc (Hons) MCOptom MCIPR is Sustainability Lead for the Association of British Dispensing Opticians (ABDO). Antonia has championed sustainability within ABDO and across the optical community and is the author of more than 20 books on business and health.

Dr Alice Clack is a Consultant in Obstetrics and Gynaecology. Alice's background is working in emergency obstetrics and clinical education in West Africa and more recently with the Centre for Sustainable Healthcare in their sustainability in quality improvement education team. She is also an active member of Health for Extinction Rebellion.

Min Na Eii is a Hospital Pharmacist in the United Kingdom and the Chief Sustainability Officer's Clinical Fellow 2023/2024. She is the Vice Chair of Sustainability at the Guild of Healthcare Pharmacists and the lead author of the Royal Pharmaceutical Society's Greener Pharmacy guides for hospital and community pharmacies.

Dr Tamsin Ellis is a salaried GP working in London. She is Co-chair and Director of Greener Practice and an Associate at the Centre for Sustainable Healthcare where she helped develop the sustainable primary care course. Previous work includes sustainability and education roles with the Royal College of General Practitioners, Health Education England, and North Central London Integrated Care Board (ICB).

Dr Ilona Hale is a Family Physician from rural British Columbia, Canada, doing a Planetary Health Fellowship with Health Quality BC. Ilona has recently led the production of a Canadian guide to Planetary Health in Primary Care and is working on incorporating environmental sustainability into quality improvement in British Columbia.

Dr Richard Hixson is a Consultant in Critical Care Medicine, Physician, Environmentalist, Member of the UK Ocean Decade Committee, and Co-founder of Healthcare Ocean. Richard's interest is the United Nations Global Goal 14, Life Below Water; he works with healthcare providers, supplier industries, and non-governmental organisations to improve the health of the ocean ecosystem.

Ben Holt graduated in 1994 with a degree in management science. He worked in the energy sector in both nuclear and oil and gas. He set up an award-winning net-zero consultancy in 2009. Ben lives in Manchester, England, and has recently managed an energy reduction project across Salford GP surgeries.

Dr Helen Kingston, a General Practitioner in Frome, Somerset, co-founded Compassionate Frome, a project designed to improve support for, and connections with, patients. As part of Green and Healthy Frome, Helen promotes community well-being and an understanding of the link between our own health and the health of our planet.

Dr Tessa Lewis is an experienced GP driven by safe, effective, quality care to support a viable, sustainable NHS. Clinical interests include medicines and care of older people; chair roles include NICE Infection guidelines. As a Medical Adviser, she works with colleagues nationally to support issues including antimicrobial stewardship, anticoagulation, and polypharmacy.

Professor Neal Maskrey has been a GP (20 years), Medical Director of the National Prescribing Centre, and Director of the Medicines and Prescribing Centre at NICE. He is now Visiting Professor of Evidence-Informed Decision-Making at Keele University and develops and evaluates programmes to support shared decision-making in consultations.

Dr Sinead Millwood qualified as a GP in 2021. She works for Hope Citadel, a community interest company in Manchester running GP practices in areas of deprivation. She is passionate about campaigning for clean air, which she sees primarily as a social justice issue.

Dr Frances Mortimer qualified in 2003, becoming a trainee physician before taking the position of Medical Director of the Centre for Sustainable Healthcare (CSH) in 2008.

Frances focuses on enabling health professionals to lead a transformation to sustainable clinical care through developing concepts and tools such as Sustainability in Quality Improvement and CSH's Sustainable Specialties Programme.

Dr James Morton is a GP in Glasgow. He has an interest in social prescribing and the climate, including as RCGP's co-representative for Sustainability and Climate Change. He sits on the council for the Scottish Intercollegiate Guidelines Network. He's not a bad baker.

Clare Murray is a Lecturer (Education) with a specialist interest in the teaching of independent prescribing skills at the undergraduate and postgraduate levels. Prior to academia, Clare worked in primary care, assuming leadership and clinical roles in the GP setting, working as a Generalist Independent Prescriber, and she has community pharmacy experience.

Dr Hannah O'Hara is a GP and Clinical Lecturer in the Centre for Public Health at Queen's University Belfast. Hannah's research interests lie in improving metabolic health, and she recognises the importance of addressing the environmental determinants of health in doing so. Hannah co-chairs the Northern Ireland Greener Practice group.

Ciara O'Kane is a Community Dentist based in London and was a Chief Sustainability Officer's Clinical Fellow in 2022/2023. Ciara is a clinical advisor for the development of the Greener Impact for Dentistry Toolkit and works as a Specialist Advisor for Sustainability at Care Quality Commission.

Dr Sean Owens is a GP based in Dundalk, Ireland. Sean's passion for lifestyle medicine and inclusion healthcare led him to planetary health. As Chair of the Irish Climate and Health Alliance, Sean sees environmental drivers of health as the key to a healthier, sustainable future.

Abi Page has three decades of experience as an Optician and co-owns an independent optician. Her passion for making a difference is expressed through writing articles about sustainability, being a member of the Association of British Dispensing Opticians Social Ethical and Environmental (ABDO SEE) working group, and roles working with ABDO, Local Optical Committee Support Unit (LOCSU) and Sightcare. She is Vice Chair of her local optical committee.

Prof. Sharon Pfleger is a Registered Pharmacist and Public Health Specialist and works as a Consultant in Pharmaceutical Public Health in Scotland. She was a founding member and NHS lead of the One Health Breakthrough Partnership (https://ohbp.org/), which is focussed on the more sustainable use of medicines, reducing antimicrobial resistance and microplastics. She sits on Scottish government committees to tackle health care's impact on climate change. Sharon is Visiting Professor at the School of Pharmacy and Life Sciences, Aberdeen.

Dr Judith Pinnick completed GP training in Tayside in 2017 and currently works as a salaried GP in Irvinestown, Northern Ireland. She's involved in undergraduate medical education and Co-chairs the Northern Ireland Greener Practice group. Judith is interested in the development of greener, more integrated approaches to health creation and healthcare.

Dr Emma Radcliffe is a GP in East London. She is a Primary Care Net-Zero Lead for NHS North East London. She is a trustee of the UK Health Alliance on Climate Change. She has worked with Greener Practice to set up a national network of leads who are trying to "green" primary care at ICB level.

Davinder Raju established an eco-friendly dental practice in the United Kingdom, Dove Holistic Dental Centre, and founded the Greener Dentistry Global accreditation programme. For his leadership in delivering sustainable oral healthcare, he has been awarded the title of fellow of the International College of Dentists.

Dr Matt Sawyer qualified as a GP in 2005. He gained an MSc (distinction) in environmental management in 2019. He spends all his time working to reduce planetary harm from delivering primary care. This includes carbon footprinting tools, decarbonisation guides for practices, and delivering Carbon Literacy training via SEE Sustainability.

Denise Smith is a Practice Manager at Merepark Medical Centre in Cheshire, with over 20 years of healthcare management experience within General Practice. Previously, she spent 10 years in the banking industry. She has a deep-rooted passion for teamwork and leadership, as well as belief that communication and networking are key to achieving success.

Dr Becki Smith-Taylor is an Anaesthetist with an interest in sustainable healthcare and is a former Chief Sustainability Officer's Clinical Fellow. As a Certified Coach, Becki specialises in supporting sensitive healthcare professionals working in climate change to rediscover their joy and make a difference without burnout.

Dr Georgie Sowman is a sessional GP in Northeast England and is Physical Activity Clinical Champion with Sport England. She has worked in healthcare environmentalism for five years. She co-founded Healthcare Ocean, which aims to ensure that nature and oceans are not left behind on our journey to a more sustainable future.

Dr Munro Stewart completed GP training in 2017, studied International Health at Copenhagen University in 2018, and has been working on healthcare sustainability since. Munro received a fellowship from the RCGP in 2023 and works with Tayside Pollution Research Group, NHS Tayside, Greener Practice, the University of Dundee, and the Scottish government.

Dr Mike Tomson is a clinically retired Sheffield GP. Mike is interested in using clinical cases to raise interest in planetary health in primary care. He is a trustee for CSH, co-wrote the RCGP's population and planetary health curriculum chapter and has been a Director of Greener Practice.

Wendy Tyler-Batt is a Clinical Pharmacist and Sustainability Lead for a group of GP practices in Gloucestershire. An active member of Pharmacy Declares, Greener Practice, Gloucestershire ICS sustainability group, the Greener PCPA, and the Pharma Pollution Hub, she communicates and facilitates sustainable improvement in all areas of primary care.

Dr Lydia Vogelaar-Kelly is a GP and qualified lifestyle medicine physician, passionate about inspiring colleagues and patients towards holistic well-being. As an environmental advocate developing sustainability plans for her primary care network, she firmly believes that optimising health through lifestyle changes is crucial for our future planetary well-being.

Dr Malcolm White qualified in 2010 and spent a decade specialising in internal medicine. He became invested in environmental activism with "Extinction Rebellion" in 2018. In 2019, he combined his energy, medical experience, and passion for public health by joining air pollution charity "Global Action Plan" as a clean air specialist.

Dr Sarah Williams' main role is as mum of two young children. She co-founded Greener Practice Wales, is the RCGP Wales' Climate and Sustainability Lead, and currently works for Green Health Wales connecting and transforming sustainable healthcare.

Dr Angela Wilson is a part-time sessional GP in Oxfordshire. Angela co-founded Oxford Greener Practice and set up the Greener Practice Nature and Health group. She was the first RCGP Thames Valley faculty lead for climate and sustainability. She works in environmental advocacy and co-founded the local nature recovery network.

Richard Yin, a retired General Practitioner in Perth, Australia, is a long-term member of Doctors for the Environment Australia (DEA). He was an early pioneer for sustainability in primary care and climate and health advocacy. Richard now works full time in environmental advocacy within DEA and the Conservation Council of Western Australia.

Foreword by Rachel Stancliffe

Everyone working in primary care needs to read this book! Climate change poses a huge and urgent threat to our whole society, but the changes we need to make are opportunities that align with many other pressing issues in healthcare today: tackling inequalities, redressing the balance for prevention, and prioritising "more staff less stuff" so that we have adequate time to treat whole people rather than medicating individual symptoms.

It is critical that everyone working in the health system understands enough about sustainability not only to be able to make informed personal changes but, perhaps more importantly, to take part in the transformation we need in the system. This wonderful book fulfils both of these with an amazing ease, as it is so well written with a very engaging style. I picked it up to skim read and found it hard to put down! The case studies in the book really bring it to life and show how applicable this is to everyday practice. I found Chapter 7 on achieving appropriate investigation, prescribing, and treatment very interesting and the chapter on behaviour change is also very powerful.

Primary care is on the frontline of the effects of climate change and environmental degradation on health, dealing with everything from eco-anxiety to the effects of polluted air and water on the most vulnerable in the community.

Primary care can also lead the way in transforming health. As personally connected trusted healthcare professionals, GPs, nurses, dentists, pharmacists, and optometrists can model best practices in sustainable care with their managers, and the whole team can also help us all to look after ourselves and build our resilience and well-being for both physical and mental health.

Sustainable healthcare is not "nice to have", an addition to our current services; it is integral to good quality care for our patients now and in the future. If you want to understand more about what it is and how you can start taking action for better healthcare, then this is the book for you.

Rachel Stancliffe founded and leads the Centre for Sustainable Healthcare which works to inspire and empower people with the knowledge, skills and tools to play their part in the transformation to sustainable healthcare. Her background is in public health and in improving evidence for all in healthcare.

Foreword by Richard Smith

Primary care practitioners are well positioned to be leaders in countering climate change and the destruction of nature, the major threats to global health. We need radical change at every level: global, national, regional, within health systems and our organisations, and professionally and personally. Primary care practitioners, who are the most trusted group and who are everywhere, can act at every level, and this inspiring, comprehensive, clearly written, and practical book will be an essential guide for that action.

Health professionals are internationally connected in a way that many professions are not. WONCA, the World Organisation of Family Doctors, has members in 111 countries representing half a million family doctors who provide care for 90% of the world's population. The global influence of health professionals is well illustrated by the work of International Physicians for the Prevention of Nuclear War (IPPNW), which won the Nobel Peace Prize for reducing the risk of nuclear destruction during the Cold War.

National political action is essential, and primary care practitioners have called on the UK government to prioritise action on climate change and the destruction of nature through bodies like the Royal College of General Practitioners, the British Medical Association, and the UK Health Alliance on Climate Change. Other groups of primary health practitioners and other countries have their own bodies calling for action.

Primary care practitioners should never underestimate their influence within their regions, cities, and local communities. They can join community groups working on renewable energy, healthier transport, improvements in the supply of healthy and environmentally friendly (mostly plant-based) food and carbon literacy.

The UK Health Alliance on Climate Change has 11 actions that it asks its members, including the Royal College of General Practitioners, to commit to. These include measuring the organisation's carbon footprint, developing and publishing a plan to reach net-zero, and reviewing travel and food policies to reduce emissions and waste.

Primary care professionals have been leading the way in reducing the emissions and waste from their practices, and Greener Practice is a community of healthcare professionals working together to inspire sustainable primary care, many of whom are involved in this book.

It is perhaps in their contact with individuals that primary care professionals have the most scope to lead in countering the climate and nature crisis through their millions of interactions with patients every day. They are naturally reluctant to discuss the climate and nature crisis with every patient, but because what is good for the planet and the individual go together, there is lots of room, even an obligation, to do so. It makes sense to discuss physical activity and diet with the many patients with cardiovascular disease, air pollution and climate-friendlier inhalers with patients with asthma, and visiting green spaces with patients with depression. It's a small step to point out that what will benefit the patient will also benefit the planet. This book discusses how primary healthcare professionals can take what may feel like a radical step and raise these issues in consultations.

As with everybody, primary care professionals can also change personally – driving and flying less, walking and cycling more, adopting a largely plant-based diet, using a renewable energy supplier, consuming less, changing banks to ones that don't fund fossil fuel companies, and much more. We know that action begets action, and taking what may be a small action as an individual is likely to lead to bigger actions collectively.

Famously, doctors played a big part in reducing smoking levels when evidence emerged in the 1960s of the extremely harmful effects of tobacco. In a very short period of time, the smoking prevalence among UK doctors dropped from about three-quarters to one-quarter. Doctors led the way, and patients followed. The same can happen with primary care professionals taking personal actions to improve their health and reduce harm to the planet.

Richard Smith is chair of the UK Health Alliance on Climate Change, an alliance of 48 organisations of health professionals that works to mitigate the harm from the climate and ecological crisis, encourage adaptation, and promote the benefits that flow to health from the changes we need to make. Previously he was the editor of the BMJ and the chief executive of the BMJ Publishing Group.

Introduction

Who is this book for? Anyone working in primary care! If you are a doctor, nurse, dentist, optician, pharmacist, or other primary care clinician, a member of the admin or management team, and are interested in what you and your colleagues can do to reduce the harm caused to the natural living world from providing primary healthcare or the changes to healthcare caused by the climate and ecological emergency, then this book is for you. The primary care team has expanded over time to include mental health workers and social prescribers, as well as physiotherapists and paramedics. All are part of the primary care team the book addresses.

What is this book about? Environmentally sustainable primary care involves taking the actions which provide best outcomes for patients, staff, finances, and planet simultaneously.

Planetary health is a field focussed on characterising the linkages between human-caused disruptions of Earth's natural systems (e.g., climate change, biodiversity loss, pollution) and the resulting impacts on public health. It is concerned with making sure our civilisation is sustained while ensuring equitable, efficient, and sustainable resource consumption.

The concept of planetary health is based on the understanding that human health and human civilisation depend on flourishing natural systems and the wise stewardship of those natural systems.

Why has this book been written? People are aware the climate is changing, the natural living world is being harmed, and understand that human activity is driving this. Most want to take positive actions to reduce their contribution but are unsure what to do or how impactful actions are. This book aims to help show there are lots of people already doing amazing things. Rather than reinventing the wheel, we can work together to find solutions that benefit ourselves, our patients, and the planet.

This book focuses on work to both improve the quality of care and reduce the environmental impact of care in high-income/resource countries (HIC). It is a pointer for those in lower-income/resource countries to the pitfalls of the HIC approach (e.g., "industrialising the medical model" and "a pill for every ill") and how they could be avoided. In many parts of the world, primary care is practised frugally. Innovation and development are welcome, but sometimes shiny new tech gadgets or solutions are not required when simple, inexpensive interventions would have prevented the problem in the first place.

How to use this book. The chapters can be read in any order depending on each reader's preference, interests, and enthusiasm. Each chapter will offer something – whether an idea, an action, or a new approach. Make notes, tick off actions, write in the margin, lend it out, and leave it well thumbed for someone else to read. It shows what we can do, what is being done, and where hope can be found.

1

Primary care and planetary health
Tamsin Ellis and Matt Sawyer

Imagine a world where the air we breathe is clean and the water we drink is clear, where a rich variety of plants and animals co-exist and thrive alongside humans, where human physical and mental health benefits from regular access to local green spaces, where travel to friends, family, workplaces and for leisure is inexpensive, easy and does not cause harm, where physical activity, social interaction and promotion of a healthy, nutritious diet are the default, and where this is all equitable, taking into account those most vulnerable. It feels like a work of unachievable, idealistic, woolly fiction, right? Well, through this book, we will show you how small positive actions lead to big changes and how behavioural shifts and system changes are possible. Have you felt alone and not sure where to begin? etc until we reach vulnerable. **How about here?**

Introduction

We know that urgent action is needed, but is it just another thing for primary care to manage? We all live demanding lives, and knowing where to begin can feel overwhelming. Learning about climate change and its health impacts is an important first step in taking action and making change happen; it can also be a great way to improve health now and to help cope with feelings of hopelessness about the future (see Chapter 19 on managing eco-distress).

The health of the planet affects us, our patients, our families, our staff, our communities and our populations. Healthcare is contributing to environmental harm. The climate and ecological crises affect human health negatively, thus increasing patient ill-health and healthcare demand. However, there are many positives to taking action. In amending our approach and delivery of primary healthcare services, significant human and planetary health gains can occur simultaneously. Working in primary care, we are

DOI: 10.1201/9781003491583-1

in the middle of complex systems, with feedback loops between the populations we serve, the environment around us and individual behaviour.

Primary care, according to the World Health Organisation (WHO), is a model of care that supports first-contact, accessible, continuous, comprehensive and coordinated person-focused care (1). At its core should be the proactive, preventative, and protective aspects of public health services.

The impacts of a changing environmental climate are being felt by populations across the globe, and primary care is on the front line. Primary care has the responsibility to manage the impact climate and ecological breakdown have on human health while simultaneously reducing its contribution to climate change.

Climate commitments. In 2015, there was a global agreement in Paris (the "Paris Agreement"), which set nationally determined own contributions to reducing greenhouse emissions to reduce the likelihood of catastrophic temperature rises (2). In 2021, the health gains from implementing the climate commitments of the Paris Agreement were calculated (3). The annual reduction in premature deaths across the nine countries studied included 1.18 million air pollution-related deaths, 5.86 million diet-related deaths and 1.15 million deaths due to physical inactivity.

In the United Kingdom – with an annual death rate of about 667,000 in 2021 – the annual reduction in premature deaths would be 98,400 (diet changes), 3,500 (tackling air pollution) and 21,500 (reducing physical inactivity) – or nearly 20% of all deaths. The gains are greater if policies aimed at preventing ill-health – i.e., going beyond "just" current climate commitments, were implemented.

Why do something different to "business as usual"? If primary care aims to reduce health inequalities and prevent chronic diseases, a change from a reactive approach could work in our communities and at the population level. Jamul et al. calculated a 19% reduction in diabetes, 12% reduction in cardiovascular disease and 81% reduction in greenhouse gas emission with a plant-based diet compared to "business as usual" (4). Financially, over half the USD$14 trillion spent globally on damage to human health and ecosystems from animal source production could be saved (5).

What positive actions are taking place at the moment? People and staff from across primary care are coming together, seeking out like-minded people. These include the following:

- Networks of individuals are coming together through Greener Practice, Irish Doctors for the Environment, World Organization of Family Doctors (WONCA) planetary health working group, Royal Australian College of General Practitioners (6).
- Organisations such as Centre for Sustainable Healthcare have sustainability networks ("susnets") for a host of healthcare professions.
- There are declarations of a climate emergency from UK royal colleges and groups working in and between colleges by the UK Health Alliance on Climate Change (UKHACC) to ensure declarations produce actions.

- UKHACC recommended that the climate and nature emergencies be approached collectively with the launch of a report and 200 editorials published in medical journals worldwide (7).
- There are networks of health workers campaigning through non-violent direct action for action to the climate and ecological emergency and its impact on health (Health for XR) or lobbying for divestment from fossil fuels (Medact). There is lobbying to reduce inequalities and poverty and improve the social determinants of health.

Active travel, dietary changes and addressing inappropriate prescribing produce benefits to patient and population health NOW.

Pop quiz

If somebody moves from being a meat eater to being plant based, what is the reduction in their carbon footprint?

$\frac{1}{5}$

$\frac{1}{4}$

$\frac{1}{3}$

$\frac{1}{2}$

Answer $\frac{1}{2}$

What is the reduction in emissions when switching from a car to a bike for short journeys?

33%

50%

65%

75%

Answer 75%

If you do the same journey by bike, on foot or in a car, who gets the highest exposure to air pollution?

The driver

The cyclist

The walker

Answer The driver has the worst air quality. Concentrations of air pollutants in cars can be considerably higher than concentrations faced by active travellers. Commuters sitting in cars can both miss the benefits of physical activity, and the benefits of exercise in air pollution outweigh the harms (unless very vulnerable e.g., from heart or lung disease) (8).

Personal actions or system change? Individuals may feel that there is no point in each of us doing anything, and all we need to work on is system change. Health workers work with individuals and are highly trusted and so have the additional capability of influencing the behaviour of others and making small system changes. All three approaches are important and should happen in parallel with each other. Chapter 17 covers more on behaviour change and personal actions. Chapter 18 addresses working systemically across organisations.

Personal actions. The step approach (described in Chapter 17) suggests avoiding "all or nothing" thinking and starting progress in the right direction. So if a seven-day-a-week, plant-based diet isn't achievable, what about one meal or one day a week? Then two days? If living car-free isn't achievable, can part of the journey be completed by walking or cycling? Away from the workplace, there are many actions we can take to reduce our contributions to the climate crisis. Among the most impactful are the following (9):

* Live car-free or reduce car use
* Shift to a battery electric vehicle
* One less flight
* Shift to public transport
* Shift to active transport
* Eat organic food
* Use renewable electricity
* Adopt an increasingly vegetarian or vegan diet

Each of us, and each of our patients, will have different actions that are important, affordable and achievable to us. Taking individual action can empower each of us.

Practice actions. Practices have made many different changes, including changes to prescribing patterns, improving social prescribing, changing behaviour around energy use, installing solar panels and using electric cars, setting up cycle schemes and walking competitions, improving green spaces and creating practice gardens and becoming "active practices" and "park run practices". Case studies of change – e.g., in improving asthma prescribing – have caught the attention of governments and influenced new respiratory guidance – e.g., Greener Practice *high-quality, low-carbon asthma toolkit*.

System change. Systems need to change – and individuals can help drive this. For example, in our organisations, we can build sustainability into the organisational culture **and** each individual role, or when advertising for new staff or during staff induction, we can emphasise the team's ethos that "environmental sustainability is at the heart of what we do here". More details in Chapter 18. We can also address systems through work with healthcare boards or equivalent organisations, through royal colleges or through national political change.

What can I do? The final chapter summarises the actions and key points from all the preceding chapters and helps to list and rank some of the actions you can use.

Which actions inspire you?

The climate Venn diagram can help us think about how each of us is part of climate solutions by identifying individual and meaningful approaches to the climate crisis (Figure 1.1).

If you want to read more about the actions you can take, turn to

Chapter 2 for dentistry,
Chapter 3 for General Practice,
Chapter 4 for optometry practice, and
Chapter 5 for pharmacy.

Overview of the current state of planetary health. There are multiple and overlapping definitions of planetary health and linked concepts. Planetary health is the whole planet and all its interactions; one health refers to the health of all plants and species; global health is the health of humans across the planet; public health is more local community health all the way to individual personal health, as shown in Figure 1.2.

How do we affect the planet? Before the Industrial Revolution, the impact of humans on the natural living world was minimal. People used replaceable natural resources for

FIGURE 1.1 A climate Venn diagram (10).

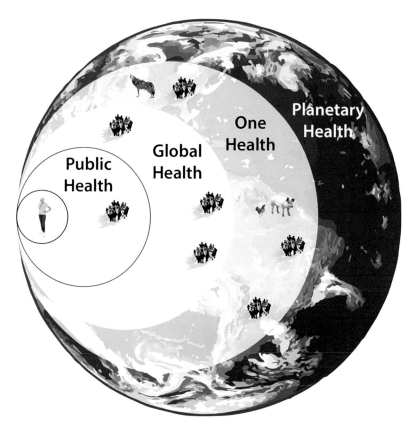

FIGURE 1.2 Planetary health and its concentric circles recognises the health of the planet as a system.

(Eric Marty).

food and to build shelters. Life expectancy was low and the burden of human disease and illness high.

With the great advances in society and civilisation that occurred with the Industrial Revolution, the impact on the world from humans rose sharply. Philosopher Francis Bacon (1561–1626) summarised the prevailing relationship with the planet as "*industry, technology, and wealth are utilised to conquer nature, to study nature, and to torment nature. Through this conquest and torment of nature our wealth and comfort is found*". Bacon's vision of nature for extraction and use, and nature as something separate from humanity is now being replaced by an awareness that humanity is part of the natural world and is dependent on it.

The Anthropocene Epoch is an unofficial unit of geologic time. It describes the most recent period in Earth's history when human activity started to have a significant impact on the planet's climate and ecosystems. This started between 1945 with the first nuclear bomb and 1950 when the "Great Acceleration", a dramatic increase in human activity affecting the planet, took off. The climate crisis is one of many impacts we are having on the natural living world around us.

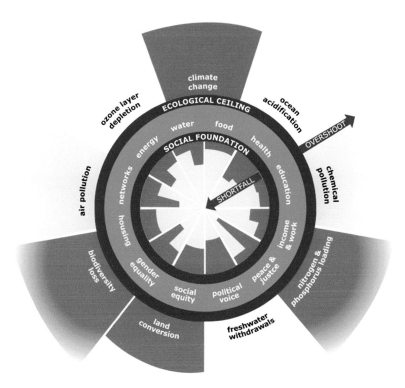

FIGURE 1.3 Planetary boundaries from Kate Raworth.

Introducing planetary boundaries. Kate Raworth (an English economist) defines these boundaries using the concept of *doughnut economics*, in which there are "ecologically safe" and "socially just" spaces for humanity to live (11).

The "doughnut" in doughnut economics consists of two concentric rings. Between these two boundaries lies a doughnut-shaped space that is both ecologically safe and socially just – a space in which humanity can thrive (Figure 1.3): a social foundation to ensure that no one is left falling short on life's essentials and an ecological ceiling to ensure that humanity does not collectively overshoot planetary boundaries.

We need the stability of planetary boundaries, such as safe drinking water, clean air, sufficient food and biodiversity, in order for humanity to survive and thrive. Exceeding planetary boundaries pushes us into dangerous territory – whether due to nutrient pollution, acidifying oceans, changing the land use or releasing forever chemicals and other novel entities into the environment. Figure 1.4 shows the increasing breaching of planetary boundaries between 2009 to 2023.

How the natural living world affects human health. The environmental impact of climate change includes rising average global temperatures, increasing wildfires, extreme events and instability. In some parts of the world, there are droughts and elsewhere floods. Vector-borne disease is also increased with heat through faster reproduction; wildfires will also increase cardiovascular diseases through increased air pollution; drought contributes to forced migration with wider distribution; wildfires and storms impact mental health.

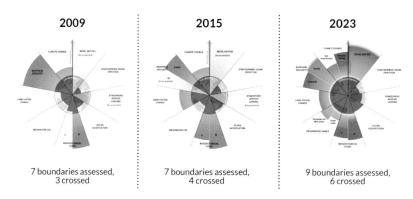

2009	**2015**	**2023**
7 boundaries assessed, 3 crossed	7 boundaries assessed, 4 crossed	9 boundaries assessed, 6 crossed

FIGURE 1.4 Planetary boundaries over time.

(Azote for Stockholm Resilience Center, Stockholm University (12)).

All these – and more – affect human health through diseases and illnesses that affect all parts of the bodies and all aspects of "good" health (Figure 1.5).

Healthcare depends on nature, from the development of new drugs, predictable procurement routes for ships, nature-based adaptation strategies, sustainable food systems, to places that humankind can rest, recuperate and play.

We have seen these health impacts in our countries and our personal lives. The figure looks at the health impacts of climate change but not air pollution, biodiversity loss, chemical pollution, etc. Sometimes, we don't recognise the impact of planetary health on our patients and clients. Clinical cases are highlighted within (almost) all of the rest of the chapters in this book and especially in Chapter 6.

Planetary health understands the links between global environmental changes, their effects on natural systems and how these changes impact human health on a local, regional and global level. Environmental exposure pathways lead to major health risks by way of the following:

- Heat stress
- Air pollution
- Food/water insecurity
- Extreme weather events
- Vector-borne illnesses
- Mental health impacts
- Social factors, including worsening inequalities

Impacts on patients and populations (13). Direct impacts include injury and death from weather events from temperature extremes (such as heatstroke, dehydration), water whether insufficient (e.g., dehydration) or excess (drowning due to flooding or cooling off in heatwaves) or physical and mental health injuries from storms and wildfires.

Indirect impacts include respiratory and cardiovascular illnesses from air pollution (which, in the European Union, causes 500,000 premature deaths annually (14)), worsening chronic disease control (cardiovascular, respiratory and diabetes (15)), changing

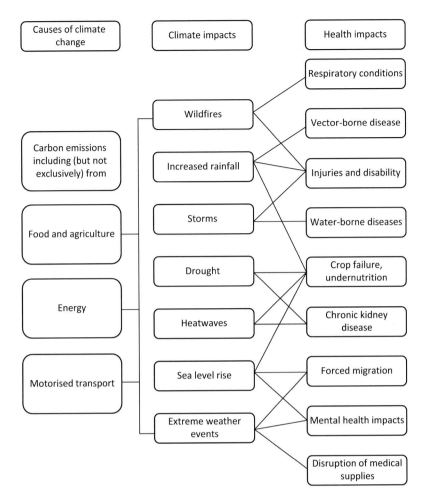

FIGURE 1.5 Human health impacts from a changing climate.

(Adapted from several sources).

infectious disease patterns (from gastrointestinal infections to malaria etc as a result of the wider distribution of vectors) and malnutrition (impact on food availability due to soil health, growing seasons, disruption to distribution networks).

Inequalities. In primary care, we are familiar with health inequalities in our communities and the importance of the inverse care law (that those who are most in need of medical care are least likely to receive it, and this effect is greater as the health system is privatised). The same is true in climate change, with many of the same drivers for health inequalities creating an inverse climate law (16). A warming planet will cause disadvantaged groups to suffer disproportionately from the adverse effects of climate change. In addition, those who suffer most are often those least responsible for emissions. In the United Kingdom, the highest 5% income households consume, on average, more than three times as many tonnes of oil equivalent annually, compared with the lowest 5%

income households (17). Moreover, making sustainable changes within healthcare has the potential to secure multiple significant co-benefits across populations, especially for those most vulnerable and marginalised. Projects that aim to improve access to green spaces, reduce air pollution, improve people's homes and help poorer families maintain good health would all tackle both inequalities and climate change.

The report "Sustainable Health Equity: Achieving a Net-Zero UK" chaired by Sir Michael Marmot lays out how policy decisions for combating climate change could also reduce avoidable health inequalities – thus promoting health equity (17).

Climate justice seeks to help us understand the links between the unfairness of climate change and the impacts being felt differently across the globe. Climate justice recognises that climate change is a social and political issue with interconnected struggles, and in fighting for solutions to the climate crisis, we may not only reduce emissions but create a fairer and more just (and healthier) world in the process (18). UN Biodiversity Conference (COP 15) recommended fair sharing of the benefits of nature and biodiversity for indigenous and local communities, and participatory mechanisms to listen and coproduce nature-based solutions with local communities (19).

"The public health case for a green new deal" (20) argues that

> both the climate crisis and the public health crisis are unmistakably rooted in an economic system that exploits human and natural resources in pursuit of profit and exponential growth. It is the marginalised who suffer the most as a result of these intertwined crises – but they are sustainable for no one.

Immediate impacts on primary care and their staff. The climate crisis affects staff performance, as extreme weather events can have psychological impacts on staff and increase job tension and workplace hostility, while higher temperatures and air pollution have negative impacts on workplace productivity and completing mental tasks (21) and can impede essential work-related decisions (22).

The interaction between the environment, society and the economy. The traditional model of sustainability is the "three-legged" model. This considers society, environment and economy separately, and the intersection is "sustainability" (Figure 1.6). This model assumes all portions are equally important and that the economy (or society) can exist outside the environment.

This model of thinking has been superseded and replaced by the "nested" model of sustainability. This recognises that society *only* exists as a subset of the environment and that the economy *only* exists as a subset of the society it is part of. We *can* have an environment unaffected by society, but we *cannot* have a society outside the environment or natural living world. The nested model highlights the importance of looking after the natural living world, as our society depends on it.

The impact healthcare provision has on the natural living world. The way that primary care is currently delivered harms the natural living world. There are effects on ecosystem quality and consumption of natural resources, and, as identified above, a significant greenhouse gas impact. Delivering healthcare is a big industry. Like all

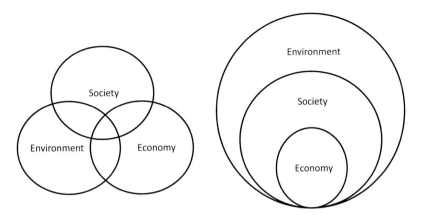

FIGURE 1.6 Three-legged model of sustainability and nested model of sustainability.

industries, it affects the health of the planet, contributes to rising levels of CO_2 and pollutants and causes biodiversity loss, which in turn damages the health of all species.

The carbon footprint of the NHS was calculated to be about 25 million tonnes CO_2e in 2019, of which primary care was 23% or 5.75 million tonnes CO_2e (23). As the footprint of the NHS is generally calculated as about 4%–5% of the United Kingdom's total, this puts primary care as 1% of the United Kingdom's total footprint, and 60% of that comes from the medications we prescribe (Figure 1.7). The nature and biodiversity impacts of healthcare are not yet fully quantified.

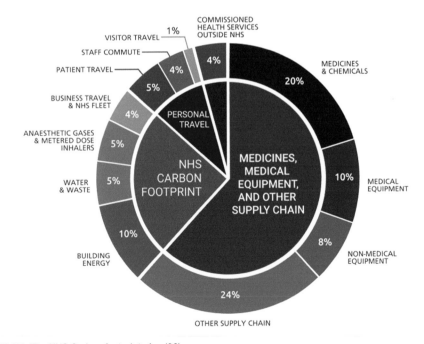

FIGURE 1.7 The NHS Carbon footprint plus (23).

Inter-connections. "Our health, wellbeing and livelihoods are dependent on nature, and yet nature is more under threat than ever" (24). Health is dependent on nature for every breath we take, safe transport systems for the goods we use, pollination for sustainable food systems, the freshwater we use every day, and the development of new medicines. We are part of nature, not separate or above it. But over one million species are now under threat of extinction, and the United Kingdom's recent "State of Nature" report defined the ongoing loss of, and threat to, species has identified us as one of the world's most nature-depleted countries (25).

There may now be a clear roadmap in some healthcare systems towards net-zero carbon, but road maps to "nature positive" are generally absent (26). Clear recommendations have now been set for governments, policymakers, and organisations that should lead to the conservation and restoration of thriving seas, land, and species (27). Healthcare can play a part in this work with a unique opportunity to start measuring its impacts and dependencies on nature, how it can collaborate to support nature recovery, and how it can support fair access to the benefits of nature.

Many indigenous healthcare systems have placed the ocean and nature at the centre of their systems and beliefs for years – seeing nature with us rather than for us. Chapters 13–15 describe those more industrialised countries in which our crucial relationship with nature has changed to one in which we have contributed to loss and become a threat to habitats and species.

> The climate crisis *is* a health crisis.
> Primary care will be affected by cumulative impacts.

If the second half of this chapter has felt full of doom and gloom, reread the first half and then move directly to Chapters 2–5.

Where to start?

Dentists – Chapter 2
General Practice – Chapter 3 and/or Chapter 6
Optometrists – Chapter 4
Pharmacy – Chapter 5

References

1 https://www.who.int/teams/integrated-health-services/clinical-services-and-systems/primary-care
2 https://unfccc.int/process-and-meetings/the-paris-agreement
3 https://www.thelancet.com/journals/lanplh/article/PIIS2542-5196(20)30249-7/fulltext
4 https://www.ncbi.nlm.nih.gov/pmc/articles/PMC7610659/
5 https://www.nature.com/articles/s43016-023-00749-2
6 https://www.racgp.org.au/getattachment/3c4c6433-b40b-4684-b5e5-50ebafd67d03/Greening-up-Environmental-sustainability-in-general-practice.aspx

7 https://ukhealthalliance.org/news-item/letter-to-political-leaders-act-on-climate-and-nature-for-better-human-health/

8 https://www.ncbi.nlm.nih.gov/pmc/articles/PMC8614825/

9 http://iopscience.iop.org/article/10.1088/1748-9326/ab8589/pdf

10 https://www.ayanaelizabeth.com/climatevenn

11 https://www.kateraworth.com/

12 https://www.stockholmresilience.org/research/planetary-boundaries.html

13 https://www.thelancet.com/journals/lanplh/article/PIIS2542-5196(20)30271-0/fulltext

14 https://www.exhaustion.eu/resources/increasing-temperatures-and-heat-waves-due-to-climate-change

15 https://health2016.globalchange.gov/low/ClimateHealth2016_02_Temperature_small.pdf

16 https://bjgplife.com/the-inverse-climate-law-a-call-for-health-equity-and-climate-justice/

17 https://www.thelancet.com/journals/lanplh/article/PIIS2542-5196(20)30270-9/fulltext (for ref https://www.instituteofhealthequity.org/resources-reports/sustainable-health-equity-achieving-a-net-zero-uk)

18 https://climate.friendsoftheearth.uk/resources/what-climate-justice

19 https://www.unep.org/un-biodiversity-conference-cop-15

20 https://stat.medact.org/uploads/2021/04/The-public-health-case-for-a-Green-New-Deal-MEDACT-April-202pdf

21 https://www.undp.org/publications/climate-change-and-labor-impacts-heat-workplace

22 https://ec.europa.eu/environment/biodiversity/business/assets/pdf/tool-descriptions/RECiPe%20and%20BioScope%20summary%20description.pdf

23 https://www.england.nhs.uk/greenernhs/

24 Final Report – The Economics of Biodiversity: The Dasgupta Review – GOV.UK (www.gov.uk).

25 State of Nature 2023 – Report on the UK's Current Biodiversity.

26 How to Produce a Green Plan: A Three-Year Strategy Towards Net Zero (england.nhs.uk)

27 COP15: Nations Adopt Four Goals, 23 Targets for 2030 In Landmark UN Biodiversity Agreement | Convention on Biological Diversity (cbd.int).

2

Dentistry
Ciara O'Kane and Davinder Raju

Introduction

A staggering 3.5 billion people worldwide, or nearly 50% of the global population, are affected by oral diseases. These diseases, which encompass dental caries (tooth decay), severe periodontal disease (gum disease), and oral cancer, are significant oral health concerns that disproportionately impact vulnerable and disadvantaged populations within and across societies throughout their lives.

The World Health Organization (WHO) identifies oral health as a key indicator of overall health, well-being, and quality of life, and emphasises that most oral health conditions can be prevented or managed effectively if diagnosed in the early stages. Yet, oral diseases still pose a significant health burden for many countries, causing pain, discomfort, disfigurement, and even death.

The treatment of these preventable oral health diseases is contributing to climate change directly through carbon emissions from delivering treatment, as well as the detrimental impact that dental materials and waste have on the environment. Therefore, as outlined by the FDI World Dental Federation in its 2017 statement, "the prevention of oral diseases and the promotion of health should be viewed as the most sustainable way to ensure optimal, accessible and affordable oral health with minimal impact on the environment". Water fluoridation is the "most sustainable option in oral health" according to WHO, and a recent research study found that water fluoridation had the lowest environmental impact compared to other community-level caries prevention programmes (8). General dental practices should have knowledge of the dental public health schemes in their area, whether they are focused on targeted prevention programmes or their local population (for example, water fluoridation schemes).

DOI: 10.1201/9781003491583-2

Dentists have an ethical and moral responsibility to manage our activities' environmental impact while ensuring optimal care is delivered sustainably without compromising safety.

> Oral health is vital for general health
> Dental care is part of healthcare

Global inequalities of oral diseases. The burden of oral diseases is not uniformly distributed across populations. Differences in oral health status are not inevitable and do not occur by chance; inequities are caused by multiple interconnecting factors, many of which are beyond individuals' direct control. Addressing oral health inequalities is essential for social justice and an ethical public health policy.

Access to oral health services is highly variable both within and among countries. Oral healthcare in most countries is a private, demand-led service rather than one resulting from a planned process which prioritises prevention. In many situations, the inverse care law applies: the provision of oral health services is inversely related to the oral health needs of the population.

Key factors contributing to the environmental impact of oral healthcare. The provision of dental care has an impact on the environment, and as a profession, we have a responsibility to address this, from how we organise and deliver care to the design of clinical pathways. Oral healthcare, as currently provided, is unsustainable as throughout the supply chain (e.g., from mineral extraction to manufacturing), high resource usage, waste generation, and CO_2 emissions occur (9).

Single-use plastics. Plastics are crucial and versatile in healthcare provision and offer a safe and cost-effective material for packaging and fabricating products. Plastics can be combined with other materials to create complex, customised devices. Appropriate single-use plastic (SUP) use gives healthcare providers and the public confidence that a new, clean, or sterile device is being used. However, plastics don't necessarily reduce infection rates – e.g., glove-wearing reduces hand washing, which can increase transmission of infection.

The dental profession in many countries operates within increasing and stricter infection prevention and control (IPC) regulatory frameworks. Fear of litigation from regulatory bodies and a lack of clear IPC guidelines encourage the use of single-use items over traditional multi-use instruments, yet substantial evidence supporting this transition is lacking.

Within the oral healthcare setting, a substantial quantity of SUP items are used, significantly contributing to clinical waste. A study conducted in the United Kingdom highlighted that, on average, 21 SUPs are used in standard adult primary care operative dental procedures (e.g., dental filling). Extrapolating from this, the authors of the study found that it is a cautious approximation that the United Kingdom annually uses about two billion dental SUPs (7). These find their way into the waste stream – ending up in landfills or undergoing incineration. Incineration of the vast amount of plastic waste generated results in the release of toxic chemicals such as dioxins, furans, and heavy metals into the environment (see Chapters 12 and 13).

To worsen the problem, the SUPs often arrive at the practice in additional plastic packaging, over 90% of which follows a linear economy and enters the waste stream.

Carbon footprint. The estimated carbon footprint of National Health Service (NHS) dental services in England is 675 kilotonnes of carbon dioxide equivalent (CO_2e; see Figure 2.1). Within NHS primary care settings in England, the main sources of carbon emissions in dentistry are as follows:

1. Travel accounts for the highest proportion of emissions. Patients and staff commuting to and from care centres account for around two-thirds of the carbon footprint of NHS dental services. Vehicle emissions also release harmful air pollutants (see Chapter 11).

2. Procurement: The oral healthcare industry acquires clinical and non-clinical products, and environmental pollution is an issue at every phase of the product-procurement process. CO_2e from procurement within primary oral healthcare services can be

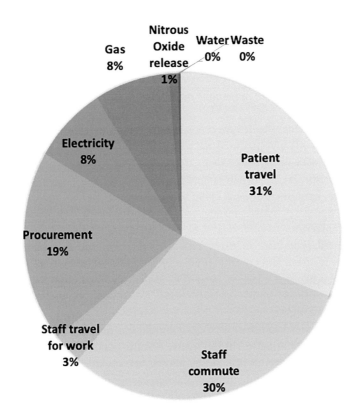

FIGURE 2.1 Main sources of carbon emissions: Total annual carbon footprint of dental services in England – 2013/2014 (1, 2).

subdivided into three main sectors: administrative (31%), material (34%), and laboratory service (35%). Unfortunately, dental materials and devices are produced, used, and discarded in the current linear economy, leading to significant waste generation and resource depletion. For more details, see Chapter 12.

3. Energy use: The energy consumption of dental equipment and facilities accounts for 15% of the carbon footprint. Understanding the impact of energy consumption in dental care is essential for recognising the broader implications of oral healthcare on planetary health. More information in Chapter 10.

What action can I take? As an examination, scale, and polish are carbon intensive because of the travel emissions of staff and patients, so it is appropriate to review the intervals between oral health reviews. Making appropriate review periods and personalised recalls continues high-quality dental care but with patient and environmental considerations valued. NICE Clinical Guideline 19 Dental Checks: intervals between oral health reviews support this individualised, risk-based approach to recalls (10).

Restorative materials and their impact on the environment. The choice of dental material that is used for restoration will have an environmental impact. Next, we have outlined the two main dental materials used for direct-placement restorations and their impact.

Dental amalgam

What is it? Dental amalgam contains approximately 50% mercury. It has been widely used for over 150 years as a filling material for dental cavities; it remains a common restorative material today and is the second most common use of mercury within the European Union.

How does it affect the environment and our health? Dental amalgam can release mercury into the environment through discharge via wastewater from dental facilities and into the soil, water bodies, and the atmosphere. Mercury – a potent neurotoxin – can accumulate in the food chain, posing risks to human health and the environment. The accumulation of mercury can cause reproductive problems, liver and kidney damage, and neurological defects in birds and mammals.

What can be done in practice? In dental surgeries, amalgam waste is generated during filling placement and also during its removal when fillings need replacement. Amalgam separation units filter and collect the waste amalgam, and the waste (including any extracted teeth with amalgam fillings) is managed appropriately by certified waste management facilities. Dental amalgam separator technology, which removes 95% of waste amalgam, has been recommended as best management practice and is a Care Quality Commission (CQC) requirement in the United Kingdom (3).

What can be done to change the system? Despite the concerns about its mercury content and environmental impact, dental amalgam remains widely used due to its durability, technique insensitivity, and cost-effectiveness. However, it's important to note that progress is being made towards more sustainable restorative practices in dentistry. The Minamata Convention on Mercury is a global, legally binding treaty aimed at reducing environmental pollution from mercury, including a phase-down of dental amalgam use. As part of this commitment, efforts are being made to explore alternative restorative materials and techniques, ensuring a less environmentally harmful and more sustainable approach to dental care.

Resin-based composite (RBC)

What is it? RBCs are commonly used as filling material and are a suitable alternative to amalgam. They are plastic, tooth-coloured restorative materials which consist primarily of an inorganic filler phase within an organic resin-based matrix phase.

How does it affect the environment and our health? RBCs have been identified as an environmental concern due to their release of RBC particulates and monomers into the environment both during manufacture and clinical placement. The impact of this is lesser known than that of amalgam, and further research is needed on RBCs to identify the true environmental impact (14).

What can I do in my dental practice?

Prevention and Minimum Intervention Oral Healthcare:
It's Good for Patients, and It's Good for the Environment

Prevention of oral diseases is the pinnacle of care. The best strategy to curtail environmental harm lies in reducing the necessity for invasive treatments.

Prioritising preventive dentistry, including comprehensive oral health education, holds promise in reducing the demand for resource-intensive interventions.

The evidence overwhelmingly shows that nearly all dental and periodontal diseases can be averted with preventive measures, incurring minimal environmental costs. Therefore, an ethical and moral obligation exists for the dental profession to proactively prevent avoidable conditions, refrain from unnecessary clinical interventions by ensuring appropriate patient care, and advocate for policies that limit sugar content in food and beverages.

Alarmingly, sugar-sweetened beverages contribute to 30% of the added sugars in the diets of children up to 3 years old, and this figure rises to over 50% by late adolescence. The introduction of the UK "sugar tax" in April 2018 has been linked to a decrease in tooth extractions among children up to 9 years old, as reported in 2023 (6). This correlation underscores the effectiveness of systemic preventive measures in reducing health issues related to sugar consumption.

A growing body of research also supports the connection between periodontal (gum) disease and systemic health issues such as cardiovascular disease, colorectal cancer, diabetes mellitus, and Alzheimer's disease. Preventing periodontal disease improves long-term quality of life and diminishes the overall environmental impact by reducing oral disease-related systemic conditions (11).

For caries (tooth decay), fluoridation is the most sustainable intervention option available, but where preventive measures have proven insufficient, and disease management becomes necessary, a minimally invasive approach should be adopted, focusing on effectively reversing the disease process. When fillings are required, any restoration placed should meet high-quality standards, thereby minimising the chances of premature failure and the need for replacement, which would incur an added environmental burden

Unfortunately, a substantial aspect of general dental practice revolves around managing failing restorations, and the management options are also intertwined with environmental consequences. The approach to addressing failing restorations can be encapsulated in the 5 R's seen in Figure 2.2.

In embracing a proactive preventive and minimally invasive approach to patient care, oral healthcare professionals achieve a dual benefit: reducing environmental impact and delivering less invasive treatments to their patients. This alignment underscores the importance of prioritising sustainable practices in oral healthcare, ensuring a healthier future for both individuals and the planet.

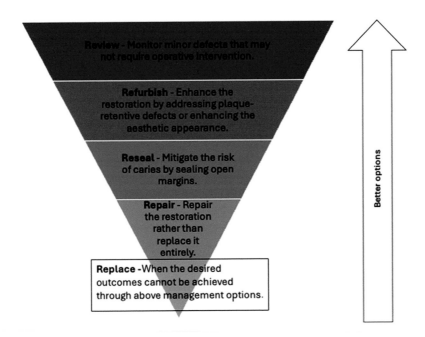

FIGURE 2.2 Least environmentally harmful options in dental care.

Reducing carbon footprint from travel

Dental practices can significantly contribute to reducing their community's carbon footprint arising from travel-associated emissions (2). The dental team could reduce travel emissions by ensuring that family members' appointments are booked together or by combining operative procedures to avoid multiple visits (see Chapter 11 for general ideas).

Recall based on risk status. Implement a recall system that schedules appointments based on the patient's risk status, avoiding unnecessary travel and appointments for those at lower risk.

Incorporate tele-dentistry. Avoid physical visits by using tele-dentistry for consultations, follow-ups, and preliminary assessments where appropriate.

Case study

Rather than booking an appointment for a treatment review, such as dentures, patients can discuss their symptoms virtually, and if there are concerns, the clinician can book an appropriate appointment in person (12).

Sustainable procurement (see Chapter 12)

Sustainable procurement in dental practices involves a strategic approach to sourcing and purchasing that minimises environmental impacts while maintaining safety and providing high-quality patient care. Tangible steps for dental practices include the following:

Prioritise reusables over single-use. Choose reusable dental instruments and devices wherever possible to reduce waste generation. Reusable items can be autoclaved and used for multiple patients, decreasing the need for frequent purchases and disposals.

Energy in dental practices (see Chapter 10).
Adopting energy-efficient practices lowers operational costs and demonstrates a commitment to environmental sustainability.

Incentivising sustainability initiatives in dental practices. Most dental practices are independent businesses owned by individuals or private corporations.

In the United Kingdom, community oral healthcare services are facilitated predominantly through private and NHS-aligned dental practices. The latter work within the NHS framework but are independent contractors to the NHS rather than employees. Dentists working in NHS dental practices provide treatments to patients at rates predetermined by the NHS. In Australia, the government does not pay for most dental services (apart from some children's services for those on benefits), so most provision is through insurance and private providers. Canada, too, has private provision with, from 2024, an insurance-linked system for lower-income residents to provide basic care.

Private dental practices represent a significant portion of the dental landscape internationally and are responsible for delivering oral healthcare to their clientele. In the United Kingdom, these practices function outside the direct purview of the NHS, determining their own fee structures and treatment offerings. Elsewhere, dentists practise under their own countries' regulations.

As most dental practices are independent businesses, the successful integration of sustainability initiatives necessitates financial sense; consequently, any investments in sustainability measures must be economically viable within the constraints of the practice's financial structure. See Chapter 15 for the business case for embracing sustainability.

Regulatory compliance and cost mitigation. Compliance with environmental regulations is vital for any business, including dental practices. Sustainability initiatives aid in meeting environmental regulatory requirements, averting potential fines, penalties, or legal issues that could result from non-compliance. Financially, this translates to savings that would otherwise be expended in rectifying regulatory infractions.

Enhanced reputation, competitive edge, and patient loyalty. Embracing sustainability enhances a dental practice's image, attracting environmentally conscious patients. Members of the public increasingly appreciate and choose goods and services from ethical, sustainable brands and are even prepared to pay more. Dental practices that showcase a commitment to sustainability may gain a competitive advantage by attracting and retaining a broader patient base and a positive reputation, fostering patient loyalty and, ultimately, benefiting the financial stability and growth of the practice.

More engaged and fulfilled teams. Besides reducing their environmental impact, sustainable businesses cultivate an engaging work atmosphere that resonates with employees. This engagement heightens job satisfaction and translates to financial gains by lowering turnover rates and the expenses of recruiting and training new team members. A cohesive and committed team, inspired by the practice's sustainability ethos, not only contributes to a positive workplace but also fuels innovation, ultimately benefiting patient care and operational effectiveness.

Balancing financial feasibility with environmental stewardship is key to driving the adoption of green initiatives within the dental care sector.

Influencing change: promoting sustainable dentistry across stakeholders. The primary care oral healthcare team can be pivotal in fostering and advocating sustainable dentistry within the larger dental organisational system.

Lead by example. Demonstrating sustainability within a practice sets a powerful example for others. When the oral healthcare team showcases the successful integration of sustainable measures, it inspires peers and instigates interest in adopting similar practices.

Education and awareness. The oral healthcare team members can serve as educators, enlightening peers and patients about the importance and benefits of ustainable dentistry. By sharing knowledge about sustainable practices and their positive impacts, they raise awareness and encourage a shift in mindset. The General Dental Council in the United Kingdom has recently included sustainable oral healthcare in its learning outcomes for dental professional education, ensuring future dental professionals understand the principles of sustainable healthcare. The newly agreed curriculum, The Safe Practitioner: A Framework of Behaviours and Outcomes for Dental Professional Education, takes effect from September 2025.

Leveraging authority bias for patient education and engagement. The primary care oral healthcare team members are trusted figures. By presenting credible information, expert recommendations, and clear guidance on sustainable home practices, patients are more likely to embrace these eco-friendly approaches. Using waiting room displays, educational materials, and workshops endorsed by dental professionals can further inspire patients to adopt responsible oral care practices.

Advocacy and policy engagement. Engaging with professional organisations and relevant authorities allows the oral healthcare team to advocate for policy changes that promote sustainable dentistry. Providing input on regulations, guidelines, and incentives can drive systemic shifts towards sustainability – e.g., around infection control regulations.

Leveraging manufacturers for sustainable dentistry. Dental manufacturers need to prioritise product and packaging recyclability. Focusing on designing easily recyclable products and emphasising the recovery of these items for subsequent recycling is essential. Manufacturers can adopt eco-friendly materials, promote circular economy principles, and facilitate recycling processes to minimise waste and contribute to a more sustainable dental industry. Collaboration among manufacturers, industry stakeholders and policymakers is crucial to drive concerted efforts to meet this requirement, forging a greener and more responsible dental product ecosystem.

What can I do?

There are resources available to support individuals and teams across the oral health and dental care system to embed environmental sustainability, some of which are identified at the end of this chapter. It will be crucial to remain up to date with evidence-based research in this developing area. For example, the Cochrane review of electric and manual toothbrushes highlighted that there is no evidence that any type of toothbrush is superior for caries prevention (4), and another research paper (5) showed "that a toothbrush which comes from recycled plastic is the most environmentally friendly option" with the next being a bamboo toothbrush.

It is important for members of the dental team to always be curious as to where meaningful change can happen and consider how challenges can be made to procedures or policies to include environmental considerations alongside high-quality, safe care. For example, a 2022 paper published in the *British Dental Journal* which evaluated HTM 01 05, the infection control framework for primary dental care in England, through an environmentally sustainable lens. This paper presented challenges to the use of single-use equipment, identified how to ensure autoclave use has the lowest environmental impact, and identified more sustainable decontamination practices (13).

Conclusion

Achieving the goal of making dental services more environmentally sustainable will require collective actions of individuals, oral healthcare teams, the dental industry, regulatory bodies, and policymakers to ensure success. There needs to be a shift towards preventive dental care, empowering patients to reduce their risk of disease and systemic action to ensure population-wide access to services. Oral healthcare teams need to work together to ensure that when treatment is necessary, they consider how to ensure it is safe, effective, high-quality, and environmentally sustainable care. They should use their trusted voices to drive meaningful change and demand that policymakers consider sustainability when designing dental services.

My pledge

What actions am I going to do in my practice?

1.
2.
3.

Where next?

Chapter 9 to learn about sustainable quality improvement
Chapter 10 for energy and estates
Chapter 11 for travel and transport
Chapter 12 for procurement of goods and services

References

1 Public Health England 2018 *Carbon Modelling Within Dentistry: Towards a Sustainable Future*, London https://assets.publishing.service.gov.uk/media/5b461fa2e5274a37893e3928/Carbon_modelling_within_dentistry.pdf

2 Duane, B., et al. Environmental sustainability and travel within the dental practice. *Br Dent J* **226**, 525–530 (2019). https://doi.org/10.1038/s41415-019-0115-z

3 https://www.cqc.org.uk/guidance-providers/dentists/dental-mythbuster-1-use-disposal-dental-amalgam

4 https://pubmed.ncbi.nlm.nih.gov/24934383/

5 https://www.researchgate.net/publication/344225187_Incorporating_sustainability_into_assessment_of_oral_health_interventions

6 Rogers, NT et al. Estimated impact of the UK soft drinks industry levy on childhood hospital admissions for carious tooth extractions: Interrupted time series analysis. *BMJ Nutrition Prevention & Health*, e000714 (2023). doi: 10.1136/ bmjnph-2023-000714

7 https://www.sciencedirect.com/science/article/pii/S0300571222000057

8 https://www.nature.com/articles/s41415-022-4251-5

9 https://www.fdiworlddental.org/sites/default/files/2021-09/Sustainable%20Oral%20Healthcare%20and%20the%20environment-Challenges%20%28June%202021%29_1353961014.pdf

10 https://www.nice.org.uk/guidance/cg19/resources/dental-checks-intervals-between-oral-health-reviews-pdf-975274023877

11 https://www.nature.com/articles/s41467-022-35337-8

12 https://networks.sustainablehealthcare.org.uk/resources/remote-consultations-dentistry

13 https://www.nature.com/articles/s41415-022-4903-5

14 https://www.nature.com/articles/sj.bdj.2018.229

Resources

Sustainable Dentistry: How-to Guide for Dental Practices. https://sustainablehealthcare.org.uk/dental-guide

- Sustainability in Dentistry –FDI World Dental Federation. https://www.fdiworlddental.org/sustainability-dentistry
- Sustainable Dentistry Foundation Course. https://sustainablehealthcare.org.uk/courses/sustainable-dentistry
- Greener Dentistry Accreditation Programme. https://greenerdentistry.global/
- Green Impact in Dentistry. https://toolkit.sos-uk.org/greenimpact/dentistry/login
- Environmental Sustainability in Dentistry – Free Module. https://portal.e-lfh.org.uk/Component/Details/810983
- Clinical Guidelines for Environmental Sustainability in Dentistry. https://cgdent.uk/wp-content/uploads/securepdfs/2023/09/OCDO-Clinical-guidelines-for-environmental-sustainability-in-dentistry-Version-11.0-Jan2023.pdf
- College of General Dentistry Sustainable dentistry – College of General Dentistry. cgdent.uk
- Delivering Better Oral Health: An Evidence-based Toolkit for Prevention – GOV.UK. www.gov.uk
- https://www.mercuryconvention.org/en/about

3

General Practice
Veena Aggarwal, Ilona Hale, Hannah O'Hara, Sean Owens, James Morton, Judith Pinnick, Munro Stewart, Sarah Williams, and Richard Yin

Overview

This chapter reflects on how General Practice/family medicine is practised in different ways in different places and the effect of politics and systems on its environmental sustainability.

To look at how clinical care is changing as a result of planetary health changes, visit Chapters 6 and 7.

What does General Practice do to our climate and environment? In high-income countries, around 4.6% of a country's carbon emissions come from healthcare, with primary care responsible for about 25% of this total. Prescribing medication and inhalers contributes around 60% of the emissions from primary care and 20% of the NHS's total emissions (1). Other significant carbon emissions are from the energy used, transport, and procurement of goods and services. The nature footprint of primary care has not yet been quantified but is likely to include the harm to habitats and species from pharmaceutical water pollution, plastics and microplastics, air pollution, shipping and noise pollution from procurement, and nature loss from primary care estate management and development.

DOI: 10.1201/9781003491583-3

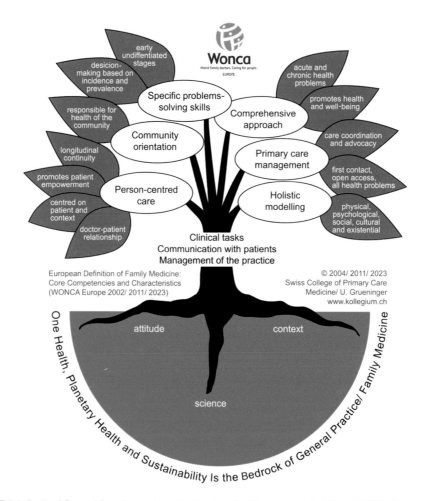

FIGURE 3.1 Basis of General Practice, one health, planetary health, and sustainability (WONCA) (3).

Currently, the situation regarding sustainability and General Practice is as follows:

1. Primary healthcare, like the majority of modern Western living, lives in a fictional world of limitless resources and negligible waste. Countless longitudinal reports (Intergovernmental Panel on Climate Change (IPCC), Intergovernmental Science-Policy Platform on Biodiversity and Ecosystem Services (IPBES), EAT-Lancet, etc.) tell us this is simply not true, nor is our way of life compatible with a habitable planet or productive future.

2. "Follow the evidence base" is the central theme driving healthcare policy. Healthcare professionals understand that often the best available evidence is of moderate to low quality. So, when strong evidence, such as IPCC reports, is available, we should listen and pay attention to this signal. We should act. Of the ten action points in the 2019 WONCA Declaration for Planetary Health, seven relate to advocacy, whether at a practice or political level (2). See also Figure 3.1.

3. Health Care Without Harm calculates healthcare as one of the top producers of emissions globally, circa 5% of global emissions. Most of this is from expensive and unsustainable procedures, investigations, therapeutics – the evidence base for which is often questionable. In healthcare, we like to *do* things, and this causes harm. Julian Tudor Hart's inverse care law may well get a second life. Those who most need medical access are least likely to have access *and* the most likely to pay the environmental bill for those that do.

4. A paradox is that the healthcare delivered today is contributing to the climate, ecological and health crisis of tomorrow. There is an added ethical onus to decarbonise and reduce our overall environmental footprint. First, second and third, do no harm.

5. While we are making noises of progress and acknowledging that strategy and governance structures do take time, we are simultaneously transgressing many planetary tipping points and entering a runaway breakdown of existing natural systems. One of the main gaps is the true sense of urgency and ability to see past bureaucracy and barriers. The response to COVID demonstrated this need not be the case.

6. However, there are major gains, such as addressing emissions at a procurement level and hot spots, particularly metered dose inhalers and appropriate prescribing.

7. The largest gains, as described by the UK Centre for Sustainable Healthcare, are in prevention. Leaner healthcare models are needed, but on their own are not enough. The lag in identification reporting of diseases such as, say, diabetes (where 6% prevalence (likely an underestimate) consumes 10% of health spend already) and faced with, for example, an extra 100,000 cases of dementia by 2050, means disease prevention provides multiple gains: less impact on climate and nature, economic gain, and patient health improvements.

8. Hence the need for an honest conversation (minus industry influence) about sustainable plant-based diets, safe urban AND rural transport, physical activity and industry-free conversation about our relationship with tobacco and alcohol.

9. The harder parts of addressing sustainability in our healthcare systems relate to addressing social deprivation and social inequalities.

How is the changing environment affecting the epidemiology of General Practice?

Workload is anticipated to rise due to climate and ecological breakdown.

- The climate and ecological crisis is no longer a future policy consideration or special interest topic; it is a present-day reality rapidly undermining the health of people and the future viability of the healthcare system.

- Rising global temperatures, sea level changes, drought, fires, floods, reduced crop yields, pest and disease spread and reduced habitable land are increasing migration and, in all likelihood, increasing the chances of civil and international conflict, all of which will impact our social fabric. The IPCC estimates that there will be 200 million climate refugees by 2050 (4): impacts on primary care are unpredictable and uncertain.

- More intense rain, flooding, drought and other extreme weather events have direct health impacts on staff and patients locally and will increasingly cause harm to healthcare facilities, thus affecting our ability to provide healthcare.

- Disease patterns are changing. Lyme disease has become endemic in the United Kingdom in recent decades; tick-borne encephalitis virus has been identified; cholera is expected to be seen in Scotland before 2100; dengue may spread from France to the United Kingdom.

- Air pollution is a significant factor in the generation of some illnesses, including respiratory conditions and links to diabetes, depression, ischaemic heart disease, developmental delay, dementia and many more (see Chapter 13).

What can we do? People trust healthcare workers. Nurses and doctors are consistently judged amongst the most trusted messengers to tell the truth (5). In the United Kingdom alone, General Practice clinicians complete over one million consultations daily. The potential for influence shouldn't be underestimated.

Primary care staff work in anchor institutions embedded into their communities and already perform vital roles to inform public opinion. As role models, they use their substantial voices – personally, politically and within their professional organisations. In America, even amongst conservative Republicans, primary care doctors are the second most trusted influence on global warming (6).

In an age of abundant misinformation, where the fossil fuel industry has huge resources to protect its vested interests, primary care voices framing *environmental issues as health issues* are vital to shift narratives. The debates can be moved on from threats to freedom and conspiracy theories.

Escalating carbon emissions, biodiversity loss, and air and water pollution have now reached a point where healthcare institutions can no longer stay silent. Unless drastic actions are taken immediately across all sectors and all areas of our society, an increasing number of lives will be lost and the most vulnerable in our society will suffer the most extreme health consequences. The evidence is clear: we need to act on environmental issues now. Should primary care not lead by example?

Cause for optimism. There are strong signs of progress, as seen in Chapter 1.

Everybody can get involved. An ever-growing network of enthusiasts is driving work on environmental issues throughout primary care. There are local, national, and international groups of environmentally focused clinicians welcoming non-experts to join organisations like Greener Practice. Some choose to work with professional bodies, others express themselves through personal actions of walking or cycling to work and then share how great that feels.

The inner optimist sees the potential seeds for large-scale change. The possibility that, with health as a common goal and healthcare professionals as trusted messengers, health workers can help people realise that society's dominant myth – that happiness and health are obtained through excessive consumption of our planet's finite resources – is false and unsustainable. The myth contributes to greater poverty, inequality, disparity, poor health, and environmental degradation.

General Practice can use its voice at every opportunity to advocate in the interests of our patients for better public health measures and spending.

Australia

The situation in Australia – a country with one of the highest per capita emissions thanks to its fossil fuel exports (7) – is quite tough regarding environmental sustainability. The Climate Council has called for Australia to reach net-zero emissions by 2035, with a 75% reduction by 2030. The federal government's commitment is for a 43% reduction by 2030 and net zero by 2050.

Despite the Australian healthcare sector's estimated 7% contribution to the country's total carbon emissions, there remain no mandated federal health sector targets and no coordinated approach across jurisdictions to reduce health sector emissions. The Australian Medical Association (AMA) and Doctors for the Environment Australia (DEA) have called for the Australian healthcare sector to reduce its carbon emissions to net zero by 2040, with an interim emission reduction target of 80% by 2030.

Amongst the states, New South Wales has a small Climate Risk and Net-Zero Unit to drive change, with a target of a 50% reduction in emissions by 2030 and a net-zero target by 2050. Western Australia also has a small Sustainable Development Unit with limited staffing. Neither has a focus on primary care.

The landscape may change with the development of the National Health and Climate Strategy. This strategy – to both prepare for the health challenges presented by climate change and reduce emissions from the health sector – remains in development (2023).

Frustrations remain with a government that continues to allow new fossil fuel projects – e.g., the greenlighting of fracking in the Beetaloo Basin. Emissions from this project are expected to be equivalent to three times the health sector's annual emissions. Environmentally harmful options of this sort make a mockery of the attempts within the health sector to reduce their emissions.

In 2019, the Royal Australian College of General Practitioners (RACGP) produced a position statement recognising the important role GP plays in mitigation and adaptation strategies, but it has no net-zero target for primary care.

Primary care sustainability initiatives have been driven largely by members within the Climate and Environmental Medicine Specific Interest Group of the RACGP, with strong support from the college. A resource base is being developed to support non-clinical, clinical and advocacy actions with a RACGP web page on climate change. A more extensive website to provide a centralised resource is being developed by individuals with the hope of getting it funded through sponsorship. A lack of funding and time has hampered progress.

In Australia, General Practices are private businesses and doctors sole traders. As of 2023, there are neither incentives nor regulatory frameworks to drive change. Nonetheless, a recent small survey by practice owners suggested that most are willing to spend up to six hours annually to get themselves a voluntary sustainability accreditation, with the majority willing to pay up to $40/month.

The Australian Commission on Safety and Quality in Health Care recently drafted a Sustainable Healthcare Module. In the future, sustainability as part of quality in healthcare may become mandatory and be part of practice accreditation.

Centralising resources on climate change and health, sustainability in General Practice, and primary care advocacy may overcome what a qualitative study by Pavli (8) identified as barriers, including *lack of knowledge about initiatives with the highest impact and lack of understanding described by staff of evidence behind particular initiatives.* Enabling factors within sustainable practices were identified as being "*leadership,*" "*staff engagement and workplace culture,*" and "*concomitant benefits*".

Funding towards the development of resources, implementation of strategies (e.g., reducing the use of MDIs), and processes to improve efficiencies and reduction of waste within the hospital-primary care interface is required to drive systemic change. Primary care should be at the centre of a sustainable health sector with better integration with allied health, the community, and the hospital sector.

Positives

- Strong support from RACGP
- Very active Climate and Environmental Medicine Specific Interest Group
- A Disaster Management Specific Interest Group
- Some evidence of the willingness of practice owners to spend up to six hours/year on environmental sustainability "accreditation" for their work
- Some evidence for practice owners willing to engage with support for pro-environmental actions – e.g., through an online portal or online carbon footprint calculator

Problems faced

- Lack of mandated health-sector-specific targets
- Lack of staff expertise and availability of data and resources
- Lack of knowledge of climate health impacts by general practitioners (GPs)
- Lack of staff to drive change agenda
- Lack of partnerships across geographical areas covering health providers, local authorities and other partners

Canada

Canada is a country known for its natural beauty and vast expanses of pristine wilderness. However, fortunes were built on exploiting this natural bounty, and although the casual observer will still enjoy the scenery, Canada steadily depletes its natural resources: forests, fresh water, minerals and, significantly, fossil fuels. Resource extraction plays an important role in the economy, which means that even a liberal government with a former

Greenpeace activist as minister for the environment is no match for the oil and gas industry, which seems determined to wring every last drop of oil out of the Alberta tar sands and gas deposits. Despite vast potential for hydro, solar, wind and geothermal energy, Canada has the notorious distinction of being the only G7 country to have failed to reduce emissions below 1990 levels. All of this is difficult to appreciate for the average Canadian who still looks outside and sees forests, prairies, oceans, and snow-capped mountains. Everything appears to be okay! As a result, the general population is not appropriately alarmed, and massive over-consumption by individuals and institutions continues. Widespread disinformation has made it difficult to know who the real enemy is.

Canada's healthcare system finds itself in a similar paradox. Despite pride in, and commitment to, a universal healthcare system, Canadians are heavily influenced by a culture of waste and excess and the for-profit medical industry of America, as well as their media, marketing, and supply chains. Although Canada continues to achieve excellent health outcomes on par with European countries, it does so at a much higher cost to the environment, second only to America.

There have been some recent (barely perceptible) movements towards recognising the importance of the environmental impacts of the healthcare system, such as signing on to the Health Programme at CoP26 in 2021.

- *Cascades* (9) – an excellent federally funded organisation – has been established through the partnership of several academic groups working towards reducing healthcare's impact. They have produced multiple playbooks and educational resources, and host regular webinars and conferences on key priority areas (10).
- The longstanding *Canadian Coalition for Green Healthcare* is a partnership between health professionals and industry with resources for hospitals, medical leaders and practitioners, including the Green Office Toolkit for primary care (11).
- The *Canadian Association of Physicians for the Environment* provides support for physicians, particularly in the area of advocacy; runs powerful campaigns to counter industry lobbyists, whether it is oil and gas or pesticides; and helps political leaders understand the serious health implications of their decisions (12). They have produced an excellent Climate Change Toolkit for Health Professionals.
- Quality and safety organisations like Health Quality BC (HQBC) recognise the importance of environmental sustainability in healthcare and quality improvement. HQBC has recently launched its Low-Carbon, High-Quality Care Initiative (13).

Until recently, much of the efforts towards reducing the carbon footprint of the Canadian health sector has been focused on waste generated in hospitals in the perioperative space, with little attention paid to primary care where our "waste" is diffused across many smaller sites. Two recent publications helping raise the profile of the importance of primary care are

- A framework for sustainable healthcare created by Dr Andrea MacNeill and colleagues that identified two keys to a sustainable system, health promotion and adequate supply of primary care providers (14), and

- *Planetary Health for Primary Care*, which introduces a new and different approach to understanding the important role of primary care clinicians (15). This expands on the UK Centre for Sustainable Healthcare's principles and helps clinicians understand how a difference can be made by addressing overuse, shifting towards prevention and health promotion, empowering patients through shared decision-making and self-management and adopting principles of "slow medicine" and team-based care. It provides practical examples and tips for providers.

The *Hamilton Family Health Team* is a primary care organisation with many excellent resources (16).

It is encouraging to see a steadily growing number of other health groups and individuals heeding the call and adopting existing practices or piloting new initiatives.

Ireland/Eire

Where is the carbon in Irish healthcare? Where the carbon lies in Irish healthcare is unclear due to a paucity of contemporaneous data about the activities of the service. There is duplication of services between public and private, such as double investigations and consultations, as there is no unique patient identifier to follow the patient. There is no real-time data on what is being prescribed and no reliable methodology to determine if this coincides with what is being dispensed, hoarded, or wasted. Addressing and fixing these issues shouldn't be considered an onerous green agenda but thought of as necessary to fix healthcare and represents spectacular potential savings for the public purse.

A significant proportion of the carbon footprint of healthcare can be linked back to clinical decisions. Therefore, evidence-based models of consultation – e.g., Calgary Cambridge – are important not only in postgraduate training but also in continual professional practice. The consultation is the ubiquitous tool that all healthcare professionals have access to, yet it remains undervalued. Two critical parts of the consultation that require attention are screening (or setting the agenda) and self-care. When rushed or when agenda screening is dropped, clinicians prescribe or investigate their way out of consultations, leading to overdiagnosis and overmedicalisation (see Chapter 7). A sustainable healthcare system needs healthcare professionals who are at their best. Self-care and doctors' health are critical issues that affect retention rates, workforce attrition, quality of care and patient safety. The importance of self-care as a carbon mitigation tool is not yet well understood or recognised (see Chapter 8).

How has sustainability in primary care in Ireland evolved? Primary care healthcare professionals in Ireland already deliver quality planetary health. Rural doctors providing house calls, "Deep End" doctors and nurses setting up makeshift clinics in areas of social deprivation, outreach to migrant communities, and bespoke addiction clinics are already leaders in planetary health. Long-acting contraception providers, chronic disease management, journal clubs to stay abreast of the evidence base are all core parts of quality planetary health.

In 2019, a group of like-minded Irish healthcare professionals came together to investigate the connections between unhealthy and unsustainable diets, the crisis in evidence-based medicine, too much medicine, and overdiagnosis. The Sustainability Working Group within the Irish College of General Practitioners (ICGP) began when a motion for planetary health was proposed for the 2019 college AGM. A motion from several faculties, based on the 2019 WONCA declaration on planetary health, for the college to incorporate planetary health in its activities and organisations was passed. This was timely as, in May 2019, Ireland became only the second country in the world to declare a climate and biodiversity emergency. The health sector has finally awoken from its slumber and published a net-zero strategy with an implementation plan in development.

The ICGP has published its own toolkit to aid practices in starting their sustainable journey and point the way to net zero (17).

Future plans. Collaboration is the key to moving forward through offering to work with the Health Service Executive (HSE) to deliver an implementation plan. This involves frequent meetings, document sharing, collaborations, etc., and is the perfect way to cross-pollinate ideas and have the chance to drive change. There is recognition within the HSE that much work has already been done.

Work continues with NGOs such as Irish Doctors for the Environment, the Climate Health Alliance, and academic and professional bodies (e.g., Royal College Surgeons, ICGP) on a joint declaration or manifesto regarding sustainability. The hope is to use this as leverage to hold decision makers to account, when they might otherwise be too busy or distracted, as an outward statement but also to exert pressure for in-house change.

As a primary function of the ICGP is on the training of trainees, the Sustainability Working Group aims to frequently present at regional GP training scheme educational sessions and has published a Continued Medical Education module that disseminates an approved educational package.

England

In England, the NHS contributes about 5% of the country's carbon emissions, with primary care estimated to be responsible for around 20% of this total. The Greener NHS programme, a team within NHS England (the commissioning body), was established in 2020 as an expansion of the Sustainable Development Unit. The NHS was the first health system in the world to commit to reaching net zero, with targets to reach net zero for directly controlled emissions by 2040, and by 2045 for indirect emissions.

Initially led by Dr Nick Watts, the Greener NHS has been exemplary in its attitude to the climate crisis: "We *are* decarbonising…we *won't* do business with you unless you come along…here are the timelines that you must adhere to". They see healthcare as having a leadership role beyond buying or procurement power and with the societal value of healthcare taking ownership.

England's NHS is divided into seven regions, which were subdivided into 42 smaller Integrated Care Systems (ICS) in 2022. Each ICS, as well as each hospital trust, is mandated to have a green plan, but no such mandate for primary care exists.

General Practices in the NHS are generally self-employed businesses with a contractual system of payment. There is a "core" contract with "additional" and "enhanced services" which practices can opt into providing. In addition, performance targets exist, such as the *Quality and Outcomes Framework* (QOF), which incentivises practices to, for example, perform annual asthma reviews. In 2022, four incentives were introduced to help clinicians improve asthma care and reduce the environmental impact of inhalers; however, despite significant success in some areas these were removed in 2023 when the government prioritised patient access in that year's contract. COVID-19 pandemic backlogs and workforce pressures remain a challenge in making sustainability a priority in practice.

Incentives towards sustainability, including contractual funding, and inclusion of sustainability in the framework of regulation, could be important levers for change. Currently, much of the work is driven by passionate individuals on a voluntary basis; in the future, funded roles for clinicians to drive sustainable quality improvement and develop resources will be key for systemic change.

Several organisations exist to educate and support clinicians to deliver sustainable healthcare:

Greener Practice started in Sheffield in 2017. It is a grassroots network with over 30 local groups and several national special interest groups, such as *Respiratory* and *Clinical Care* or *Education* run mainly via WhatsApp. One group – *Working with Other Organisations* – coordinates those working to achieve change in their ICBs. In 2022, Greener Practice produced the NHS England-approved *high-quality, low-carbon asthma toolkit* to help practices reduce the environmental impact of inhalers with a range of quality improvement projects and linked resources.

The Royal College of General Practitioners (RCGP) declared a climate emergency in 2019 and supports the sustainability agenda. It has a web page listing resources, a net-zero hub (18) with e-learning modules, and trained clinical advisors to assist practices to reach net zero. It has a clinical sustainability leadership team. Each faculty is asked to choose a sustainability or green lead which collectively forms a group of regional representatives who influence the local branch of the college, as well as contribute to national discussions. In 2023, the chair of council identified building sustainability as one of the four pillars of her time as chair.

The Green Impact for Health (GIFH) Toolkit is a Students Organising for Sustainability product supported by the RCGP (19). Practices complete tasks and can achieve a variety of awards.

Northern Ireland

Northern Ireland passed its Climate Change Act in 2022. This sets a target for the achievement of net-zero greenhouse gas emissions by 2050, with bridging targets, including a 48% reduction in emissions by 2030. The Act requires all civil service departments to deliver reduced emissions. However, as of winter 2023, no detailed strategy on decarbonisation has been created or put into motion by Northern Ireland's Department of Health. Specific legislation has been set out with a stipulation that the Department of Infrastructure must develop sectoral transport plans with a minimum spend on active travel of 10% of the overall transport budget. This is relevant to the health of the population. The devolved government in Northern Ireland has had a turbulent recent history – collapsing in 2017 and again in early 2022, two years after reforming, due to fallout over post-Brexit trading arrangements.

As well as keeping the health service in Northern Ireland running without a government in place, Northern Ireland's Department of Health is facing a budget deficit and the longest per capita waiting lists of any UK region. It is therefore not very surprising that the strategy on decarbonisation has not progressed as far as in the rest of the United Kingdom or the Republic of Ireland.

There is, however, some positive activity. The School of Medicine, Dentistry and Biomedical Sciences at Queen's University Belfast set out a strategic priority within their most recent academic plan that planetary health and the United Nations Sustainable Development Goals will be core to all curricula. Consequently, social accountability and sustainable healthcare are specified subthemes which run longitudinally throughout the undergraduate medical curriculum within the central theme of Global and Population Health. The university ranked as the fourth highest university in the United Kingdom in the Planetary Health Report Card scheme in 2022/2023, recognising engagement in planetary health research, outreach activity, and student-led initiatives in addition to curriculum changes (20). The new postgraduate School of Medicine at Ulster University also aims to develop sustainability into a formal curricular theme.

In primary care, the QOF (see Chapter 16) included an indicator in 2022/2023 incentivising practices to reduce the carbon emissions associated with the prescription of salbutamol inhalers, leading to a fall in inhaler-related emissions across the province.

The RCGP in Northern Ireland has appointed a climate and sustainability lead within its council and arranged an online discussion on the impact of the climate crisis on primary care in Northern Ireland in October 2023.

Under the umbrella of the UK-wide Greener Practice Network, a group has been set up and meeting online since January 2023 – providing peer support for GPs interested in sustainability and taking steps to promote awareness of planetary health and sustainable healthcare amongst colleagues and medical students in primary care and beyond.

Scotland

Primary care sustainability enthusiasts have collaborated in a number of different spheres of influence within Scotland.

Greener Practice. There are strong and growing networks of healthcare workers around Scotland, ensuring medical school teaching and curriculum coverage and working with health boards.

RCGP. A local member has taken environmental papers to the East Scotland Faculty Board, Scottish Council and UK Council, which have each been received well, including asking for broad engagement and more specific action on issues like fuel poverty. This was driven by the challenge of *"If I don't do it, who will?"*, and *"Which is worse – feeling uncomfortable at presenting to colleagues or failing to even try to make a change?"*

It has been encouraging to see that experienced GPs are open to engaging with the evidence and not intimidated by either the scale of the task or the potential dilution of limited resources in the college. Quicker action would be preferable; however, progress has been better than initially expected.

At the same time as the first faculty paper, a group of GPs led by Dr Aarti Bansal, Dr Terry Kemple, and others took a paper to the RCGP's UK Council, which would be supported by practitioners across the country, leading to the college's Climate Emergency Advisory Group.

The health board. The next scale of operations is the health board, of which there are 14 in Scotland. A GP – collaborating with Dr Nick Watts – took the plunge and presented "A Grand Rounds Slot" to NHS Tayside in 2020 (21). This was based on the 2019 Lancet Countdown report and aimed to hang on to the coattails of recent rapid changes to the delivery of healthcare in response to COVID. Since then, progress has been slower than through COVID, in part due to "crisis fatigue" and the reality that everyone is on a different stage of the journey towards net zero.

The Grand Rounds became a good platform to approach joining the local sustainability group within NHS Tayside, which is a combination of managers who are responsible for risk and clinician volunteers who are true grassroots pioneers, especially from the anaesthetics department. Work on desflurane has been inspirational and gives an insight into how change can be driven from the bottom up. These local leaders who take the initiative through a determination to make a difference have been able to drive national change. In Scotland, with our small population and greater manoeuvrability than some of our neighbours, individuals and small groups have great opportunities to have a high impact.

NHS Tayside Sustainability Group reacted well during the COVID crisis. A network of local makers coordinated by Rod Mountain produced extra scrubs for the health services in an incredible example of community buy-in (22). Health board "buy-in" and engagement are rapidly improving due to the 2040 NHS net-zero target and the NHS Scotland Sustainability Strategy.

SIGN. The council of the Scottish Intercollegiate Guidelines Network (SIGN) makes Scotland's guidelines akin to NICE in England and Wales and are globally respected. Volunteering to sit on this council enabled asking, "What could our national guideline body do for environmental sustainability?" and led to a GP chairing a working group to devise how Scotland might incorporate these issues into clinical guidance.

Identifying the "great and the good" in the area, using the esteem of the organisation and the importance of the task got people on board. Listening to each group member about what really mattered to them, including several lived-experience public partners, culminated in a set of principles that would guide future decision-making.

The problem was whether there was actually any evidence. Advising clinicians to consider social prescribing as an alternative needs published scientific proof that this is categorically better for patients and the planet. The challenge was to find proof of ways to reduce health inequalities, improve health, and protect the environment..., for less money, and to then integrate this through the clinical guidance SIGN provides to clinicians.

This evidence exists and is growing, but there is a lot of doubt from the people traditionally in the know: the guideline methodologists who just cannot compute trying to tackle more than one variable at a time.

The benefits are there. While SIGN works hard to commission the guidance, clinicians cannot delay. Individual interventions that can make a difference are known (see Chapter 8), so we should do what we can now, in good faith, for our patients.

No alternative other than to try. There are a lot of opportunities: reviewing what funding is available; disseminating knowledge and passion through published articles to highlight available support; meeting with fellow local GPs who are ahead of the curve, and, for example, using e-bikes at their practices; and starting conversations with colleagues, stakeholders, leaders and interested parties such as those working in green health prescribing locally.

Making it easy for busy people. Those working in sustainability are conscious that the clinicians, GPs, managers, and admin staff are often already beyond capacity. It can be difficult to push extra things that General Practice "should" be doing. So, it's important to work to make *doing the right thing the easy option*. Examples include the Greener Practice Glasgow network sharing best practice or the Greener Practice *high-quality, low-carbon asthma toolkit*.

Recognising forward steps taken. The 2022 and 2023 Chief Medical Officer's reports include climate and sustainability (23). It shows how grassroots work can quickly become the case studies which the leaders refer to for driving national change. This offers encouragement to anyone passionate – however small the subject – that if they can make a change, describe it, and share it, this could drive much wider change across Scotland and beyond.

RCGP Scottish council chairs David Shackles, Chris Williams, and vice chair Catriona Martin made climate and sustainability their executive priority for three years, with funded time for joint leads to work through a broad action plan, which has been continued and renewed by the latest chair Chris Provan. This positive outcome encourages and enthuses other college activists to go further and be more involved. Success is contagious! GPs have good communication channels with the government and have tabled parliamentary questions and presented at parliamentary receptions for members of the Scottish parliament (MSPs) on how climate and health interact and on positive examples of collaborations, such as that with the Royal Pharmaceutical Society on sustainable prescribing.

Wales

Dod yn ôl at Fy Nghoed. There's a beautiful phrase in the Welsh language; its literal translation is "coming back to my trees", but it's translated as "returning to a balanced state of mind".

Welsh communities have long adapted to changing scenery and resources using community spirit to survive the landscape. Aneurin Bevan, founder of the NHS, was born in Wales. GPs, family doctors, sit in the political and financial category of "primary care" in Wales, alongside community pharmacies, optometrists and dentists. Welsh GP surgeries are essentially NHS financed and have similar training systems to everywhere else in the United Kingdom. There is a huge mixture of urban and largely rural surgeries.

The Well-Being Future Generations Act 2015 Deddf Llesiant Cenedlaethau'r Dyfodol (Cymru) 2015. With this Act, Wales acknowledges the importance of fairness and community spirit. The Future Generations Act has a commissioner within the Welsh government to check that every public body assigning new and existing projects must ensure that they secure a sustainable future for children. They need to breathe clean air, have clean water and access sustainable food supplies and medical care. With the changing climate, increasing global emissions, polluted air, polluted water and unsustainable food supplies, our children cannot continue to survive and thrive as they have done previously without action from the top.

Green Health Wales Iechyd Gwyrdd Cymru is the main driving force for sustainable healthcare in Wales. The values of Green Health Wales are "connect", "learn", and "transform".

The Welsh government worked with the Carbon Trust to design the Welsh NHS Decarbonisation Strategy 2021, which was a largely secondary care–led document. In response, speciality leads interested in sustainable healthcare, from primary and secondary care, came together to forge a multi-professional group called Green Health Wales. This grassroots collaborative group uses cross-boundary leadership across multiple communities of practice and encourages interested NHS staff to join in sustainable healthcare communities unrelated to pre-existing structures and enables new connections and creates communities of practice with different specialities. This energy in collaboration connected masses of NHS staff, some in task and finish groups working for Welsh government and others in green groups developed in health boards across Wales.

Greener Practice Wales 2020 Iechyd Cynaliadwy Cymru 2020. Drs Sarah Williams and Richard Thomas initiated work to spread and scale sustainable healthcare amongst GP surgeries in Wales. They developed and grew a network and held regular meetings. They started campaigning for policy changes nationally and locally. Dr Sarah Williams worked with Green Health Wales alongside secondary care colleagues to expand their influence on national and governmental levels.

Richard and Sarah decided that affiliation with Greener Practice United Kingdom would aid sustainable healthcare, and their network became Greener Practice Wales. At the same time, Green Health Wales was developing momentum, developing resources and developing a website hosting all the green groups and leads from different areas of the NHS. Through the Green Health Wales platform, all the Welsh communities of practice feed into green groups, which encourages efficient dialogue with Welsh government policy. Top-down policy and grassroots delivery have become more connected than ever.

One Health Wales Iechyd Cyfuno Cymru. The Hwyel Dda Health Board has been innovative in ensuring a one health approach is embedded within system-wide issues, incorporating climate and health action within wider policy and programmes of work. It has promoted working on biodiversity and sustainable development, liaising within primary, secondary, and veterinary care. The work focuses on bringing together partners from the human, animal, and environmental sectors to work on issues that intersect, including the food system, education, threats from infectious diseases, and the environment and climate priorities.

Green Health Wales and Greener Practice Wales – the Green Health Wales Prescribing Hub – looking backwards to go forwards. In 2024, Green Health Wales launched "The Green Health Wales Green Prescribing Hub" for the NHS community and patients. The website aims to connect people to local community programmes and non-pharmaceutical options, offering social, blue, green, and lifestyle prescribing in a bid to reduce pharmaceutical consumption. This platform aims to normalise and prioritise non-pharmaceutical management options as first line.

Green prescribing case studies across Wales have been rapidly developing with community programmes, linking GP surgeries to organic growing, rewilding projects encouraging biodiversity and green spaces to restore well-being, all working to reduce the risk of diabetes and cardiovascular disease. Seminal projects linked to Green Health Wales and Greener Practice Wales have been the Fathom Trust – building in ecotherapies to support mental health, well-being, and multiple medical needs through community projects. Cynon Organics is a site using social prescribing, organic food growing, a Celtic roundhouse, and medical flower growing to connect local patient health back to nature.

Greener Primary Care Framework and Award Scheme 2021 until present 2024 Fframwaith a Chynllun Gwobrwyo Gofal Sylfaenol Gwyrddach Cymru. The Primary Care Division of Public Health Wales adopted the GIFH Toolkit in 2021. In the first year, nearly one in four Welsh surgeries joined.

Greener Primary Care Wales has rolled out the programme to include the four pillars of primary care in Wales. They have developed the toolkit with yearly evaluation and development of ongoing actions included.

Greener Primary Care secured funding from the Welsh government to deliver a six-month pilot in which a green champion promoted the toolkit to all four pillars of primary care in each health board. This process identifies actions and decarbonisation possibilities across Wales in all pillars of primary care. The development of the awards and sharing of "quick wins" has allowed places to identify streamlined decarbonising areas to focus on. GP clusters and health boards have now started to write these into their long-term visions and integrated medium-term plans.

Green Inhalers Wales Mewnanadlyddion Gwyrddach Cymru. Before the introduction of the Green Inhaler Quality Assurance and Improvement Framework (QAIF), about 96% of inhalers prescribed annually in Wales were pressurised meter dose inhalers (pMDIs). The Welsh NHS decarbonisation plan set a target to reduce MDIs to 25%. A Green Inhaler QAIF incentivised payment scheme was bought into the Welsh General Medical Services contract. The Institute of Clinical Science and Technology developed a suite of educational posters, apps, learning, and video support materials. The apps – only accessed by NHS patients in Wales – promote good quality asthma care and the need to switch to dry powder inhalers (DPIs). The charity Asthma and Lung UK supported this campaign across the nations, providing multi-language translations. The All Wales Toxicology and Therapeutics Centre Decarbonisation Dashboard developed a decarbonisation dashboard allowing data on all inhaler prescriptions to be analysed from a health board, cluster, and GP surgery level. Visit https://www.gov.wales/sites/default/files/publications/2023-02/green-inhaler-phase-2-quality-improvement-project.pdf and https://networks.sustainablehealthcare.org.uk/resources/susqi-project-turning-blue-inhalers-green-high-quality-low-carbon-asthma-care for more information.

What can I do/what can my practice do?

- **Have a "green meeting"**. Appoint a lead/coordinator/networker to stay up to date, set regular updates and meetings to track progress, celebrate successes, and be kind to yourselves; being green in an environment that isn't conducive to being green isn't easy, and it isn't perfect!

- **Find tools to help**. Download the GLAS toolkit (from ICGP.ie), or GIFH toolkit. Pick an action, pick an audit, pick a quality improvement (QI) project, and work towards a goal. Publish your work, involve trainees, share the successes with peers and other practices.

- Have a meeting to consider how your practice will mitigate the effects of climate change. Is your practice open to migrants and climate/conflict refugees? How will your practice run in the event of water or energy shortages, flooding, or fires?

- *How do my actions help patients, practice, and the planet?* Like much of prevention, the direct benefits are hard to see, the rewards of a stroke prevented, or a fall or fracture saved can be difficult to quantify. Those endorsing planetary health see a happier, healthier, and more vibrant patient population and community of which we are all part.

Summary

Each country and healthcare system has its own challenges. However, there is a lot of overlap and lessons which can be learned from one another. Highlight the passages in the text and make a list for you to use and try where you are.

Pledges

Pledge – from this chapter, I will pledge to...

1.

2.

3.

Where next?

Chapter 6 for linking planetary health in General Practice
Chapter 8 for how lifestyle medicine can solve both patient and planetary problems
Chapter 9 to learn about sustainable quality improvement
Chapter 10 for energy and estates
Chapter 11 for travel and transport
Chapter 12 for goods and services

References

1. https://www.england.nhs.uk/greenernhs/
2. https://www.wonca.net/site/DefaultSite/filesystem/documents/Groups/Environment/2019%20Planetary%20health.pdf
3. https://www.woncaeurope.org/kb/european-definition-gp-fm-2023
4. https://www.unicef.org.uk/policy/climate-migration-and-education/
5. https://www.ipsos.com/en-uk/ipsos-veracity-index-2022
6. https://climatecommunication.yale.edu/publications/politics-global-warming-april-2022/
7. https://ourworldindata.org/per-capita-co2#:~:text=Australia%20has%20an%20average%20per%20capita%20footprint%20of,which%20in%202017%20was%204.8%20tonnes%20per%20person
8. https://academic.oup.com/fampra/article/40/3/465/7083935
9. https://cascadescanada.ca/about/
10. https://cascadescanada.ca/resources/
11. https://greenhealthcare.ca/clinics/green-office-toolkit/
12. https://cape.ca/
13. https://healthqualitybc.ca/improve-care/low-carbon-high-quality-care/
14. https://pubmed.ncbi.nlm.nih.gov/33581064/

15. https://view.publitas.com/5231e51e-4654-42c2-accd-b722e21f3093/primary-care-toolkit_en/page/1
16. https://www.hamiltonfht.ca/en/what-we-offer/green-office-initiative.aspx
17. https://www.icgp.ie/speck/properties/asset/asset.cfm?type=LibraryAsset&id=C5CBED4C%2D364E%2D4CFB%2DB4321E4091A7799D&property=asset&revision=tip&disposition=inline&app=icgp&filename=ICGP%5FGlas%5FToolkit%5F2%5Fv5%2E2%2Epdf#:~:text=The%20toolkit%20may%20inform%20your,%2C%20antibiotics%2C%20and%20medication%20reviews
18. https://elearning.rcgp.org.uk/course/view.php?id=650
19. https://toolkit.sos-uk.org/greenimpact/giforhealth/login
20. https://phreportcard.org/
21. https://www.youtube.com/watch?v=aGhBhDF75E8&ab_channel=DundeeUniversityandNHSTaysideGrandRounds
22. https://www.youtube.com/watch?v=gS8CxBo5Y8&ab_channel=DundeeUniversityandNHSTaysideGrandRounds
23. https://www.gov.scot/publications/realistic-medicine-doing-right-thing-cmo-annual-report-2022-2023/

Resources

Australia

Sustainable General Practice https://www1.racgp.org.au/ajgp/2023/may/sustainable-general-practice

RACGP Position Statement – https://www.racgp.org.au/FSDEDEV/media/documents/RACGP/Position%20statements/Climate-change-and-human-health.pdf

Doctors for the Environment Australia https://dea.org.au/

Greening Up: Environmental Sustainability in General Practice www.racgp.org.au/FSDEDEV/media/documents/Running%20a%20practice/Security/Reducing-the-environmental-impact.pdf

National Health and Climate Strategy https://www.health.gov.au/our-work/national-health-and-climate-strategy

Canada

https://view.publitas.com/5231e51e-4654-42c2-accd-b722e21f3093/primary-care-toolkit_en/page/1

Scotland

https://www.youtube.com/watch?v=aGhBhDF75E8&ab_channel=DundeeUniversityandNHSTaysideGrandRounds

https://www.gov.scot/publications/cmo-annual-report-2022-realistic-medicine-fair-sustainable-future/pages/4/

Wales

https://www.gov.wales/sites/default/files/publications/2021-09/a-healthier-wales-our-plan-for-health-and-social-care.pdf

General resources

https://www.science.org/doi/10.1126/science.abn7950 tipping points

WONCA Revision of Planetary Health

https://www.woncaeurope.org/file/0dce3f9f-e60f-4416-b257-4698590bd0c9/WONCA_European_Definitions_2_v7%20(1).pdf page 25

https://pubmed.ncbi.nlm.nih.gov/15489066/

https://www.ncbi.nlm.nih.gov/pmc/articles/PMC6404899/

4

Optometrists and opticians
Antonia Chitty and Abi Page

Case study – Disposable contact lenses

Emma, a 47-year-old daily disposable contact lens wearer, attends for an eye examination and contact lens check. She has worn lenses since age 13 and wants to continue, as she has a public-facing job where she wants to look good. She has two teenage sons. She suffers from anxiety and is particularly anxious about climate change and plastic waste. She is concerned about her sons' futures and worries that daily disposables are not environmentally friendly.

Things to consider:

* What options are available to meet her clinical and ethical needs?
* How would you reassure her?

Actions

Emma is not alone in her concern about plastic use in the world of eyecare and eyewear. Plastic is used in packaging for contact lenses and lens solutions, as well as outer packaging for transport. Additionally, the industry depends on plastic for spectacle frames, spectacle lenses and contact lenses. While some plastics can be recycled, optical waste often includes mixes of different plastic types, as well as plastics mixed with metal, which makes recycling much harder to achieve.

Good vision from the right eyewear is critical for everyone, at school, at work and at home. Emma may be reassured by research showing that full-time contact lens wear represents just 0.20%–0.26% of the 412 kg of household waste generated per person per year in the United Kingdom and that manufacturers are looking at solutions to diminish the environmental impact of all types of eyewear.

DOI: 10.1201/9781003491583-4

If Emma wants to continue to wear contact lenses, she can recycle the lenses at an optical practice that offers this service. Alternatively, she could look at some of the wide range of spectacles made from reclaimed plastics and discuss the most sustainable lens options with the practice dispensing optician. She may consider making changes in other parts of her life, such as with an audit of her home plastic use to reduce her waste.

Case study courtesy of Elaine Grisdale, FBDO, FAOO.

Resources

Smith, S. et al. An investigation into disposal and recycling options for daily disposable and monthly replacement soft contact lens modalities, *Contact Lens and Anterior Eye*, Volume 45, Issue 2, 2022.

Introduction

Eyewear is essential for many people, whether for visual correction, safety eyewear or protection from the sun.

Moving towards more ethical eyewear. Manufacturers now offer frames made from wood, bamboo, plastics reclaimed from the ocean, used bottles and more. Research is being done on developing a circular economy for both spectacles and contact lenses, looking at both logistical and technical challenges. There is frequent news of innovations in this field.

As prescriptions change, as children grow, old spectacle frames and lenses are generated. Consumers ask practices whether they collect old frames. Sightsavers is clear that sending old frames to countries in the global south is **not** an option (1). It aims, instead, to support countries to develop their own infrastructure for eyecare and eyewear. Old frames and lenses must, therefore, be recycled, but this is a complex challenge.

Take a look at your own glasses. If you wear glasses, take them off for a moment and take a look: the plastic lens is made from a different type of plastic to the spectacle frames. The sides of a plastic frame often have a metal core to ensure they are robust and can be adapted to a patient's face, along with a metal hinge for strength and flexibility. Metal frames have plastic tips and nose pads. Many different types of plastics are used in frames and lens manufacture. The supply chain shows that a large part of optical manufacturing takes place in China. Manufacturers can source low-cost products – but there are emissions from travel, whether by boat or plane. If a customer orders a designer frame from Italy, that frame may be flown in. Lenses from China are cut down or glazed into frames; this is a process that creates wastewater mixed in with ground plastic particles which have to be filtered and separated.

Take a look at your contact lenses. Contact lenses raise similar issues to spectacles. The lenses are made from plastic. Soft lenses are supplied in a solution so they remain hydrated. The lens is contained in a tray (constructed from another type of plastic) with a foil and plastic lid. For daily disposables, each month's supply is usually contained in a cardboard box. Daily disposable lenses are the most popular modality of wear currently: although this may seem like a wasteful way to correct eyesight, there is not such a significant difference when compared to monthly soft lenses or rigid gas permeable lenses as both these options require contact lens solutions, bottles and packaging. The amount of plastic used in contact lenses is a fraction of an adult's daily plastic use.

Environmental impact on the eyes. The environment affects eye health.

- Indoor air pollution from environmental tobacco smoking, heating, cooking, or poor indoor ventilation is related to several eye diseases, including conjunctivitis, glaucoma, cataracts, and age-related macular degeneration (AMD).
- Outdoor pollution can lead to ocular surface changes, which researchers have tied to discomfort, allergic conjunctivitis, and retinopathy (2).
- Climate change can worsen these conditions. Increasing UV radiation exposure, rising air pollution, and warmer, drier conditions all increase the risk to human eye health (3).

People living in the most deprived communities are more likely to experience poorer environmental quality than those in the least deprived areas (4). The Royal College of Ophthalmologists has highlighted the link between poverty, health inequalities and increased risk of eye disease (5).

Eye care services. In primary care, eye care principally takes place in local optical practices, often seen on the high street and in shopping centres. These practices face a range of challenges at a time when fuel bills are rising, adding financial pressure to the environmental need to reduce greenhouse gas emissions. Practice owners and managers face outmoded buildings with poor insulation in locations where cars are often the primary way that staff and patients can access them. Simultaneously, the will to tackle climate change amongst eye care practitioners (ECP) and their professional bodies is clear, as evidenced by the Association of British Dispensing Opticians' *Thinking Green* campaign (6) and SEE Summit on the Environment (7) launched in 2021.

Eye health services can be resource intensive, with consumables, energy consumption and travel requirements contributing to rising GHG emissions. In this context, it is imperative to support ECPs, managers and support staff to take actions to deliver sustainable eye care.

Is progress being made? Many manufacturers, suppliers and ECPs have made a start on improving the system. In 2022, a number of UK optical bodies came together to issue the following statement (8):

> The top sustainability priorities for the optical sector are to reduce greenhouse gas emissions, to reduce waste and develop sustainable ways of practice.

Optical bodies will join together to help inform, educate and support their members, and review their own activities, in order to stimulate rigorous and immediate action to reduce greenhouse gas emissions within the optical sector in line with the current UK commitment of 78 percent by 2035 (compared to 1990). We will also develop targets to reduce waste, develop sustainable ways of practice, and deliver a healthier, fairer zero carbon world.

A promising start, yet, like all sectors, eye care has several challenges. In the United Kingdom, the way primary eye care is funded presents a challenge. The historically low level of funding for the NHS sight test has led to the cross-subsidy of clinical care with spectacle sales. While professional bodies and practitioners are working on initiatives to remedy this, the current situation means that practitioners need to sell products to balance the books in the majority of primary eye care settings.

There are plenty of initiatives to make frames from reclaimed and recycled plastics. Frames made from plant based materials such as wood and bamboo can be bought, and sustainable products feature large at optical trade shows. In 2023, the first lens made from bio-based plastic was launched. Manufacturers have developed water-free methods of glazing lenses into frames, as well as looking at how to cut emissions across their output. Researchers are looking at how to create a circular economy within eyecare. Suppliers are cutting back on packaging, using more sustainable and reusable materials and combining multiple orders into single deliveries.

What can ECPs do? In practice, ECPs are taking significant steps to play their part. There are a number of opticians' practices where sustainability is the top focus, attracting staff and patients who want a more sustainable approach to eyewear. Smarter use of utilities is driven by sustainability as well as cost, a sensible choice for business owners and managers, combined with staff initiatives to switch off and use less where possible.

Simple ways to make the optical world more sustainable. Sustainability is an ongoing journey for us all. Recognising every individual action is vital in contributing to an overall reduction in emissions and environmental harm.

Carbon footprinting. Calculate the greenhouse gases emitted by your business – either through online calculators and/or sustainability consultants – to determine your carbon footprint (9).

Once the practice footprint is known, actions can be prioritised. If there is an area of high emissions, this may be the best place to start. Others start with the easier tasks so they feel they are making progress.

In a study which examined the carbon footprint of a sight test at five locations, travel was found to be the leading cause of emissions, followed by energy use, emissions from procurement, waste, and, finally, water (10).

How to travel sustainably. Making travel more sustainable is something that you, your team, your patients and your customers can be involved in together for maximum results (see Chapter 11).

How to save energy at work. Actions optical businesses can take to save energy and cut costs are found in Chapter 10.

Moving towards sustainable purchasing. In addition to ideas in Chapter 12, optician-specific ideas include the following:

- Stock sustainable frames.
- Look for companies that offer paperless billing or consolidated billing through a buying group such as Sightcare.
- Consider using glazing labs that are local to the practice to cut down on transport emissions.
- Offer free or discounted refills of glasses cleaner.

Is zero business waste possible? The waste hierarchy is explained in Chapter 12. It emphasises rejecting excessive packaging and single-use items wherever possible. While recognising some packaging is essential to protect the product, inappropriate packaging is unacceptable.

Encouraging patients to reuse their own frames and cases is important but also presents challenges. Many practices rely on frame sales to offset clinical costs. Beyond this, there can be a risk of breakage in reglazing older frames. If reglazes are offered, make sure to explain the risks (and benefits) to the patient and have an open and transparent policy about what happens if things go wrong.

As an industry, lens waste is a big issue. How can old spectacle lenses be reused? Can the plastic sleeves be reused in some way? Are contact lenses and lens packaging recycled? What information is available in the practice and on the website about recycling for patients and customers? Guidance for patients to help them recycle spectacles, contact lenses and lens packaging could have a big impact.

Some items are harder to recycle, but some specialist schemes exist. Up-to-date lists of recycling schemes for old spectacles and spectacle cases can be found online.

Use your influence – and be creative! Artwork has been made from old and dummy lenses. Practices have upcycled items for exciting window displays. One practice said,

> We gifted a giant cardboard cutout Belle from Beauty and the Beast that was previously used in a princess frame themed window display to a local children's community group and we regularly gift boxes from large deliveries to locals for moving house.

What can I do this week?

- Can you start a conversation with the suppliers who are providing over-packaged or packaging products in excess plastic? Will they take back the packaging for reuse?

- Look at single-use items across the practice and consider sourcing reusable alternatives.
- Review the frame stock policy to avoid wastage. For example, get frames on consignment; try not to buy more frames in a year than are sold.
- Review all sundry stock policies to reduce wastage. For example, make sure expiry dates are reviewed regularly and that older stock is sold first. If product sales are managed, stock levels can be improved and waste cut.

What other ideas can you think of to reduce your environmental impact? Consider personal practice and wider influence on the system

1.
2.
3.

Going solo for sustainability. There are plenty of activities an individual can do. One very important action is becoming a sustainability advocate. Those moving from practice to practice can share ideas and good practice across different teams. This can help start a sustainability conversation by, for example, sharing details of local schemes for recycling with practices that have yet to start. As a locum, assist each place in finding one thing they can do to be more sustainable.

Build a sustainable community. A key part of sustainability is working together, ensuring that everyone has access to what they need. Being part of the wider community can help improve the environment, and it can build the business network and reputation too. Becoming more sustainable is a marathon, not a sprint. Everybody can make changes for the long term.

If you haven't done so already, why not

- take part in community litter picking,
- join a community water bottle refill scheme,
- take part in community vegetable growing,
- set up community composting,
- look for a drop-off point for community recycling, or
- encourage staff to participate in volunteering.

Make a great start in sustainability. There are lots of resources to support you in your sustainability journey. Visit the ABDO website (11) and explore their SEE Hub, where links to resources for ECPs and optical businesses are found. You can

- watch a video on initial steps to becoming a sustainable practice,
- download a template sustainability policy for your practice,

- find links to a range of sustainability standards,
- download some sustainability resources for your practice,
- complete the sustainability self-assessment tool and opt-in for three months of emails to help you make changes, or
- download the European Council of Optometry and Optics(ECOO) environmental sustainability guidance (12).
- submit a case study about your journey to sustainability.

There are schemes that you might want to take part in, such as Green Mark (13), Investors in the Environment (14) and Net Zero Optics (15).

Table 4.1 lists recommendations based on *The Annual Carbon Footprint of NHS Sight Tests at Five Optometry Practices* (10) – a place to start becoming more sustainable.

TABLE 4.1 Recommendations for action within optometry practices in the short, medium, and longer term.

		QUICK WINS	MEDIUM WINS	LONGER TERM WINS
General	Collect baseline carbon footprint data	*		
	Set up a green team	*		
	Collaborate beyond the practice		*	
	Monitor progress via self-assessment tools		*	
	Share results across the practice	*		
Travel	Carry out a travel survey of staff	*		
	Car-free day	*		
	Car sharing	*		
	Promote and enable active travel		*	
	Carry out a travel survey of patients	*		
	Consolidate/combine patient appointments	*		
	Promote sustainable travel options to patients		*	
	Consolidate deliveries		*	

(Continued)

TABLE 4.1 (Continued) Recommendations for action within optometry practices in the short, medium, and longer term.

		QUICK WINS	MEDIUM WINS	LONGER TERM WINS
Energy and water	Change energy supplier to 100% renewable	*		
	Switch off campaign	*		
	Install a smart meter	*		
	Check for water leaks	*		
Procurement	Procure most energy-efficient equipment			*
	Paperless office and sight tests	*		
	Only sustainable spectacles		*	
Waste	100% reusable or recyclable packaging		*	
	Carry out a waste audit	*		
	Recycle frames		*	
	Contact lens (and solution) recycling		*	

Pledges

Pledge – from this chapter, I will pledge to…

1.

2.

3.

Where next?

Chapter 9 to learn about sustainable quality improvement

Chapter 10 for energy and estates

Chapter 11 for travel and transport

Chapter 12 for goods and services

References

1 https://www.sightsavers.org/wp-content/uploads/2021/07/Sightsavers-Refractive-Error-Strategy.pdf

2 The Adverse Effects of Air Pollution on the Eye: A Review. *Int J Environ Res Public Health*. 2022 Jan 21;19(3):1186. doi: 10.3390/ijerph19031186. PMID: 35162209; PMCID: PMC8834466.

3 World Health Organisation. *Climate Change and Human Health Risks and Responses.* 2003. 001–017. https://www.who.int/publications-detail-redirect/climate-change-and-human-health---risks-and-rzesponses

4 Michael Marmot, Peter Goldblatt, Jessica Allen, et al. *Fair Society Healthy Lives.* 2010. https://www.instituteofhealthequity.org/resources-reports/fair-society-healthy-lives-the-marmot-review

5 Inequalities in Health Alliance calls on the PM to take action to "level up" health https://www.rcophth.ac.uk/news-views/inequalities-in-health-alliance-letter-to-pm/

6 https://www.abdo.org.uk/regulation-and-policy/abdo-policy-2/environmental-sustainability-policy/

7 https://www.abdo.org.uk/dashboard/see-hub/see-summit/

8 Press Release: Optical Bodies Collaborate to Release Statement of Intent on the Environment Association of British Dispensing Opticians. 2022. https://www.abdo.org.uk/about-us/media-centre/press-release-optical-bodies-collaborate-to-release-statement-of-intent-on-the-environment/

9 https://www.abdo.org.uk/dashboard/see-hub/see-hub-2-2/see-hub-cf/

10 The Annual Carbon Footprint of NHS Sight Tests at Five Optometry Practices. https://www.abdo.org.uk/wp-content/uploads/2022/03/The-Annual-Carbon-Footprint-of-NHS-Sight-Tests-at-Five-Optometry-Practices_1.pdf

11 www.abdo.org.uk

12 https://www.abdo.org.uk/wp-content/uploads/2023/01/ECOO-guidance-on-sustainability-January-2023.pdf

13 https://greenmark.co.uk/

14 https://www.iie.uk.com/

15 https://www.netzerooptics.com/

Resources

Visit www.abdo.org.uk to browse the SEE Hub for an extensive list of resources.

There are a number of companies now offering recycling of optical waste including:

- Recycline – spectacle frames – https://www.recycline.co.uk
- Refactory – spectacle frames – https://myrefactory.com/
- Terracycle – contact lenses – https://www.terracycle.com/en-GB/brigades/acuvue
- MyGroup – plastics – https://mygroupltd.com/recycling-box-schemes/
- Sightcare – https://www.sightcare.co.uk

5

Pharmacy
Min Na Eii, Clare Murray, and Wendy Tyler-Batt

Case study – Anticholinergic side effects

Brian, a 68-year-old obese retired archaeologist, visits his local community pharmacy to discuss his medication. He has chronic pain from his osteoarthritis. He takes co-codamol 8/500 mg (with some extra codeine at night) for pain and paroxetine for depression. He has chronic gastric reflux, which is well controlled by cimetidine. He has dermatitis and uses creams – betamethasone RD and Oilatum – and a nightly chlorphenamine 4 mg tablet. His diabetes is no longer diet controlled, and his friend suggests he should be on metformin tablets.

Things to consider:
- Do you think that each of his medications is justified individually?
- Is there good evidence for using each of them?
- What side effect patterns do these medications have in common?
- What ways could we support him to manage his conditions better?

The planetary health issue is the volume of medication being prescribed. In his case, he is prescribed medication which is an overload of drugs with an anticholinergic burden (ACB). A high score on an ACB Score calculator (38) or over 3 increases his risk of confusion, falls, and death. His ACB score is 9 before prescribing metformin (codeine = 1, paroxetine 3, cimetidine 2, chlorphenamine 3, metformin 1).

Both betamethasone and Oilatum are derived from oil and have an impact on water. Ask how often he is washing and whether he is using soap or (even worse, from a planetary health perspective because of the amount used each time he washes) shower gel. Soaps remove natural oils and normally exacerbate dermatitis.

Several of these drugs are prominent in the water supply due to excretion and non-clearance by sewage plants.

DOI: 10.1201/9781003491583-5

Anticholinergic burden. Certain medicines have antimuscarinic (anticholinergic) effects, which include constipation, dry mouth, dry eyes, urinary retention, falls, dizziness, sedation, confusion, agitation, delirium, and cognitive impairment. This can lead to an increased risk of hospital admission [and is a particular concern for people with existing cognitive impairment (39). Medicines commonly involved include certain antidepressants, antihistamines, antipsychotics, and urinary antispasmodics. Co-prescription of these medicines increases the anticholinergic burden and risk of adverse effects. Online calculators can help to identify the burden of individual medicines and combinations of medicines (38). Consider tapering when stopping these medications to avoid withdrawal effects, which may include nausea and sweating (39).

Actions

There are a number of alternative treatment options which can help reduce his medications:

- Obesity can improve with diet changes and increased physical activity.
- Depression can be managed with social or green/blue prescribing.
- Reflux may be improved through weight loss.
- Pain from osteoarthritis can be improved through weight loss.

There are some positive wins that can be had by reviewing ineffective drugs, as over-medication is a planetary health risk as well as being bad medical care:

- Eight milligrams of codeine is ineffective except to cause side effects.
- The effectiveness of Paracetamol for chronic pain is dubious.
- Alternative anti-reflux medication is available with lower ACB side effects and addressing obesity could make a big difference to this (as does raising the head of the bed).
- Antihistamines can exacerbate heat-related illnesses, as they reduce sweating for some.

Introduction

Medications, including inhalers and anaesthetic gases, form a significant proportion of the carbon footprint, a source of potential waste and environmental pollution in any health system. In the United Kingdom, the carbon footprint is estimated at about 25% of the NHS carbon footprint (see Figure 1.7 in Chapter 1). Although the primary care nature footprint has not yet been quantified, pharmaceutical pollution of water and land is likely to be one of the main sources of harm (1) (see Chapter 14).

There were an estimated 1.14 billion prescription items dispensed in England in 2021/2022 – an increase 6.4% from 1.07 billion items in 2014/2015 (2). Contributing factors include an ageing population, inactive lifestyles, and poor diet, leading to an increase in obesity, type 2 diabetes, and heart disease. Most (75%) prescribing takes place in primary care and with this comes a huge responsibility for ensuring every medication is appropriately prescribed.

There are negative health impacts and a significant financial and environmental burden, with an estimated 10% of prescriptions being unnecessary. Overprescribing is a serious problem internationally with complex cultural and systemic causes, and the adverse effects of medicines are linked to one in five hospital admissions (3). Previous research has found that between 30% and 50% of medication is not taken as intended (4). People experiencing health inequalities are less likely to seek help and advice and more likely to be prescribed medication inappropriately (5).

Primary care pharmacy teams. Pharmacy teams in primary care are broadly split into two sectors: working in General Practice as part of the wider healthcare team and in community pharmacy.

GP pharmacy team. Pharmacy teams have become an integral part of the wider General Practice team in the United Kingdom. The role has moved from a remote supportive and cost-saving function to patient-facing, with the ability to inform and influence patients on all aspects of medicines. In England, it is stipulated as part of the NHS long-term plan that the clinical pharmacist role is patient-facing (6). In Northern Ireland, it forms an integral part of the plan to transform General Practice into a sector capable of delivering multidisciplinary care close to patients' homes and reducing the overreliance on secondary care (7).

Community pharmacies. The traditional model of a community pharmacy is a retail outlet with qualified healthcare professionals providing a ready source of advice and support around medicines, and some clinical services for minor acute illnesses or for ongoing long-term conditions. A small minority in the United Kingdom operate online or as distance-selling pharmacies that don't typically provide one-to-one services but deliver their service obligations under contract for the NHS. Community pharmacies are encouraged to operate sustainably as part of their corporate social responsibility initiatives. A net-zero pharmacy may appear more attractive to customers or patients and improves the organisation's reputation in a competitive market (8).

The advent of split training posts across the sectors (9) bodes well for better future communication and collaboration with an increasing overlap in roles with opportunities to employ the following quick wins:

Recognise current practice. As pharmacy professionals, much of current practice, such as medicines optimisation, medication review, patient counselling, lifestyle advice, and cost savings, is already inherently positively contributing to sustainability and greener health and care. This is reassuring and empowering for teams and individuals managing the potential stressor of yet another addition to the "to-do"

Pressurised metered dose inhaler
London to Coventry – about 100 miles

Dry Powder inhaler
London to another bit of London – about 2 miles

FIGURE 5.1 Carbon footprint of metered dose inhaler versus dry powder inhaler.

list. Minor tweaks to messaging in written and verbal communication to patients are impactful (examples include texts, labelling, letters, posters, counselling).

Changing conversations. It is appropriate with everyone, colleagues and patients alike, to weave environmental impact into discussions about medicines and prescribing to prompt thinking from an additional perspective – the lens of sustainability for better patient and planetary health.

Carbon literacy. Becoming "Carbon Literate" is probably one of the most important actions for communicating an understanding of the widely used term "carbon footprint" – e.g., using a meaningful analogy to patients, such as car journeys to an inhaler carbon footprint. The Carbon Literacy Project has healthcare-specific Carbon Literacy training (10). Figure 5.1 provides a useful pictorial representation which could be incorporated into conversations with patients.

Medication reviews. Medication reviews are fundamental to the pharmacy team's role and cover all aspects of medicines optimisation – ensuring clinically effective and cost-effective prescribing. Reviews may be planned or opportunistic, and many frameworks and templates are available in GP practice systems for detailed reviews known as "Structured Medication Reviews" (SMRs) in England. The inclusion of sustainability and consideration of environmental impact is not yet widely included outside respiratory care templates.

Top tip: Establishing a patient's knowledge and beliefs at the outset is essential to tailor a consultation

Remote consultations. The CONSULT guide is a very useful tool to help structure remote consultations and ensure that pharmacy teams approach them consistently and safely for all patients (11).

Since COVID-19, there has been a substantial rise in the number of consultations across primary care conducted over the telephone or through video software technologies. Remote consultation methods have the advantage of reducing the carbon footprint of journeys to the practice. However, the appropriateness of the remote consultation must be determined. If deemed more appropriate to have a one-to-one appointment, this should be offered and perhaps may be linked to another appointment (e.g., for blood tests) to reduce the number of visits to the practice.

The opportunity to follow up consultations with written communication via a text message has become routine practice since its adoption during COVID-19. A standard message such as, *"Please ensure all unwanted medication and inhalers are returned to a pharmacy for safe disposal to protect the environment"* can be sent. Information and guides on the carbon impact of inhalers are available (12, 13).

Care must be taken to ensure that the health and digital literacy of all patients is respected. Those who do not have or are unable to use the full IT facilities of a mobile phone should not be disadvantaged. They should be supplied with information in an appropriate format, including those who are not able to read/whose first language is not English.

Discussion of sustainability and environmental impact in the consultation notes is another way of raising awareness among the practice team members, who may subsequently read the notes.

A follow-up phone call to establish the success of a prescribing recommendation with notable environmental impact should always be documented. Patients are often very motivated by sustainability and feel very empowered when taking positive action for environmental impact, whether it is reducing/stopping their medication, changing to a lower-carbon alternative, or returning medication to the pharmacy.

Housebound/post-discharge patients. Another opportunity that needs to be seized is a review of post-hospital discharge and housebound patients. Medications may be started during a hospital admission with uncertainty about whether or not continued prescribing is necessary in the community. In England, hospital, community, and GP pharmacy teams can utilise the NHS Discharge Medication Service, which is an integrated approach to support patients with medicines reconciliation and optimisation following discharge (14). The capacity for home visits from the practice pharmacy team may be limited, but some good work has been done showing the value of this intervention with the assistance of the wider healthcare team simultaneously addressing sustainability and health inequalities (Deb Gomperz – *"Show me your meds"* [15]). Housebound patients should receive a holistic review inclusive of medication, ideally involving a member of the pharmacy team.

Repeat prescribing protocols. A huge potential source of waste, cost, and environmental impact is the overordering of medication. There are many reasons for this – patients are concerned that if the medication is not ordered regularly, it will be removed from the repeat medication list; medication review has not been effectively carried out; repeat prescriptions ordered on behalf of patients who might not be taking them anymore; patients order because they believe this is what the prescriber expects.

General Practices should aim to have a robust repeat prescribing protocol. This will help to reduce the waste associated with inappropriate supply of medicines on repeat by ensuring the following:

i) Repeats are linked to a defined medication review date.

ii) Only the patient is responsible for ordering new prescriptions (e.g., by use of the NHS app in England). Where this is not possible, the practice should have robust processes in place to ensure the requests are reviewed.

iii) Good communication exists between the practice and community pharmacy team.

iv) Re-issue of prescriptions flags up over- or under- ordering.

v) Fifty-six-day prescribing is used where appropriate for patients whose medication is stable, and there is a positive history of adherence. This guidance followed research in Wales (16) that has shown this to be a realistic balance for waste (and therefore sustainability) for suitable patients.

vi) Good relationship and communication between GP and community pharmacy teams – e.g., use of Accumail, which documents exchanges in the patient record (17).

Where available, practices should promote online ordering of medicines to improve safety but also to reduce paper waste generated or unnecessary journeys to the surgery. Continuing telephone repeat prescription lines aid elderly patients in ordering their medications.

Elsewhere, while awaiting the introduction of electronic prescriptions, General Practice should aim to have robust relationships with designated local pharmacies. Good lines of communication around the processes involved in the generation of repeat prescriptions related to timelines and managed collection times will ensure that unnecessary journeys are not made by community pharmacy colleagues to collect prescriptions from neighbouring General Practices.

Using the Centre for Sustainable Healthcare's four principles of sustainable healthcare (18), the following explores how community pharmacies can promote environmental sustainability (see Chapter 9).

Four key elements:

1. Better at preventing illness
2. Patient empowerment to self-care
3. Leaner service design and delivery
4. Use lower-carbon alternatives

1. **Better at preventing illness**
   Non-pharmacological alternatives to medication should be the first consideration for **all** pharmacy teams before any medication is prescribed or offered as an over-the-counter remedy and then again at reviews (see Chapter 8).

   Community pharmacies are in the heart of communities, ideally placed to promote the public health services they provide, offer lifestyle advice and signpost to local health and well-being services. These can include weight or hypertension management, smoking cessation, travel, and flu vaccinations. Through shared-decision making and person-centred care, Healthy Living Pharmacies can tackle the wider social determinants of health to keep their communities healthier based on local priorities to address health inequalities.

Pharmacy staff can signpost patients to health and well-being coaches or social prescribers, or they can signpost 'link workers' available through their GP practices for a range of local, non-clinical services. An example would be green social prescribing, where people are supported to engage in nature-based interventions and green/blue activities to improve their mental and physical health, reduce loneliness and promote pro-environmental behaviours. Patients may be referred to local walking schemes, community gardening projects, conservation volunteering, green gyms (all "green" – land-based activities), open water swimming (a "blue" activity that involves water), or arts and cultural activities which take place outdoors. The lack of widespread timely access to mental health services or social prescribing continues to encourage the early prescribing of antidepressants.

2. **Patient empowerment to self-care**
   Hospital admissions have a significant carbon footprint. Appropriate prescribing and review will help keep patients well and out of hospital. It is essential that patients know what to do when there is a change of circumstance, e.g., a personalised asthma management plan for an exacerbation of asthma; follow "sick-day rules" (19) in the event of extreme dehydration due to a heat wave/illness and certain medications, e.g., diuretics, ACE-inhibitors/ARBs, metformin, or non-steroidal anti-inflammatory drugs (NSAIDs); and have an infection and are prescribed steroids.

   Community pharmacies' presence on many high streets and within large supermarkets, often on a walk-in basis, makes them easily accessible for treatment advice for minor ailments and self-care.

   Community pharmacies can also support medication adherence at home by issuing medication reminder charts for patients and carers, and moving away from dispensing single-use plastic dosette boxes (see next section). Patients should be coached to use digital healthcare applications on their smart devices to better manage their long-term conditions which require regular tracking to improve management. Efforts should be made to reduce unequal health access for patients who are not digitally literate to order their repeat prescriptions online and only order items when required without stockpiling at home.

   Multi-compartment compliance aids (MCCAs). MCCAs (or a limited seven-day supply in individual boxes) may be suitable where it is deemed clinically unsafe for a patient to have access to a large supply of medication – e.g., where there is a risk of overdose. Evidence to support increased patient adherence with the implementation of a weekly supply of medication in a "compliance aid" is limited (20). Some community pharmacies have procured biodegradable single-dose pill pouches or boxes to support medication taking at home for those who will benefit the most – e.g., those with increasing frailty. A robust assessment process is the first step after a request for an MCCA has been made – very often, the request is not from the patient but a family member, social care, or another healthcare professional. This presents an ideal opportunity to review medication, not just what is prescribed but to simplify regimens to once daily wherever practical. This or another adjustment, such as large print labels or counselling on linking administration to a daily activity – e.g., cleaning teeth – is often all that is needed.

Supply of medication in MCCAs results (21) in the following:

1. Increased workload to prepare and supply
2. Not all medication is suitable for supply in a compliance tray (22)
3. Medicines, once removed from their original packaging, become unlicensed
4. MCCAs carry significant risk of harm to patients, especially at points of care transition, for example, following discharge from hospital
5. A request for seven-day prescriptions (increase NHS costs)
6. Lack of ease and flexibility to change doses and stop/start medication without the return of the MCCA to the community pharmacy
7. Patient adherence may not improve, as patients may "cherry-pick" and choose to take some medications over others
8. Patients and carers may experience difficulty in identification of individual medications not in their original packaging
9. MCCAs are not a solution for patients with poor sight, unable to read, or with dementia
10. MCCAs disempower patients
11. Increased waste. Some MCCA packaging may be recyclable, but if any medication is remaining, the MCCA in its entirety has to be disposed of as waste medication

All of the above have the potential for a negative impact on environmental sustainability.

The New Medicines Service (NMS) is a free service offered by community pharmacies in England to help patients who have been prescribed a new medicine for certain long-term conditions, e.g., checking the technique of inhalers prescribed for asthma or COPD to assist adherence, e.g., to prevent excessive use of Short-Acting Beta Agonists (SABAs such as salbutamol) and reduce disease exacerbations and related emergency attendances to healthcare settings due to poor disease control.

Medicines disposal. The acceptance of unwanted/expired medication by a patient to any community pharmacy is a contractual obligation (23). However, many pharmacies have limited storage facilities and may need further financial support for increased waste collections from waste providers to ensure this is positively encouraged. Patients and carers should be counselled to return any unused or expired medication and all inhalers to a pharmacy for safe disposal and avoidance of environmental pollution. An informal survey showed only 16% of patients knew that returning their inhalers to the pharmacy was the most environmentally friendly way to dispose of their inhalers; however, 96% said they would be happy to do so. Between 30% and 90% of medicines taken orally are excreted and enter the waterways (24) as "pharmaceuticals in the environment" (PIE). These drug residues are not removed by wastewater treatment plants and have known antimicrobial resistance (AMR) and possibly other unknown environmental impacts (15).

A further consideration is the disposal of the packaging: blister packs, dry powder inhalers, and plastics (e.g., disposable insulin pens). In the United Kingdom, there are no comprehensive, widely available recycling schemes. Where applicable, community pharmacies have taken part in pilot medication recycling schemes (e.g., blister packs, inhalers, insulin), but this required significant coordination with multiple stakeholders, such as private companies, local councils, and communications teams, to effectively promote the uptake of the scheme, and approved clinical waste carriers. All those that are, or have been, available are restricted geographically and for a limited number of products.

There is potential for reducing the obligatory paper information leaflets currently included in every dispensing pack of medication. The option to include a QR code on the box for patients to scan would reduce this waste considerably. Some packs are unnecessarily large and banded together with plastic outers. Another source of waste and potential confusion is the supply by the manufacturers in 28-day or 30-day packs. A decision made by the industry to provide packs of one or other size would help with waste, cost, and the inevitable cumulative misaligning of patient medication supply over time with packs of 28 needing 13 prescriptions per annum and those of 30, 12 per annum.

Antimicrobial resistance (AMR). AMR is a global health and environmental challenge (25) and is a consequence of overuse and incorrect disposal of antibiotics, as well as poor infection prevention and control. GP pharmacy teams have an education role with the wider healthcare professionals (HCPs) team to prevent antibiotics being prescribed inappropriately – e.g., use of the FEVERPAIN tool (26), delayed prescriptions, or not prescribing before analysis of sputum/urine samples unless a delayed prescription might represent a serious threat to the health of the individual. Community pharmacy and GP pharmacy teams have an important role in educating the general public in self-care and the expected trajectory of recovery for many common ailments. Despite public health campaigns, patients still demand antibiotics inappropriately.

Patients should be advised to

- only use antibiotics when prescribed for them;
- to complete a prescribed course in full;
- never share antibiotics with another patient or use leftover antibiotics prescribed for another patient;
- prevent infections by regularly washing hands, preparing food hygienically; and
- dispose of unwanted antibiotics via the community pharmacy.

Activity. There are many educational resources available, including videos for waiting rooms (27).

Patients should also be encouraged to be active/made aware of the benefits of active travel and how this improves the health and well-being of themselves and the community. Walking, cycling, or taking public transport to the pharmacy will reduce air pollution, the overall costs, and the carbon footprint associated with motor vehicles used to deliver medications to people's homes if they can walk or cycle to their local pharmacies. The message is more powerful if the pharmacy team has made changes to walk or lift share.

3. **Leaner service design and delivery**

Community pharmacies should adopt digital technological solutions where applicable to minimise paper use, such as having electronic records for controlled drugs and private prescriptions. A community pharmacy in Sheffield has succeeded in adopting a paperless dispensing system, which saves printing 16,000 Electronic Prescription Service paper prescriptions monthly (28). Digital solutions should also be adopted by GP practices to send prescriptions electronically to community pharmacies to save time and travel for patients or consolidate prescriptions in order to reduce the number of visits to various healthcare settings.

Community pharmacies should also have sensible ordering practices where they adequately stock the store's most dispensed items to ensure ready access for patients to avoid signposting to another pharmacy and reduce the number of deliveries from wholesalers required. Efficient inventory management with regular expiry date checking and stock rotation can reduce medicines waste and also improve timely patient access to treatments required.

Collection of prescribed items. As part of the collection process, as automatic as checking the patient name and address for correct identification, we should be asking the patient to check their medications before they leave the pharmacy premises. Any medication that does not leave the pharmacy can then be reused. This generates potential cost and environmental savings, and an opportunity to refer patients for a medication review if the medication that has been prescribed is not wanted or not taken for a number of reasons, with a further benefit of improving health outcomes.

4. **Use lower-carbon alternatives**

Community pharmacies should regularly liaise with and be updated by their local medicines optimisation team (e.g., Integrated Care Boards in England) about formulary and guideline changes to ensure they adequately stock lower-carbon alternatives. This avoids leaving patients a duration gap between ordering and receiving their repeat medications and reduces unnecessary doubling of their visits to their pharmacy.

Choosing drug formulations. Liquid medication has a higher carbon footprint than solid formulations (packaging, transport, shelf life, volume of production). It is prescribed where there are perceived or real swallowing difficulties – e.g., in children and stroke patients. There are often alternatives, such as crushing tablets or orodispersible formulations, which are often less costly and have a lower-carbon footprint (29). It is often assumed that children will not be able to swallow tablets, even when the liquid alternatives (e.g., some antibiotics) are often refused because they are found to be unpalatable.

Help is at hand with some recent initiatives (30); clinicians made clear use of the techniques advocated by the KidzMed project so that parents and children could be supported to swallow solid dosage forms. The use of solid dosage forms in place of liquid medicines is not only beneficial for the environment but also clinically safer, more convenient, and cost-effective (Figure 5.2).

FIGURE 5.2 Kidzmed poster demonstrating the technique to teach children to swallow pills.

(Authors Emma Lim, Ailsa Pickering, Great North Children's Hospital for content and artist Becky Stephenson).

Case study

KidzMed project teaches children and young people how to swallow pills

Most medicines are in pill form, and swallowing pills is an important life skill for children to learn; training has been developed to help HCPs and carers teach children and young people how to swallow pills. In addition, their website (31) contains resources to help you set up pill-swallowing training at your local centre.

Greener pharmacy guide and toolkit. In 2023, the Royal Pharmaceutical Society (RPS) was commissioned by NHS England to develop a guide and self-accreditation web platform for hospital and community pharmacies to benchmark their sustainability status. The actions listed in the guide and toolkit are similar to what has been outlined earlier in "Greener Community Pharmacy", where there are three levels of community pharmacy actions. GP Practice or PCN Pharmacists were encouraged to use the RCGP's Green Impact for Health Toolkit (32) for similar accreditation of GP surgeries, and the community pharmacy staff in Wales were encouraged to undertake the Greener Primary Care Wales Framework and Award Scheme from Public Health Wales (33). Further development of the guide and toolkit are tailored to community pharmacies in Scotland and Northern Ireland.

Completing the toolkit brings multiple co-benefits, such as increasing productivity through time, cost, and resource-saving actions, improving staff and population health, reducing waste, and promoting a circular economy. Simple actions such as not having single-use plastic cutleries or cups in the pharmacy tea room reduce global plastic pollution, switching off lights or electrical devices when not in use, and operational building changes such as switching to all LED light bulbs and installing light sensors in low use areas reduce energy use and businesses' running costs. Where possible, community pharmacies can work with organisations such as NHS Forest to create green spaces (e.g., gardens, green roofs) which can benefit mental health and well-being for staff and patients, promote biodiversity, and provide natural shading or insulation.

Pharmacy education. Given that we need all pharmacists to be both engaged and motivated to practise greener pharmacy, our undergraduate and foundation year teaching has a significant role to play. Embedding the principles of sustainability into pharmacy education was officially endorsed by the Pharmacy Schools Council in the United Kingdom in June 2023. The Sustainability in Pharmacy Education group produced a document, *Environmental Sustainability in Pharmacy Education*, mapping sustainability to the General Pharmaceutical Council (GPhC) learning outcomes provided within the Standards for the initial education and training of pharmacists (34). These Standards must be attained by all pharmacy students prior to their registration with their professional body. Their goal is to ensure that all future pharmacists have the necessary knowledge, skills, understanding, and professional behaviours to provide patient care from their first day on the register.

For pharmacy educators and educational supervisors, the document provides useful ideas and strategies for informing teaching on environmental sustainability. The document ensures a consistent approach across the 31 schools of pharmacy within the United Kingdom. The document also provides useful case studies from universities across the United Kingdom and how they have successfully embedded and implemented sustainability into their undergraduate degree programmes. Examples include the use of scrubs for placements and practicals to avoid the use of single-use plastic aprons, ethical debates focusing on the reuse of patient-returned medicine, and the mapping of course learning outcomes to the UN SDGs.

The Association of Pharmacy Technicians UK has committed to the education of its members on their role in environmental sustainability and addressing the climate emergency. As an organisation, they have moved to holding meetings and training via online platforms to reduce travel.

Qualified pharmacists and pharmacy technicians have many opportunities available to them for postgraduate Continuing Professional Development (CPD) related to the topics, extending from short one-hour online modules to postgraduate masters focused on sustainability in healthcare.

Barriers and enablers to sustainable pharmacy practice

Prescribing by carbon footprint. The availability of the carbon footprint and environmental impact of medicines would represent a huge step forward in informing prescribing choices. Research in progress has established that approximately 80% of the carbon footprint of medicines is attributable to the manufacturing process of the "active pharmaceutical ingredient". NHS England announced at COP28 that they are working with the British Standards Institute to agree on a methodology for the carbon footprint calculation (35).

Remuneration model/incentivisation. The current community pharmacy remuneration model is skewed towards dispensing volume with no financial incentive not to dispense medication. This is not in the interest of patient or planetary health; it leads to poorer health outcomes, wastage and pollution, and greater expense to the health system. Incentive schemes for community pharmacy review and stopping medicines would change this culture. A place where influencing and working with commissioning bodies is essential.

Access to GP records. In the United Kingdom, community pharmacies do not have access to the patient's GP records. This limits the advice and support the community pharmacist can offer a patient. International provision of access to local GP records by community pharmacists would help reduce waste and the inappropriate supply of medications, such as at points of care transition – e.g., discharge from hospital.

Medicines reuse. Legal barriers (such as Medicines and Healthcare products Regulatory Agency (MHRA) regulations) currently exist for the reuse of medicines that left the pharmacy premises after dispensing to named patients and returned to them by patients. It is considered unethical to reuse patient returns – including medication that is returned unopened and in-date – a disincentive for patients to return medication. Research has been carried out by exploring stakeholder views of medicines reuse by Reading University (36). Heat-sensitive barcode technology exists which could be employed to check exposure to adverse temperatures (37).

Medicines supply shortages. This is an ongoing issue in the United Kingdom, exacerbated by Brexit through reduced purchasing power and compounded by pressure from the NHS to procure medicines at the lowest price; it has resulted in system inefficiencies, including increased communication to procure supplies for individual patients, alternatives not being acceptable, less time to spend with patients counselling and reviewing medication, and potential poorer health outcomes. There are increased financial costs in terms of labour, alternative product procurement, and increased wastage with an environmental impact.

Health inequalities. Patients with a low income or who are unemployed live in poorer housing associated with poorer insulation, often with less access to green spaces, and in areas with the highest air pollution. They are often less likely to seek out health services and yet are likely to have the greatest needs. This is likely to be the case for some ethnic minorities – e.g., those without English as a first language, with widely different cultural beliefs. Pharmacy professionals need to be aware of and empower these groups where at all possible, including encouragement to seek access to services/council for home improvements, signposting to community services, and lifestyle interventions that the individual can act on – e.g., smoking cessation, healthy eating.

Better communication. Historically, communication has been problematic between community and General Practice pharmacy teams. This has improved with the use of software embedded in patient records – e.g., Accumail. Furthermore, split posts where pharmacy team members work in both settings generate understanding, flexibility, and goodwill, which is happening now in England (UK-wide) as part of trainee pharmacist training and apprentice technician schemes.

Workforce. There is a global-wide shortage of pharmacy professionals which has implications for continuity of patient care, patient safety issues, and communication across pharmacy sectors.

Pharmacogenomics. Pharmacogenomics is the study of how a person's genes affect their response to a medicine. It combines the pharmacist's key foundational knowledge in pharmacology with an understanding of genomics. The overall goal is the development of and prescribing of medicines tailored to the person's genetic makeup. This therefore has the potential to reduce the inappropriate prescribing of medicines to patients and to reduce medicines waste consequentially. However, it would be inappropriate not to consider the environmental impact drug development has in its own right. Considerable environmental impact is derived from molecule development and ongoing drug development processes. Pharmacogenomics is also a highly data-driven process, with the digital sector contributing 2.1%–3.9% of the global carbon emissions. We need an ongoing commitment to work with the pharmaceutical industry to ensure that this emerging sector of medicine is developed and expanded with a focus on the environmental impact.

Conclusion

The pharmacy sector in primary care has been proactive in raising and spreading the communication of sustainability and greener healthcare with medicines. This has been augmented with supporting organisations such as Greener Practice, Pharmacy Declares and the Greener PCPA. The inclusion of sustainability throughout the undergraduate and postgraduate curricula will ensure sustainability and that greener healthcare is an automatic consideration in all clinical and prescribing decisions. Split training posts across community and General Practice bodes well for better communication and teamwork in the future.

Pledges

Pledge – from this chapter, I will pledge to…

1.
2.
3.

Where next?

Chapter 9 to learn about sustainable quality improvement
Chapter 10 for energy and estates
Chapter 11 for travel and transport
Chapter 12 for goods and services

References

1   https://www.thelancet.com/journals/lanplh/article/PIIS2542-5196(22)00309-6/fulltext
2   PCA England nhsbsa-opendata.s3.eu-west-2.amazonaws.com
3   https://assets.publishing.service.gov.uk/government/uploads/system/uploads/attachment_data/file/1019475/good-for-you-good-for-us-good-for-everybody.pdf
4   https://www.nice.org.uk/guidance/qs120/chapter/Introduction
5   https://www.nice.org.uk/about/what-we-do/nice-and-health-inequalities
6   NHS Long-Term Plan "Clinical pharmacists vital to patient care in five-year GP deal". https://www.england.nhs.uk/2019/01/clinical-pharmacists-vital-to-patient-care-in-five-year-gp-deal/
7   Pharmacist Workforce Survey 2022 doh-pharmacy-workforce-review.pdf health-ni.gov.uk

8   Public Health Wales. Time to Talk Public Health. https://phw.nhs.wales/topics/time-to-talk-public-health-panel/time-to-talk-public-health-panel-publications/publications/time-to-talk-public-health-june-2023-panel-survey-findings/

9   https://www.pharmacyregulation.org/sites/default/files/document/gphc-pharmacist-foundation-training-manual-2021-22.pdf

10 https://carbonliteracy.com/toolkits/healthcare/

11 https://pharmaceutical-journal.com/article/ld/remote-consultations-how-pharmacy-teams-can-practise-them-successfully

12 https://www.prescqipp.info/umbraco/surface/authorisedmediasurface/index?url=%2fmedia%2f6213%2finhaler-carbon-footprint-comparison-tool-21.pdf

13 https://humberandnorthyorkshire.org.uk/wp-content/uploads/2023/09/HNY-Asthma-Guideline-Final.pdf

14 https://www.england.nhs.uk/primary-care/pharmacy/nhs-discharge-medicines-service/

15 https://www.bgs.org.uk/bgs-green-issues-show-me-your-meds-please

16 https://pure.southwales.ac.uk/ws/portalfiles/portal/5948986/FINAL_REPORT_Review_of_dispensing_volumes_in_CP_March_2021.pdf

17 https://www.accurx.com/accumail

18 https://www.rcpjournals.org/content/clinmedicine/10/2/110

19 https://www.gov.uk/government/publications/hot-weather-and-health-supporting-vulnerable-people/supporting-vulnerable-people-before-and-during-hot-weather-healthcare-professionals

20 https://doi.org/10.1002/psb.1865

21 https://www.bmj.com/content/362/bmj.k2801

22 https://www.sps.nhs.uk/home/tools/medicines-in-compliance-aids-stability-tool/

23 https://cpe.org.uk/national-pharmacy-services/essential-services/disposal-of-unwanted-medicines/

24 https://pharmaceutical-journal.com/article/feature/pharmaceuticals-in-the-environment-a-growing-problem

25 https://www.nature.com/articles/s41579-021-00649-x

26 https://cks.nice.org.uk/topics/sore-throat-acute/diagnosis/diagnosing-the-cause/

27 https://medsdisposal.eu/pharmaceuticals-and-the-environment/

28 https://cpe.org.uk/our-news/it-case-study-pharmacy-in-sheffield-goes-paperless/

29 https://www.newtguidelines.com/

30 https://www.e-lfh.org.uk/programmes/kidzmed/

31 https://www.nenc-healthiertogether.nhs.uk/parentscarers/medicine-children/pill-swallowing-kidzmed

32 https://greenimpact.nus.org.uk/green-impact-for-health/

33 https://primarycareone.nhs.wales/topics1/greener-primary-care/

34 https://www.pharmacyregulation.org/initial-training

35 https://www.sustainable-markets.org/news/global-healthcare-leaders-advance-sector-decarbonisation-ahead-of-cop28/

36 https://www.mdpi.com/2226-4787/8/2/58

37 https://jamanetwork.com/journals/jamaoncology/article-abstract/2811990

38 https://www.acbcalc.com/

39 https://bmcgeriatr.biomedcentral.com/articles/10.1186/s12877-022-03235-9

Resources

https://www.greenerpractice.co.uk/information-and-resources/clinical-considerations/prescribing-and-deprescribing/

https://www.arthritis.org/health-wellness/healthy-living/nutrition/weight-loss/weight-loss-benefits-for-arthritis

6

Planetary health in a GP surgery
Mike Tomson

How does planetary health relate to the patients that are seen across primary care every day? The majority of the chapters in this book start with a person seen in primary care. This chapter is an example of clinical cases seen during a "morning surgery" in General Practice, during a heat wave, in the United Kingdom.

8:30 a.m. – Flu-like illness

Hamza, a 36-year-old bank clerk, recently flew back to the United Kingdom from a weekend break to Southern France and presented with a flu-like illness. He describes feeling exhausted with a fever, rash, and vomiting. He tells you he had lots of mosquito bites when in Southern France and feels just like on his gap year when lots of his friends got unwell in Southeast Asia.

Things to consider:

- What are the likely or possible causes?
- Which types of mosquitoes are involved?
- What is the effect of planetary health changes on the distribution of mosquitoes?
- Does increased heat affect the speed of the reproduction or the amount mosquitoes feed or bite?

In this case, the best fit is dengue – although Zika also causes flu-like symptoms and can cause a rash. Malaria can also have skin signs, though these are rarer.

DOI: 10.1201/9781003491583-6

Changing patterns of infectious diseases mean "tropical" diseases will become more common. This is for several reasons:

- The vectors that transmit them are surviving better in a broader band of countries.
- Rates of reproduction speed up as it gets warmer, and the vectors get hungrier if hot and so bite more and grow faster.
- Only female mosquitoes bite.
- The Aedes aegypti mosquito is reported as endemic in London and East Anglia. It is a mosquito linked to dengue, Zika, and yellow fever, but not malaria.
- Malaria is endemic, though, in Spain, and mosquitoes capable of spreading West Nile fever are found as far north as Finland.
- Malaria (Plasmodium) is spread by Anopheles mosquitoes.

What actions can reduce the risk?

Prevention would be either primary through reducing mosquito reproduction or secondary through nets or clothing, with insect repellent as a last line.

Resources

https://dermnetnz.org/topics/malaria-and-its-skin-signs

8:45 a.m. – Stroke symptoms

Archie, an 80-year-old retired postman, presented with a sudden onset, one-sided weakness of his face and slurred speech. He lives with his similarly aged wife in a deprived neighbourhood. He has been on treatment with a thiazide and calcium channel blocker for hypertension. He was otherwise fit and well.

Things to consider:

- How does heat make people more likely to die directly and through its effects on the cardiovascular system?
- Will his drugs have made this more or less likely?
- Should "drug holidays" in hot weather be considered?
- Is living in a deprived neighbourhood relevant to the stroke (and if so, how?)?
- Do you normally consider planetary health when you see somebody with a stroke/transient ischaemic attack (TIA) or heart attack and it's hot or when they live in a deprived neighbourhood? Should you?

Strokes (and heart attacks) are much more common in extreme heat due to cardiovascular overload, with an increased incidence of death in the over 65s.

Living in a deprived neighbourhood makes poor air quality more likely, which further increases the risk of ischaemic heart disease or stroke. The World Health Organization

(WHO) identified air pollution as the second-greatest preventable cause of death behind smoking, but with a bigger effect than alcohol and other causes.

Planetary health impacts are not usually considered when people present with a stroke or heart attack.

In the United Kingdom, the number of deaths from heat waves is much lower than the number killed due to cold weather, though prolonged heat waves are a new cause of additional mortality.

Action

The United Kingdom has an adverse weather and health plan: does the practice have a plan? Review the patient's medication:

- Thiazides might be expected to increase dehydration.
- Peripheral vasodilation drugs like Ca channel blockers will increase cardiac load if it is hot: there is not currently UK advice to take a drug holiday from particular drugs when it is hot, though there is advice that some drugs will make heat-related morbidity more likely. Warn patients in advance what to do in the event of a heat wave with their medication.

Practices can sign up for local heat and health impact alerts within the United Kingdom at https://www.gov.uk/guidance/weather-health-alerting-system.

Resources

https://www.greenerpractice.co.uk/information-and-resources/clinical-considerations/prescribing-and-deprescribing/

https://www.gov.uk/guidance/weather-health-alerting-system

Report on impact on NHS https://static1.squarespace.com/static/6391e85d016fa00803f1c14d/t/649aec54f32c912fa7c343bb/1687874667248/NHS+OVERHEATING+-+Round+Our+Way+report+-+June+2023+-+FINAL.pdf

https://www.nidirect.gov.uk/conditions/heat-exhaustion-and-heatstroke

9 a.m. – Difficulty coping

Alannah, a 30-year-old woman, is seeking asylum. She presents with poor sleep, poor concentration, and angry outbursts which have been present since her long journey to the United Kingdom. She tells you she is struggling to cope.

Things to consider:

- What diagnosis is likely here after the journey she has had?
- What could be done?
- If the country she has moved from is much less habitable due to increasing heat and drought, and as the largest contributor to climate change is the global west, then are "we" collectively responsible for her?

"Climate migration" is migration caused by climate change.

Several factors include heat waves (globally, there have been twice as many days over 50° C as 30 years ago) and flooding (currently, 600 million people live within 10 m of sea level globally). Additionally, increasing global population plus less habitable space results in more migration.

She is likely to suffer from post-traumatic stress disorder (PTSD) and mental health issues. How well recognised is PTSD across cultural barriers and via interpreters? In the United Kingdom, all those registered with a GP are entitled to full NHS free primary care services, including mental health provision in primary care (and legally patients don't need an address or paperwork to register with a GP).

The global north is responsible for the majority of emissions causing the climate crisis. This is a combination of burning fossil fuels and deforestation. The link between rising CO_2e levels and temperature changes was first identified in 1859 (by Dr John Tyndall – https://tyndall.ac.uk/). Is it our responsibility to support those affected by climate change?

Actions

Assess for PTSD, depression, and anxiety.

What support networks are available locally which can help with meeting the basic needs (shelter, food, water, healthcare, etc.)?

What opportunities for implementing lifestyle medicine exist, and how can they benefit the patient?

Resources

https://www.doctorsoftheworld.org.uk/safesurgeries/safe-surgeries-toolkit/
Benefits of green/blue prescribing are varied but significant
https://www.greenerpractice.co.uk/information-and-resources/clinical-considerations/
    nature-and-health/
https://www.carbonbrief.org/analysis-which-countries-are-historically-responsible-
    for-climate-change/

9:15 a.m. – Skin lesions

Jimmy, a 60-year-old agricultural labourer, comes in asking whether the changes on his face are skin cancers. He has had a basal cell carcinoma in the past.

Things to consider:

- What are the worrying lesions that he may have?
- Are there more benign skin lesions to consider too?
- How do we prevent these?
- Should skin protection be more available on the NHS?

Both malignant melanomas and squamous cell carcinomas (SCCs) and non-malignant basal cell carcinomas (BCCs) have a higher incidence with sun exposure and sun damage. Cases are expected to rise over the coming decade.

Prevention is by avoiding skin burning. Some sun exposure is required to allow vitamin D creation, but the safe amount of time in the sun depends on how easily the individual's skin burns and how well covered the person is.

There are over 16,000 new melanoma diagnoses in the United Kingdom annually. It has been calculated that 4,000 of these are linked to poverty and the unaffordability of sunscreen. The cost of treating each melanoma is about £2,500 – or a total of £180 million in 2020. Other countries – such as the Netherlands – provided free sun cream during recent heat waves. Some governments think it is worthwhile.

Actions

For a GP – dermatoscope +/− dermatology advice and guidance/opinion and check for other signs of solar damage – e.g., solar keratosis.

Advice for the patient on avoiding sunburn – e.g., "slip, slop, slap" (slip on a [long sleeve] shirt, slop on [factor 50] sunscreen, slap on a [wide-brimmed] hat and sunglasses) between March and October.

Suggest they talk to their friends, relatives, (ex)work colleagues about being vigilant, take photos of areas to establish if there are changes, and get checked if there are signs of skin changes.

Resources

https://www.nhs.uk/conditions/non-melanoma-skin-cancer/
https://www.cancerresearchuk.org/about-cancer/skin-cancer
https://www.nhs.uk/live-well/seasonal-health/sunscreen-and-sun-safety/
https://melanomafocus.org/for-professionals/educational-resources/resources-
    for-your-patients/
https://www.nhs.uk/livewell/summerhealth/documents/concensus_statement%20_
    vitd_dec_2010.pdf

9.30 a.m. – Respiratory problems

Constance, a 31-year-old care worker, works in an asylum hostel. She presents with cough and haemoptysis. She is a non-smoker. She's aware that some of the asylum seekers living where she works have chronic coughs and have been losing weight.

Things to consider:

- What is the most likely diagnosis?
- What prevention does the UK population have for the prevention of this illness?
- What factors make the spread of this illness more common in asylum seekers?

As well as malignancy, the differential should include tuberculosis (TB), although Legionnaires' disease can also cause a cough and loss of appetite.

Illnesses will travel with people who must travel because of persecution or because their homes have become uninhabitable. Overcrowding during transit is extremely common, increasing the opportunities for spread.

It commonly takes years for asylum cases to be addressed, during which time poverty and poor access to good food are widespread. If cases are initially rejected, most applications win on appeal, but during this period in the United Kingdom, there is no access to benefits.

The United Kingdom no longer provides routine TB vaccination (known as the "BCG") for most people, so prevention depends on testing and limited use of BCG in high-risk communities. In the United Kingdom, there is a TB Action Plan (running from 2021 to 2026) and a latent TB infection testing and treatment programme (see resources for links).

Actions

Check the patient's BCG status. Vaccinations of adults aged 16–35 who are at risk of TB through their jobs – such as healthcare workers – should be arranged via the local occupational health department.

Discuss whether other staff have symptoms.

Make a referral to a specialist for final diagnosis, clarifying the infective likelihood.

Raise awareness of the latent TB infection testing and treatment programme with the hostel and/or public health.

Resources

https://www.nhs.uk/conditions/vaccinations/bcg-tuberculosis-tb-vaccine/
https://www.england.nhs.uk/ourwork/prevention/tuberculosis-programme/
https://www.england.nhs.uk/ourwork/prevention/tuberculosis-programme/
    national-latent-tuberculosis-infection-testing-and-treatment-programme/

9.45 a.m. – Hay fever

Mollie, a 25-year-old literary agent, comes saying that she's extremely worried her wedding will be ruined by the impact of her hay fever. She sneezes; her nose runs; she has swelling around her eyes. Ten years ago, when living in the Lake District, she barely had any allergies or hay fever and feels they now "ruin her life".

Things to consider:

- Why is hay fever more common, and how does this link to planetary health?
- Is this a medical problem that GPs should be addressing?
- What non-medical inputs improve hay fever?

Occurrences of hay fever are increasing in many parts of the world with "longer seasons of discontent".

Pollen levels have risen, resulting in an increase in severity, intensity, and length of season with earlier symptoms. Different pollens occur at different times of the year, with trees in the spring, grasses in the later spring/summer, and weeds in late summer/early autumn.

Pollen production is influenced by average temperatures and the amount of rain. Grass pollen increases in warm but wet springs but decreases if it's very hot and dry. Some trees produce more pollen if the previous year had a hot summer.

Pollen is spread on warm days with gentle or moderate winds, while rainy days can clear pollen from the air. Conversely, heavy rainfall and flooding can increase mould growth in damp buildings, triggering symptoms from different allergens.

Allergen and air pollutant co-exposure has been shown to exacerbate allergic rhinitis symptoms and induce changes in the allergic immune response.

All parts of primary care could receive people with symptoms, from GPs to pharmacists (OTC medication requested), optometry (allergic conjunctivitis and eye symptoms), and dentists (oral symptoms from pollen food syndrome).

Who has responsibility for hay fever, whether this is over-medicalisation of normal life, and what should a health service offer for diagnosis and treatment are areas for discussion and may reflect different assumptions about what health systems in the United Kingdom and other countries should offer.

Actions

Pollen avoidance tips include the following:

- Shower and wash your hair after arriving home and change your clothing.
- Avoid drying washing on a clothesline outside when pollen counts are high, and note that as temperatures drop, the pollen will settle on clothes.
- Apply an effective allergen barrier balm around the edge of each nostril.
- Do not cut grass or walk on grass.
- Do not spend too much time outside in the middle of a sunny day.
- Use dark glasses.

Resources

https://www.nhs.uk/conditions/hay-fever/
https://www.allergyuk.org/types-of-allergies/hayfever/
Hay fever treatment
https://www.allergyuk.org/resources/frequently-asked-questions-about-allergy-medications-factsheet/
How to use your nasal spray – https://www.allergyuk.org/wp-content/uploads/2022/06/Nasal-Spray.png

10:00 a.m. – End-stage kidney disease

Sharif, a 45-year-old man of Southeast Asian background, comes to see you about his chronic kidney disease. He worked in construction on large projects and was involved in building the World Cup stadium in Qatar. He often worked long hours in very hot conditions, carrying out strenuous, demanding physical labour. Sharif describes living on-site as cramped. Visits to healthcare facilities for monitoring were difficult. He returned to the United Kingdom for short periods each year. He has visited a kidney specialist who has said he needs a transplant.

Things to consider:

- How is this related to planetary health?
- Do you know how to clarify what services people are entitled to in the NHS and know to ensure your services are appropriately welcoming?

Chronic kidney disease is a recognised complication of dehydration related to working in high temperatures. Other countries – such as Nepal – report a high rate of kidney failure in workers returning from the Gulf countries.

The high death rate from unknown causes in migrant workers in the Eastern Mediterranean/Gulf area is probably related to dehydration and working conditions but is incompletely assessed. Working conditions in Qatar involved low-quantity and low-quality drinking water, and dehydration due to physical labour in high temperatures.

Economic inequalities are key as the most affected by climate change are those who contribute the least harmful emissions. The world's richest 10% contribute to approximately 50% of the world's carbon emissions, while the world's poorest 50% of people contribute approximately 7% of global emissions.

Just 100 companies are responsible for 71% of all global emissions from fossil fuel, agribusiness, cement and concrete, and mining industries.

There is no access to acute or chronic secondary care for asylum seekers, and they are billed if they do use it. Sharif has eligibility for GP care in the United Kingdom. See *Patient, not Passport* campaign (details below), for more information.

Actions

Assess kidney function; actions depend on this and its rate of change.
Protect kidney function through diet, exercise, and other lifestyle interventions.

Resources

https://www.patientsnotpassports.co.uk/support/advocacy-guide-for-healthcare-workers
https://www.theguardian.com/sustainable-business/2017/jul/10/100-fossilzfuel-companies-investors-responsible-71-global-emissions-cdp-study-climate-change

10:15 a.m. – Wild camping holiday

Three members of the McDonald family come in with diarrhoea, stomach cramps, vomiting, fever, and signs of dehydration after a wild camping expedition. They used water from the river to drink.

Things to consider:

- What are the likely causes of this family's symptoms?
- How clean is the water in the rivers and around the coast of England?
- Does climate change make it more likely that sewage systems and water treatment works get overwhelmed?
- Wild camping is a choice. Do most people who have diarrhoeal diseases on the planet get them through choice or through poverty or exclusion?

Classically, this could be Cryptosporidiosis or other diarrhoeas, including Giardia or Salmonella. There is no mention of blood in the diarrhoea, so, although possible, Shigella or Campylobacter are less likely. Salmonella might also be expected to cause bloody diarrhoea.

In 2022, nearly 400,000 discharges of raw sewage entered UK waterways, and 75% of UK rivers posed a serious risk to human health. Additionally, a House of Commons Committee report on the state of UK rivers concluded that no river in England was free from chemical contamination. Concerns include pollution from chemicals – insecticides (such as imidacloprid), antibiotics (such as clarithromycin), anti-inflammatory medication (such as diclofenac), and hormones (such as oestrogens) – nanoparticles, and (micro) plastic pollution.

In 2016, the UK government reported 14% of rivers, 16% of lakes, and 20% of estuaries achieved "good or better ecological status". Water companies have made poor progress in sewage management for many years, resulting in many spills and poor-quality freshwater swimming in the United Kingdom.

Globally, most people with diarrhoeal disease will get these due to poverty rather than from a wild camping expedition. The impact is greatest on the youngest and oldest – i.e., those least able to fend for themselves.

Waterborne infections are more common due to global climate change due to extreme weather events and increases in air and water temperatures. For example, a 1° C rise in temperature was associated with a doubling in cholera cases in Zanzibar, and a study in Bangladesh found that the number of cholera cases increased by 14% for each 10 mm increase in rainfall above 45 mm.

Actions

Initial management of the family includes medical assessment and, when appropriate, investigation and treatment.

Prevention of future episodes includes personal measures (access to clean drinking water, sterilisation kits, etc., when away), local/national societal measures (lobbying for cleaner waterways and coastal regions), and global measures (access to sanitation via https://toilettwinning.org/, etc.).

Resources

https://www.sas.org.uk/water-quality/water-quality-facts-and-figures/

10:30 a.m. COPD

Constance, a 75-year-old retired choreographer, used to be a smoker. She has chronic obstructive pulmonary disease (COPD) with few symptoms, well controlled by using Long-Acting Beta Agonist/Long-Acting Muscarinic Agonist (LABA/LAMA) dry powder inhalers. She has very few exacerbations. She takes carbocysteine, prescribed when coughing a few years ago. She is worried about the plastic pollution and waste being generated from her inhalers and wonders what she can do.

Things to consider:
Poorer control tends to have the biggest environmental impacts from extra medication to treat repeat exacerbations, Accident and Emergency (A&E)/Emergency Room attendances, and hospital stays.

Although both dry powder and metered dose inhalers have an environmental impact from the plastics and metals, the greatest impact is from the gases released by pMDIs.

Actions

Optimise the fundamentals of COPD care: optimise inhaler technique, access to pulmonary rehabilitation, and address concordance and co-morbidities, smoking cessation, and vaccines, including supported self-management.

Using the message of Right Medicine (inhaled corticosteroids [ICS], not Short-Acting Beta Agonist (SABA) over-reliance) to the Right Place (observing inhaler technique and making sure people are on the right inhaler device for them, often dry powder inhalers (DPIs)) is an easy shortcut for clinicians and patients.

- Breathlessness management and techniques to control are important too. They increase sputum clearance and energy conservation. Patients can do exercises at home or online (see Asthma and Lung UK and/or NHS chair exercises) are helpful.
- Active cycle of breathing technique (ACBT) is a set of breathing exercises that loosens and moves the sputum from your airways. It is best to be taught by a physiotherapist. The ACBT exercises are breathing control, deep breathing, and huffing, which are performed in a cycle until your chest feels clear.
- An Aerobika device can be helpful for some.

Important for patients and clinicians to know when to escalate – and deescalate – treatment appropriately.

- For example, start with LABA/LAMA maintenance prn short-acting agents (usually SABA) if there is no asthma component.
- Review additional medication the patient may have ended up on – such as carbocisteine, theophylline, macrolides, etc. and STOP if not helping. This reduces polypharmacy, waste and associated side effects.
- Treatment decisions are influenced by whether patients are frequent exacerbators or symptom driven.
- Reducing exacerbations is important, as reducing hospital attendance reduces environmental impacts.

10:45 a.m. and 11:00 a.m. – Gynaecology and irregular periods

Tanya, a 14-year-old school girl, attends with heavy, erratic periods. She regularly floods the bed at night and had an embarrassing incident at school when her period started unexpectedly. She is currently using sanitary pads and needs to change every two to three hours. She has missed school as a result, as she doesn't like using the school toilets.

Things to consider:

- Can alternatives to her current sanitary pads be considered?
- Mum wonders about starting the pill. What are the downsides to this?

Melanie, her mum, who is 45 years old, attends the following appointment. Her periods have become heavier and erratic. She has completed her family but still requires contraception.

Things to consider:

- What are her options?
- What impact might these have on our natural environment?

Every year in the United Kingdom, the disposal of single-use menstrual products – pads, tampons, and applicators – generates more than 200,000 tonnes of waste. When it comes to single-use period products in particular, 90 percent of a menstrual pad is made of plastic, and menstrual products take up to 500 years to break down in landfills. Reusable products are considerably cheaper in the long run. The average cost of single use is £492/year compared to a menstrual cup at £20 that can last 10 years. Single-use tampon applicators are one of the most common items found at beach cleans.

- There are known impacts of hormones on aquatic life if using the combined pill.
- Impact on waterways – e.g., blister pack waste.
- Impact on the wider environment – e.g., from travel time for regular prescriptions vs one-off long-acting contraception, packaging associated with coil kits, and single-use coil kits vs reusable.

Action

Personalised approach – what works best for the patient? What do they prefer?

11:15 a.m. – Mental health conditions – struggling to come off medications

Colin, a 45-year-old IT worker, was first diagnosed with depression about six years ago. Due to work commitments, he has never taken up a face-to-face cognitive behavioural therapy (CBT) or mental health appointment. Since diagnosis, he has been on a variety of selective serotonin reuptake inhibitors (SSRIs) at various doses. The last time his patient health questionnaire (nine question) (PHQ9) was done was a year ago, scoring 13 (moderate depression) when he felt worse than now. He is currently taking fluoxetine. He has entered a new relationship and is having sexual difficulties. He wants to come off his fluoxetine, as he attributes his problems to this.

Things to consider:

- How likely is it that fluoxetine will be the cause of his erectile issues?
- Do best practice pathways suggest that at this PHQ9 score, he should be on an oral agent?
- From a planetary health perspective, is this possible overprescribing?
- What options might be considered for him now?

Approximately 1 in 10 people on SSRIs will get erectile issues; other side effects can also occur.

There is good evidence that in mild to moderate depression

- Antidepressants are not more effective than CBT (including online options) and
- Green and blue prescribing may be equally as effective.

In the United Kingdom, there has been a 35% increase in the prescribing of SSRIs in the six years to 2022. Prescribing of SSRIs has increased without a corresponding increase in incidence or prevalence of depression, suggesting prescribers are over-medicalising ("medicalising unhappiness") and prescribing some inappropriately.

Actions

Discussion of other ways to manage his mood, including computerised CBT and virtual or phone contact with primary care–based therapists if attending remains too difficult.

Discuss what might be underlying factors in his mood and how these are being addressed.

Discuss activity, as there is good evidence for the effectiveness of this in mild to moderate depression.

Use leaflets to gain informed consent regarding the challenges of stopping antidepressants and provide a phased withdrawal with planned review points.

Resources

https://pharmaceutical-journal.com/article/news/antidepressant-prescribing-increases-by-35-in-six-years

https://bmcprimcare.biomedcentral.com/articles/10.1186/s12875-017-0643-z

11:30 a.m. – Rehospitalisation

Betty is 93 and is living in a care home. She has severe vascular dementia and had a previous stroke. Her swallowing is poor, causing recurrent aspiration pneumonia. She is bedbound and has hoist transfers. So far this year, she has been admitted to hospital for falls, general deterioration, and infections five times and four times last year. She has a DNACPR form but no other advanced care plan. She is on 14 medications, including antidiabetic medication, antihypertensives, anticholinergics, and statins.

Things to consider:

- How much value is Betty getting from her repeated hospital admissions?
- How sustainable is Betty's end of life? And how dignified?
- Is it enough to have a DNACPR? What can be done to maintain dignity and prevent admissions?
- What are the patient and planetary implications of Betty's medications?
- How much of our NHS resources go into the last year of life? Is this successful?

It is likely these admissions are causing her harm from overdiagnosis, overtreatment, painful interventions, risk of delirium, falls, hospital-acquired infections, deconditioning, and more.

Ten per cent of NHS care is spent in the last year of life. Some interventions can be justified and are important, but some are futile and harmful. Resources can be redirected from high-carbon end-of-life care to be used more effectively for patients likely to benefit from them and more appropriate care.

Involving family, holistic, and advanced care planning is valuable. ReSPECT forms can help.

Admissions avoidance. Consider comfort and dignity rather than prolonging life at all costs, especially when quality of life may be very poor.

The Lancet Commission on the value of death is particularly interesting. The UKHACC webinar on Sustainability in End-of-Life Care is also very insightful.

It is likely that some of her 14 meds are not necessary. Some, like statins, assume a desire to prolong a good quality life; is her diabetic treatment aimed at symptom control or at reducing long-term morbidity?

Actions

Personalised care planning – what is important to the patient? Dignity rather than prolonged life perhaps.

Simplify medication to symptomatic control only with deprescribing and consideration of anti-cholinergic burden in frailty.

References

ReSPECT https://www.resus.org.uk/respect/respect-healthcare-professionals
https://www.thelancet.com/commissions/value-of-death
UKHACC Webinar https://rb.gy/8338d1

11:45 a.m. – Atrial fibrillation

Toby is a 40-year-old asymptomatic delivery driver. He doesn't smoke but is overweight and admits to drinking more than he "thinks is good for him". His older brother has recently had symptoms of palpitations and breathlessness, was diagnosed with atrial fibrillation (AF), and started anticoagulants. Toby is worried and asks if he is also at risk. If so, what could he do to reduce his risk?

Things to consider

- Could conditions such as this be avoided?
- What impacts would having a condition and medication have on other parts of his life (finance, work, travel, life insurance, etc.)
- Are lifestyle changes for managing AF effective?
- What are the effects of lifelong medication for people in their 40s?

Obesity is strongly associated with the development of AF. It also contributes to high blood pressure (which promotes structural changes to the heart), obstructive sleep apnoea, and diabetes (both independently increase the risk of AF).

Alcohol and smoking are known risk factors. Cutting back (ideally abstaining) from alcohol is effective at reducing the risk of developing AF. Alcohol-induced AF has a 10% increased risk of permanent AF. Stopping cigarettes results in a 36% risk reduction (https://www.health.harvard.edu/blog/cutting-down-on-alcohol-helps-if-you-have-atrial-fibrillation-2020030218968).

Diabetes and hypertension lead to a higher risk of AF by 40% and 56%, respectively. Both lead to structural, electronic, and autonomic changes within the heart from higher blood sugar levels and higher pressure exerting damage.

Acute sleep deprivation increases the risk over threefold. Sleep disorders such as obstructive sleep apnoea (OSA) are a risk of cardiovascular disease and AF. Worse, OSA has an increased recurrence of AF symptoms.

A 10% reduction in weight improves AF symptoms. Dietary changes contribute to weight loss and improved diabetic control, which in turn reduces the incidence of AF. The Mediterranean diet reduces the risk of AF and other cerebrovascular disorders.

Stress, emotions, and yoga have been shown to have an impact on AF, with yoga reducing AF by 24% (https://www.ncbi.nlm.nih.gov/pmc/articles/PMC6059525/).

Regular exercise prevents AF, reduces symptoms, and improves quality of life of those with AF.

Lifestyle modifications reduce the incidence of AF, induce more AF remission, and also produce successful ablation outcomes.

Review

Can you notice planetary impacts for the patients you see?
Can you bring this up with the patient?

My pledge

What actions am I going to do in my practice?

1.
2.
3.

Where next?

Chapter 7 for overinvestigating, reducing inappropriate prescribing
Chapter 8 for lifestyle medicine
Chapter 9 for sustainable quality improvement

Material from this chapter appears on https://www.greenerpractice.co.uk/
information-and-resources/planetary-health-cases/
Additional case contributions from Dr Kath Brown, Dr Veena Aggarwal, Dr Matt
Sawyer

Achieving appropriate investigation, prescribing, and treatment
Tony Avery, Tessa Lewis, and Neal Maskrey

Case study 1 – Overtesting

Mohammad, a 50-year-old man, had a battery of tests for recent weight loss. Reception advised a phone conversation with the clinician for results which was booked for mutual convenience three weeks later. By then, his weight was back to normal. However, he was advised to attend for a repeat prostate blood test (PSA), followed by examination for a slightly abnormal result. He has no prostate-linked symptoms.

Things to consider:

- How appropriate are batteries of tests?
- What are the recommendations regarding PSA tests?
- What's the link between tests and planetary health?
- How appropriate is a repeat PSA at this interval?
- Travel is part of primary care's carbon footprint. What are your reflections on the use of travel here?

Testing appropriately is important. Tests are resources which have planetary impacts and, though individually represent only a few extra emissions or resources used, cumulatively are a significant issue.

Overtesting can cause further testing. Most tests are not designed as screening tools, and the normal range is generally defined by two standard deviations from the mean, so some normal people will have tests outside the normal range *by definition*.

Recommendations for PSA tests are taking a history and discussing the inherent ambiguity in the test and the meaning of results prior to the test (see the "Resources" section).

DOI: 10.1201/9781003491583-7

The advised PSA repeat test interval is six to eight weeks, so doing it at three weeks is overtesting.

The arrangements for appointments and talking to the patient here have led to an initial visit, follow-up for a repeat test, and then a one-to-one appointment with a clinician for examination… and phone contacts in between. Is there a better system for patients, their time, and travel?

Actions

- Review the appointment system to reduce unnecessary, inappropriate, or duplicated visits/appointments.

Highlight repeat test interval recommendations to colleagues.

Resources

https://www.nhs.uk/conditions/prostate-cancer/psa-testing/

Case study 2 – Overdiagnosing

Chris, a 30-year-old carpet fitter, has a diagnosis of "asthma" and is treated with multiple short-acting beta agonist (SABA or "blue") inhalers. His symptoms are a sudden onset of shortness of breath associated with palpitations, flushing, feeling weak, pins and needles, sweating, and chest pain. He feels exhausted after each episode. His Peak Expiratory Flow rate shows no diurnal variation.

Things to consider:

- Does the diagnosis of asthma provide the best fit for his symptoms?
- What other diagnosis might be more appropriate?
- What treatment options are there if there is a better diagnosis?
- What steps might be appropriate to ensure that this overdiagnosis is not common in this practice?

The history is not suggestive of asthma. Making a diagnosis of asthma here is likely to be an **overdiagnosis**. Correct diagnosis is paramount. The details suggest the most appropriate diagnosis is panic disorder. Treatment with SABA is likely to be ineffective, inappropriate, and make symptoms worse, as well as being bad for the environment.

Remedies that could help anxiety and panic include cognitive behavioural therapy, exercise, social/green/blue prescribing, and mental health input, depending on patient choice. It is important to explore with the patient which one(s) could work best for them.

It may be appropriate to examine practice criteria for diagnosing asthma, especially in high SABA/low preventer users.

Case study 3 – Overtreating

Seventy-two-year-old Judy presents with an episode of collapse. She reports gradually worsening palpitations, often on exertion over a few months. This makes her more anxious and reduces her confidence in leaving the house. She has a background of atrial fibrillation, osteoporosis, obesity, and anxiety. Her medications include bisoprolol, apixaban, alendronic acid, calcium/vitamin D supplement, omeprazole, and sertraline. Examination shows a slow heart rate (bradycardia) with 45 bpm and irregular pulse. Her blood pressure is low, but her heart sounds normal.

Her bisoprolol is stopped. Judy is seen one week later and is delighted to report she has no further palpitations. She feels much better in herself. Her heart rate has improved to 80 beats per minute. The clinician uses this opportunity to optimise her medications, and after reviewing advice on stopping those started less appropriately, a bone scan is requested. As the result shows good bone strength, and there is no ongoing indication for treatment, her alendronic acid is stopped. She stops the omeprazole – which was started for alendronic acid induced reflux. Judy feels so well after stopping the bisoprolol that she chooses to start walking regularly and opting for healthier food options. She has reduced from six medications down to two.

Resources

Patient Information Leaflets https://patient.info/health
Osteoporosis resource https://theros.org.uk/healthcare-professionals/courses-and-cpd/osteoporosis-resources-for-primary-care/initiation/

Achieving appropriate investigation, prescribing, and treatment

Uncertainty is sometimes talked about a little in relation to health and healthcare and can hinder appropriate testing and treating. Being uncertain of a diagnosis or whether treatment will help or has helped a patient can feel a contradiction to modern ways of thinking about health and disease. Over the last three centuries, medicine has become predicated upon science and the scientific method, and those are about proof and certainty. Despite this, many accept there might be some uncertainty on occasion.

Over testing. Healthcare professionals often do not recognise that a state of certainty is frequently achieved only after the passage of time and multiple scientifically and technologically based investigations and scans. Healthcare professionals may fear that deviating from the "evidence-based" guideline-recommended investigations and treatment equates to poor medical practice and is fraught with medico-legal risk.

High-risk drug monitoring. Unnecessary testing is a source of non-essential patient visits to the GP practice and onward transport of blood samples to laboratories.

High-risk medicines with a narrow therapeutic index, such as warfarin (where a direct oral anticoagulant is not licenced or otherwise judged as not an appropriate anticoagulant), lithium, and disease-modifying antirheumatic drugs such as methotrex-ate require regular monitoring for continued safe prescribing. National guidelines (e.g., from the British Society of Rheumatology) and local shared care guidelines should define the monitoring parameters for a patient. The monitoring interval of a stable patient should be expanded in line with the shared care guideline recommendations, as this reduces unnecessary phlebotomy, reduces the risk of harm to the patient, reduces the carbon footprint and use of consumables, and increases practice capacity to review other patients.

Overdiagnosis and certainty. Sometimes clinicians will choose a diagnosis which is not ideal but stick to it despite evidence suggesting a better fitting diagnosis, failing to remember that diagnosis is best made over time. Sometimes somebody who is seen as senior has made a diagnosis, and so others fail to check its appropriateness. Sometimes a test is done and seen as infallible, ignoring evidence that it could also be normal. Achieving a certain diagnosis may be best done slowly and with the patient, not for them.

Disease risk calculators are used to try and predict who may succumb to a disease. A NICE-recommended Q-Risk calculator estimates the probability of a currently well individual having a heart attack or stroke (cardiovascular – or CV – risk) in the next ten years.

A 66-year-old, non-smoking English man of normal weight without diabetes or hypertension, with average cholesterol, has a ten-year CV risk of 14.1%.

In ten years' time, if nothing else changes, his ten-year risk goes up to 26% *just* because he is ten years older (Figure 7.1).

He might take regular exercise and eat a healthy Mediterranean-type diet, both of which ought to reduce his calculated risk. But since, like alcohol consumption, they are not included in the calculator, their effect is unknown. Once again, we seek certainty when the uncertainty is greater than many of those using the calculators realise.

FIGURE 7.1 Probabilities of a CV event comparing non-treatment with treatment.

(© 1998–2024 Mayo Foundation for Medical Education and Research).

The left-hand set (red faces) represents 100 people – before statin treatment is considered – with a 14% risk of a heart attack or stroke in the next 10 years. Equally, it could also be said that there is a 86% chance of NOT having a heart attack or stroke in the next ten years (represented by the green faces). This "positive news" or "negative news" is called "framing" and makes a big difference in how human beings can view risk.

Would telling a patient, "Good news, you have a 86% chance of NOT having a heart attack or stroke in the next ten years" lead to the same decision as being told, "Bad news, you have a 14% chance of having a heart attack or stroke in the next ten years"?

Are they being given untruthful information? Definitely not. More data and evidence will not "fix" this decision. Great consultation skills might be a good start to making decisions better.

The right-hand set represents 100 people all taking a statin daily for the next 10 years. The statin is very effective at reducing heart attacks and strokes. It reduces them *in relative terms* by 20%. Who wouldn't want 20% fewer heart attacks and strokes?

But, of course, 86 people out of the 100 were never going to have a heart attack or stroke anyway (the green faces). A policy of giving everyone with a ten-year CV risk of 14% a statin means a heart attack is prevented in three people out of the hundred (the blue faces). This means that there are still eleven people who have a heart attack or stroke (the remaining red faces) despite *all* 100 people taking a statin – and only three will get any benefit.

Empowering patients. In 2023, the Chief Medical Officer of England's annual report stated,

> It is essential that all patients, but especially those in later old age, are able to have realistic discussions with their doctors about whether more treatment will improve quality of remaining life. Some treatments may extend life but at the expense of reducing its remaining quality and independence; the decision about how to balance these should be the patient's.
>
> **(19)**

In this report, the importance of reducing treatment burden (including polypharmacy and multiple appointments) and unplanned care was recognised. This notion is supported by NICE multimorbidity guidance, *which "aims to improve quality of life by promoting shared decisions based on* what is important to each person in terms of treatments, health priorities, lifestyle and goals" (20).

Choosing Wisely UK has resources to help patients *"make the right choice for them at their healthcare appointments"* (21).

There are surprisingly few facts at clinicians fingertips on the benefits and risks of treatment and most would struggle to tell patients the likely absolute benefits and risks when prescribing medicines to them. There are sources of data on "numbers needed to treat" (for one patient to benefit) and "numbers needed to harm", including GP Evidence (22) and Scottish Polypharmacy Guidance (23). For data on the likelihood of harm from specific medicines, the Electronic Medicines Compendium (24) can be helpful.

Thinking and perspectives. How people view this depends on more than the numbers. A hospital specialist seeing lots of people with heart attacks or strokes is likely to be in favour of everybody taking a statin. A GP working in an under-doctored practice might see counselling patients about these benefits and risks, advising how to take their statin, managing attributed side effects, taking periodic blood tests, issuing repeat prescriptions, and reviewing how the patient is getting on etc differently.

Patients vary in how they view this uncertainty. Some people are not keen on taking tablets and say, "Only three people benefit? I'll take my chances". Others might say, "I remarried a few years ago; our children are young, so though it's only three out of a hundred, I want to do everything I can to see them grow up". There is a third response. "Knowing my luck, I'll be one of the eleven who'll have the heart attack despite taking tablets for years. No thanks. I'll take my chances".

What do the statin-takers who've had no events think ten years later? Do they all think the statin prevented a heart attack or stroke? What about their doctors? If it is known that 86 out of the 89 would never have a heart attack or stroke, it is not possible to predict in advance which decision works best for an individual patient. It is important to set out the probabilities and see what that individual thinks about the decision. Not everybody wants the plan with the best numbers we can find, nor are numbers necessarily the biggest factor in their decision-making.

Most patients and many healthcare professionals have become accustomed to believing that the scientific and technical aspects of medicine must be correct in all cases, and their expectation is that the test result must be right for everyone and the guideline-recommended treatment will benefit everyone. This fuels an approach which not only fails to respect individuals but also is extremely wasteful in unwanted treatment and medication. Sustainable healthcare must prioritise patient agency, and lean delivery depends on a shared diagnosis and agreed intended outcomes (which is harder to achieve in primary care!).

Overtreatment and overprescribing

Starting medications is like the bliss of marriage,
and stopping them is like the agony of divorce.

Doug Danforth

What is overprescribing?

Overprescribing is the use of a medicine where a better non-medicine alternative is available, or the use is inappropriate for that patient's circumstances and wishes (1).

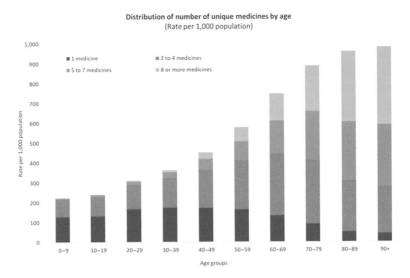

FIGURE 7.2 Distribution of number of unique medications by age (1). Footnote: population figures are mid-year estimates for England from 2019; appliances not included in numbers of unique medicines.

The extent of overprescribing is not known. The National Overprescribing Review (1) estimated that around 10% of prescriptions are likely not needed or not appropriate. Tackling overprescribing is an important way in which we can help address sustainability and help the NHS move towards its medicines' net zero goal.

Polypharmacy (taking multiple medications) is now common. Figure 7.2 shows that over half of people in their 70s take five or more unique medicines, and around 40% of people in their 80s take eight or more. For some people, all these medicines will be appropriate, but many will have "problematic polypharmacy" where their medicines may be doing more harm than good (2).

The number of prescriptions patients receive has increased over time. In 1996, the number of prescription items dispensed in primary care in England was 10 per head, and this had doubled to 20 per head in 2016. Much of this increase may be attributable to increased evidence-based indications or medications and an ageing population, but some of the increase will undoubtedly be due to overprescribing.

What are the reasons for overprescribing? Therapeutic advances mean there is a licenced medicine available for almost all the conditions encountered. Busy healthcare practitioners may find it easier to prescribe than to consider whether a medicine is the best solution or whether an alternative non-pharmacological intervention (or doing nothing at all) may be preferable.

• Increases in prescribing have been partly driven by guidelines informed by research findings. However, many of the underlying studies are based on randomised trials involving patients with single conditions, and older people are sometimes excluded. A review of NICE guidelines relevant to primary care found only 38%

of recommendations were based on evidence derived from populations typical of primary care (3). Therefore, guideline recommendations may not be applicable to all our patients, particularly those with multiple long-term conditions and the elderly.

- Clinicians often overestimate the perceived benefits of medicines while under-estimating the risks of harm (4), which further contributes to overprescribing.

- When treating people with long-term conditions, once a prescription has been issued, it can sometimes be easier to put this straight on repeat prescription rather than undertaking a careful review to check if the medicine is helping.

- If a medicine (such as an analgesic) is found to not work very well, the response is often to increase the dose or try a medicine that is perceived to be even "stronger" rather than considering alternative ways of managing the condition.

- Once medicines are on repeat prescription, research suggests that GP-led medication reviews result in little change in overall prescribing volume (5), and so any initial overprescribing tends to become a long-term problem.

The "prescribing cascade" – a concerning form of overprescribing is where medicines are inadvertently used to treat the unrecognised side effects of other medicines. In *The Book about Getting Older* by Dr Lucy Pollock (6), medical students are presented with six medicines without any additional information and asked, "What order were they prescribed in?" After some thought, the students work out that after the initial medicine, each other medicine has been added to treat the unrecognised side effects of the previous medicines.

Impact on patients. Overprescribing can have a significant impact on patients.

Firstly, there is increased risk of medication error and patient harm, including hospitalisation and sometimes death. For every extra medication a patient receives, the risk of medication error increases by 16% (7), and medication-related adverse events have been shown to contribute to 18% of hospital admissions in one UK study (8).

Secondly, patients, relatives, and carers can really struggle with managing medicines, even when they are necessary. The volume and timing of medicine taking can become extremely complicated and lead to confusion and increased risk of error. Polypharmacy is associated with increased risk of non-adherence and medicines waste. All problems are exacerbated by overprescribing.

Thirdly, patients are sometimes not fully involved in decision-making. This affects the detailed discussion of the likely benefits and risks of starting a new medicine or whether to continue medicines long-term. Where medication reviews do take place, they sometimes don't involve the patient, and where they do, there is rarely time for detailed discussion about the patient's experiences and views of their medicines. This impacts patients' autonomy around medicine-taking decisions, as they are not empowered to question whether ongoing treatment is in their best interests, especially in the case of older frail people where their priorities may shift away from life-prolonging treatment to quality of life.

Fourthly, patients may become dependent on their medicines, particularly for opioids, gabapentinoids, benzodiazepines, and 'Z drugs', and these (and other drugs such

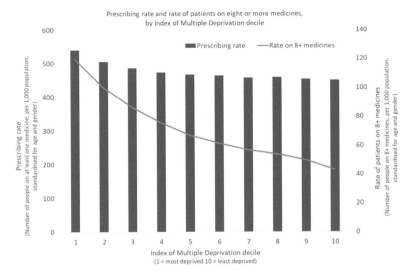

FIGURE 7.3 Prescribing rate and rate of patients on eight or more medications (1). Footnote: population figures are mid-year estimates for England from 2017.

as antidepressants) may cause problems with withdrawal symptoms. Escalating doses can increase the risk of dependence and make it more difficult for patients to come off these drugs.

Fifthly, recognition that overprescribing may be associated with health inequalities. Those living in the most deprived communities are at least twice as likely to receive eight or more medicines as those least deprived (Figure 7.3), and polypharmacy is higher in Black, Asian, and minority ethnic populations (1).

Impact on primary healthcare. While prescribing medicines may be one of the most straightforward interventions in primary care, overprescribing leads to additional work for General Practice and pharmacies with more prescriptions to process and dispense, more prescription queries, and more things that can go wrong because of the adverse effects of medicines.

There are financial costs associated with overprescribing, both from unnecessary medicines but also from dealing with the consequences of medication-related harm. Prescribing in primary care accounts for 34% of clinically significant medication errors in the NHS, and overall medication-related harm contributes to over 1,700 deaths, over 180,000 bed days, and monetary costs of over £98 million annually (9).

Tackling medicine waste is an important challenge. Back in 2010, it was estimated over £300 million of NHS medicines were dispensed but not used each year, representing £1 in every £25 spent in primary and community care pharmaceutical use (10).

Impact on the planet. It is calculated that medicines account for 25% of the NHS carbon footprint, with inhalers alone accounting for 3% of emissions (11). Figures from 2019 show that, even excluding emissions from inhalers, the supply chain for pharmaceuticals and chemicals for primary care was 2,095 kilotonnes of carbon dioxide equivalent (12).

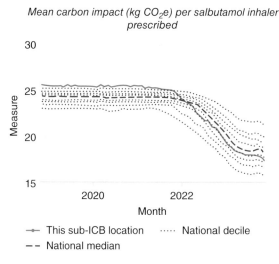

Mean carbon impact (kg CO$_2$e) per salbutamol inhaler prescribed

FIGURE 7.4 Changes in carbon impact of salbutamol inhalers for NHS Brighton and Hove (red line) compared with national data.

(From OpenPrescribing.net, Bennett Institute for Applied Data Science, University of Oxford, 2024 [15]).

Prioritised national prescribing measures support the Greener NHS policy (13). English GP practices can readily access their prescribing data for measures such as the environmental impact of inhalers and levels of seven-day prescribing for long-term conditions using OpenPrescribing data (14). Figure 7.4 shows the carbon impact reductions achieved in NHS Brighton and Hove for salbutamol inhalers.

Other OpenPrescribing dashboards provide data on prioritised measures of antimicrobial prescribing and resistance, which is relevant to greener prescribing (16). National organisations, such as NICE, also include environmental sustainability considerations in their processes (17).

What can I do, and what can my practice do?

- Consider alternatives to medicines, particularly where lifestyle changes have equivalent benefits. See Chapter 8 for details.
- Doing nothing can sometimes be the best option, particularly for minor self-limiting conditions or where patients are willing to live with their symptoms rather than risk the side effects of medicines.
- Optimising medicines is an important opportunity to support a person's well-being, address the environmental impact of medicines, and support a sustainable NHS. "Appropriate prescribing" is perhaps a better term than "deprescribing". The latter has negative connotations, particularly when reviewing medication in older people (52). Every medication review should align with the principles of medicines optimisation.

- "Think – medicines?" When a patient presents with new symptoms, it's important to consider whether these could be medication-related.

Reviewing medicines

A structured medication review is an opportunity to have a shared decision-making conversation with a patient (and/or their carers) to make sure that their medicines are working well for them, minimising the number of medication-related problems, and reducing waste. It should be undertaken at any time when a patient's health or circumstances may have changed. For example, where a patient with type 2 diabetes has made lifestyle changes, and their HBA1C is now on target or following discharge from hospital.

For patients taking relatively simple medicines regimens, GPs commonly undertake reviews in routine consultations or based on checking the patients' records and ensuring that any necessary monitoring has been done when the "review date" has been reached.

For patients with more complex regimens, reviewing medication can be daunting. However, it is likely to be an important opportunity both for patients and for a sustainable NHS.

There are numerous tools to support pharmacy teams carrying out this process. There are various approaches and several tools that can help. The key is to be systematic.

One approach suitable for GPs is the **NO TEARS** tool, designed for a ten-minute consultation (25).

NO TEARS	
Need and indication	Is the medicine still needed? Would non-pharmacological treatments be better?
Open questions	What does the person think of their medicines? Any not suiting or taken?
Tests and monitoring	Assess disease control and outstanding monitoring
Evidence and guidelines	Has the evidence base changed since starting the medicine? Is the dose still appropriate?
Adverse events	Are there medication- related side effects or evidence of the prescribing cascade?
Risk reduction or prevention	What are this person's risks, such as from falls? Are the drugs optimised to reduce these risks?
Simplification and switches	Can treatment be simplified? Do they know which treatments are important?

Another method, more commonly used by pharmacists undertaking structured medication reviews, is the **seven-steps approach** (26).

Case study – Seven-steps approach

Janata, a 49-year-old, attends her GP appointment with pain, stating her "medicines are not working". She struggles to work due to widespread pain, particularly affecting her back, left knee, and shoulder, and fatigue. She has asthma, hypothyroidism, and fibromyalgia, and a previous ankle fracture. She attended a pain clinic several years ago. A referral to physio was made nine months ago, but her records suggest that she missed the appointment. Recent blood tests were normal.

Current medication:

- Amitriptyline 10 mg tablets, one or two at night
- Fentanyl 50 mcg patch, one patch applied every 72 hours
- Gabapentin 300 mg capsules, two to be taken three times daily
- Mirtazapine 30 mg tablets, one at night
- Levothyroxine 75 mcg tablets, one daily
- Macrogol sachets, one twice a day
- Morphine sulphate liquid (10 mg/5 ml), 5 ml every four to six hours when required for breakthrough pain
- Asthma inhalers (which have recently been optimised)

Step 1: What matters to the patient? The patient wants help with her pain. Despite already taking more than 120 mg of oral morphine equivalent per day, she states the "medicines are not working". This is in keeping with the lack of evidence for opioids in chronic primary pain (27), and it may be best to explore non-pharmacological alternatives, recognising that *"chronic pain is very complex and if patients have refractory and disabling symptoms, particularly if they are on high opioid doses, a very detailed assessment of the many emotional influences on their pain experience is essential"* (28).

Getting to know the patient as an individual, including their social situation, stressful life events, substance misuse, employment, or housing difficulties, is important for doctor and patient. Therefore, time and continuity of care make it easier to understand their values, preferences, and goals and may reduce the burden of medication.

Step 2: Identify essential drug therapy. It is essential that Janata continues with levothyroxine and asthma inhalers.

Step 3: Does the patient take unnecessary drug therapy? If Janata could manage her pain with non-pharmacological approaches, she might be able to gradually withdraw from the opioids and gabapentin with support (29). Reducing or stopping the opioids may mean that she no longer needs the macrogol.

Step 4: Are therapeutic objectives achieved? Janata remains in pain despite her medication. NICE gives recommendations for exercise, psychological therapy, and acupuncture for chronic primary pain (27). Good online resources for patients include the *Ten Footsteps* programme (30). Referring back to a local pain service (especially if offering a biopsychosocial approach) may help. NICE recommends considering amitriptyline (which she is already taking) or a selective serotonin reuptake inhibitor (SSRI) for chronic primary pain; consideration could be given to swapping mirtazapine for an SSRI. It is important to consider any coexisting conditions – such as deteriorating osteoarthritis – with her chronic pain.

Step 5: Is the patient at risk of adverse drug reactions (ADRs)? High-dose opioids put Janata at increased risk of ADRs. There is a risk of dizziness, cognitive dysfunction, and respiratory depression when gabapentinoids are added to opioids (31). She is taking four medications that contribute to anticholinergic burden (32) (see Chapter 5). Janata's fatigue may be associated with several of her medicines, including the mirtazapine (which could be reduced in dose or changed to a less sedating antidepressant).

Step 6: Is drug therapy cost-effective? Given that Janata is taking numerous medications for chronic pain with little apparent benefit, these medicines are not cost-effective. Nevertheless, this would not be a reason for stopping the medicines unless she agreed.

Step 7: Is the patient willing and able to take drug therapy as intended? Many people don't take their medication as prescribed, but sometimes they are reluctant to admit this to healthcare professionals. The Innovation Network in England hosts a range of tools that can be used prior to, and during, medication reviews to encourage open discussions, and it is worth considering using these (33).

Focussing on higher-risk medicines. In patients with new symptoms or undergoing a medication review, recognising some medicines and combinations of medicines are associated with higher probability of patient harm. Some are as follows:

1. Common medicines (particularly when combined) that increase the risk of gastrointestinal bleeding. These include antiplatelets, anticoagulants, NSAIDs, oral corticosteroids, and SSRIs. Reduce risk by identifying patients through computer searches, followed by action by pharmacists (34) or other clinicians.

2. Common medicines that can cause acute kidney injury (AKI). People taking diuretics, angiotensin-converting enzyme (ACE) inhibitors, angiotensin receptor blockers (ARBs), and non-steroidal anti-inflammatory drugs (NSAIDs), particularly in combination, are at risk of AKI if they become dehydrated; this is an important cause of hospital admission (35). Consider temporarily withholding these medicines in people with diarrhoea, vomiting, or sepsis (36) and in heat waves if patients are not able to keep hydrated (53).

3. Anticholinergic burden (39). See Chapter 5.

4. Medicine(s) associated with dependence or withdrawal symptoms. NHS England has published guidance on optimising personalised care for adults prescribed medicines associated with dependence or withdrawal symptoms. These higher-risk medicines include opioids, gabapentinoids, benzodiazepines, "Z drugs", and antidepressants (29). NICE has issued guidance on the safe prescribing and withdrawal of these medicines (39).

5. Other high-risk medicines. There are several other high-risk medicines to be aware of, and often these are prescribed in shared care arrangements with hospitals, such as disease-modifying antirheumatic drugs, lithium, and amiodarone. These and other medicines, such as anticoagulants, require careful monitoring.

Reducing waste

Repeat prescribing systems in General Practice can help with the efficient supply of long-term medicines, but overordering can happen, and this can lead to waste. It is important for practices to ensure that their systems are set up to minimise risk of over-ordering and that potential overordering is considered when doing medication reviews, particularly for dependence-forming medicines.

Antimicrobial stewardship

Case study – Overprescribing of antibiotics

Margaret is 63 years old; she rings the surgery with cystitis. She describes burning on passing urine for several days. What are the sustainability and antimicrobial stewardship considerations?

Why Antimicrobial Stewardship (AMS) matters

While antibiotics can be lifesaving, overprescribing is an important driver of antimicrobial resistance (AMR). AMR has been declared by The World Health Organisation as a top 10 global public health threat, (43) and is on the UK Government's National Risk Register (44). AMR has a health and financial cost, with over 2,000 estimated deaths due to severe antibiotic-resistant infections in the UK in 2022 (45).

AMR is a complex problem, and the *One Health* approach recognises the interdependence of the health of humans, domestic and wild animals, plants and the wider environment. Primary care prescribes over 70% of NHS antibiotics in England (45) and has an important role ensuring optimal use.

In Margaret's case, a careful history may indicate her discomfort relates to thrush, a new sexual partner or post-menopausal atrophy (she may well not volunteer this information unless asked). While an infection is not to be missed, unnecessary exposure to antibiotics may increase her risks from AMR and make future infections more difficult to treat.

Clinicians and patients face the challenge and balancing of concerns about both AMS and sepsis, and considerable uncertainty. A systematic review of RCTs in non-pregnant women with UTIs found that 62% treated with antibiotics had complete symptom resolution compared with 26% of those who did not receive antimicrobials (59).

If patients receive antimicrobials and get better, those patients and the clinicians looking after them will think the antimicrobials were responsible for the improvement.

However, about a quarter of patients would have got better without an antibiotic. In most cases, managing a lower UTI will require antibiotic treatment, but this is not obligatory. Shared decision aids can help women make their own choice about whether to start an antibiotic straight away or to wait 48hours to see if the symptoms get better on their own (60).

However, there is a risk that UTIs are over-diagnosed, for example an older person who becomes muddled may be assumed to have a UTI but there are many other possible reasons: 'PINCHME' **P**ain, **I**nfection, **N**utrition, **C**onstipation, **H**ydration, **M**edication, **E**nvironment.

At the same time, the presence of bacteria in the urine doesn't always require treatment, especially if there are no symptoms.

In primary care, a clinician must weigh up a person's individual risks and benefits of different treatment options; national guidance encourages and support prescribers to <u>only</u> prescribe antimicrobials when clinically appropriate (46). Clinicians may also benefit from considering whether it is their action which makes the difference!

Top tips for antimicrobial stewardship. Useful resources to help primary care health providers with AMS include the TARGET antibiotics toolkit hub from the Royal College of General Practitioners (47). Guidelines can help identify those people most at risk of a serious infection or a resistant bacterial infection, and decision aids can help illustrate the options for patients; the NICE decision aid for sinusitis is an example (48).

Some consultation tips:

- What are the patient's expectations? When discussing possible infection, establish the patient's concerns. Studies (47) suggest that less than half are expecting antibiotics, with others worried about a more serious illness or looking for advice on symptom relief or "natural history". In Margaret's case, consider giving the TARGET UTI patient leaflet (47) to empower self-care and prevent further infections.

- Consultation location. Remote consultations may be convenient for patients or clinicians, but a study has shown that adults assessed remotely rather than face-to-face have a higher chance of being prescribed an antibiotic (49). National guidance discourages antimicrobial prescribing based on a remote assessment for suspected acute respiratory infection (50).

- Antibiotic choice and course length. Guidelines change in response to research and resistance levels. Check local antimicrobial guidelines and note that national guidance now recommends a five-day course for most respiratory bacterial infections.

- Delayed antibiotics. Where a person does not require an immediate antibiotic, "delayed prescription" for respiratory infections can be a useful option. A meta-analysis showed that delayed antibiotics achieved lower rates of antibiotic use compared to *immediate* antibiotics (30% versus 93%) (51).

Patients with frailty and medicines

What is frailty? Frailty in scientific terms describes a situation where the body's reserves are wearing out, meaning individuals are at risk of doing badly after a minor illness or stressful event (54). It is *not* an inevitable part of ageing – progression can be prevented (55). Prevention of frailty has three themes: Lifestyle factors like physical activity, smoking cessation, and alcohol limitation; activities of daily living (so consideration of sleep and eye and hearing health); and addressing medical interventions like polypharmacy. There is no pharmacological treatment which will correct loss of reserve and, paradoxically, many drugs which may worsen it. It should be suspected where

- syndrome of losing weight, strength, and energy exists with no overt cause;
- frequent infections cause functional decline;
- frequent falls; or
- confusion and functional decline.

How is frailty measured? There are multiple ways to measure frailty. The main way UK GPs are encouraged to measure is with eFI, the electronic frailty index, which is available on clinical IT systems, but patients need to be confirmed as having frailty or not by humans who know them. One alternative is the Rockwood Score (more commonly known as the Clinical Frailty Scale) (Figure 7.5).

   If six or over, then classed as a patient with moderate or severe frailty.

What abilities does a score of 6 or above relate to?

- 6 Moderately Frail – People need help with all outside activities and with keeping house. Inside, they often have problems with stairs and need help with bathing and might need minimal assistance (cuing, standby) with dressing.
- 7 Severely Frail – Completely dependent for personal care, from whatever cause (physical or cognitive). Even so, they seem stable and not at high risk of dying (within ~ 6 months).
- 8 Very Severely Frail – Completely dependent, approaching the end of life. Typically, they could not recover even from a minor illness.
- 9 Terminally Ill – Approaching the end of life. This category applies to people with a life expectancy <6 months, who are not otherwise evidently frail.

Falls, medicines, and frailty. In people with moderate and severe frailty, asking about falls and reviewing possible contributing medications is important. Numerous drugs have been implicated, including antihypertensives (optimal BP in over 75s associated with lowest mortality is 165/85 (56)), antiepileptics, anti-Parkinson agents, opioids, and psychotropic medicines (40). Deprescribing these drugs may not necessarily lead to a reduction in falls (41), but it is sensible to carefully ask what matters most to the patient and shared care decision-making with BRAIN, assess the risks and benefits of treatment, and stop medicines that clearly seem to be implicated.

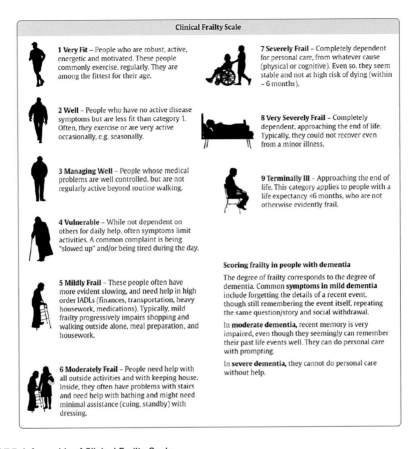

FIGURE 7.5 Infographic of Clinical Frailty Scale.

(Adapted with permission from Moorhouse P, Rockwood K. Frailty and its quantitative clinical evaluation R Coll Physicians Edinb. 2012; 42: 333–340).

Home visits. When visiting older patients in their homes, it is not uncommon to find large quantities of unused medicines (42). Dr Deb Gompertz (complex care GP and honorary secretary at British Geriatric Society) advises any health or care worker doing home visits to ask, "Show me your medicines, please?" In a three-month pilot, over 1,000 months of unused medicines were identified from just 40 patients; stopping medicines in these patients was predicted to save £3,529 over the following 12 months and prevent 549 kilograms of carbon emissions (42).

Barriers to deprescribing. Clinician and patient barriers are both perceived and real but can be overcome. Clinician anxieties can include "How will the patient/family perceive this?", "Isn't it easier to leave the status quo?", "Can I stop drugs started by specialists?", and "Will stopping cause me more work?" Undertaking training in polypharmacy can help overcome such barriers – e.g., the excellent and free to NHS prescribers (57).

Patient anxieties include current faith in their medicines (but they often overestimate benefits) and trust in their prescriber to get it right: "So why would I stop it?", and "I was told to take them 'for the rest of my life'". This may be overcome by explaining that as patients grow older, their bodies react differently to medications, and they may not be as safe to take in future.

Benefits and burdens

The benefits of prescribing medication in frail patients are often overrated, such as for preventive drugs – "Is this still appropriate?" – or for symptomatic drugs – "Are the symptoms still there?" Patients commonly overestimate the value of medication – e.g., this pill will stop me from having a stroke. Prescribers may have been complicit in this in attempts to ensure treatment adherence. There is benefit for some people in looking at the number needed to treat (NNT) (see Table 7.1) and the number needed to harm (NNH), as in the Scottish Polypharmacy guidance, *but* appreciate that most trials have been done on patients who are under the age of 80 with single conditions rather than multimorbidity, and an abundance of single condition guidelines have contributed to polypharmacy in those with multimorbidities. Therefore NNTs can vastly overestimate the likely benefit in the older person with frailty.

Burdens are often underestimated. Cumulative side effects are much more common as we grow older and worsened by "lack of reserve" in patients with frailty (25). There is a risk of errors (in prescribing or taking), more drug interactions, and acute illnesses alter drug handling abilities (8). Admissions can lead to deconditioning, falls, infections, and increased likelihood of losing independence.

Overcoming barriers. Initially, have conversations to understand the patient's opinion on the outcomes of their care. Clinicians worry about how patients may perceive stopping medications – "Has the doctor given up on them?" Have discussions about continuing to give care and focussing on achievable, patient-centred outcomes. GPs may struggle for adequate time to review long-standing medications or be reluctant to stop drugs started elsewhere by a colleague, especially a specialist. The clinical picture may have altered significantly since the initial prescription with more comorbidities, physical and metabolic changes, or adverse effects. Regular review by clinicians is expected and welcomed by the vast majority. Use the experience of practice-based pharmacists to review medications.

Principles for appropriate prescribing for patients with frailty

Principle 1 – understand

Understand the patient's priorities, goals, and fears.
Understand the non-drug burdens from treatments (blood tests, X-rays, clinics).

TABLE 7.1 How to review medication for specific diseases in severe frailty with Rockwood scores of 7–9 (58)

FOR ROCKWOOD SCORES OF 7–9 SEVERE FRAILTY	THERAPEUTIC TARGET	SUGGESTED ACTIONS
Diabetes	Symptom control Avoid hypos HbA1C only to identify risk of hypos (aim >65) Usually no BP Rx	Reduce treatment Symptomatic drugs only – stop other drugs – e.g., statins, BP Stop metformin if eGFR <30, consider stopping sulphonylureas or insulin (type 2) Watch for falling weight In EOL type 1, give low-dose, once daily, long-acting insulin
Hypertension	Usually no BP targets	Stop antihypertensives
Cholesterol	No added value	Stop cholesterol medication
Epilepsy	Treatment continues	Reduce doses if delirium Consider midazolam by syringe driver in EOL if poorly controlled
Osteoporosis	Drugs unlikely to be of value if life expectancy <1 year May still consider Vitamin D	Stopping Rx if poor life expectancy
Angina/IHD	Angina less likely if immobile	Stop aspirin and statin (NNT to prevent ischaemic event 250/yr, and no significant reduction in mortality) Stop angina drugs if asymptomatic B blocker at low dose
Heart Failure	Continue Rx to reduce risk of terminal CCF Furosemide in syringe driver EOL	Symptom management and less concern regarding renal function May continue low dose ACE and diuretic even where BP is low as long as not dizzy or syncope
Dementia	Usually stop dementia drugs (38) Memantine for behaviour problems Minimise other drugs to reduce risk of delirium	Delirium very likely Management plan for delirium Stop drugs if swallow now unreliable
COPD	Usual Rx but may be unable to use inhalers Avoid theophyllines Avoid oral salbutamol	Anticipatory care plan for managing exacerbations at home Consider palliative oxygen therapy
Pain and analgesia	Often reduce doses Risk of overtreatment with patches Abbey pain scale	Titrate doses down with weight loss Titrate all drugs down if delirium (anticholinergic burden) Assess for constipation

EOL (end of life), CCF (congestive cardiac failure)

Discuss of life expectancy expectations of all involved in care.

- Less than two years means preventive drugs unlikely to confer benefit
- Less than one year should signal advance care plans and symptom drugs only

Principle 2 – adherence

Poor adherence may have multiple causes – e.g., quality of clinician's explanation for taking, attitude to medication, cognitive impairment, understanding of medication, physical impairment preventing the ability to handle packaging with containers/inhalers. These need to be understood and accepted as part of the process.

Principle 3 – notice weight loss

Titrate down drugs (e.g., drugs for hypertension, Parkinson's, diabetes, or analgesia) as weight loss occurs (which may be part of frailty syndrome or other causes, such as cancer).

Principle 4 – side effects

If any new symptoms – think medication. Symptoms may be side effects (e.g., dyspepsia/nausea, itch, dizziness, oedema). Try to stop drugs rather than start an antidote.

See Chapter 5 for sick-day rules which are especially important in patients with frailty (and 37).

Principle 5 – most beneficial

If asymptomatic for 5–10 years, ask what matters to the patient. It may be that they no longer need medication for angina, dyspepsia, or breathlessness. There are some meds – e.g., antiepileptics and antipsychotics – for which advice from secondary care should be sought. *But*, stay on drugs giving benefit with little harm.

Principle 6 – gradually!

Usually stop one drug at a time (if in hospital or a crisis, this may be more radical, as there is daily monitoring compared with when in the community). Take the family with you and give positive rather than negative messages. Review, as this is an ongoing process.

Conclusion

When people are ill and consult a healthcare professional, the end product of that consultation is a decision or, more usually, several decisions. There will often be a diagnosis decision, a decision about treatment, about when to review the condition, or when to return for further consultation. There might be a decision made about when to come back sooner if certain things get worse.

Knowing the science about the disease and its treatment is necessary but not sufficient for decision-making. For great decision-making regarding testing, diagnosing, and treating, there is a need for healthcare professionals to understand how they arrive at decisions and how other people arrive at decisions, and then why those decisions might legitimately be very different. Only then can appropriate decisions be made by and for individual patients – decisions that are appropriate for them.

Pledges

Pledge – from this chapter, I will pledge to…

1.

2.

3.

Where next?

Chapter 8 for lifestyle medicine
Chapter 9 for sustainable quality improvement

References

1 Good for you, good for us, good for everybody. A plan to reduce overprescribing to make patient care better and safer, support the NHS, and reduce carbon emissions. https://www.gov.uk/government/publications/national-overprescribing-review-report

2 Duerden M, Avery T, Payne R. *Polypharmacy and Medicines Optimisation: Making it Safe and Sound*. King's Fund, 2013. https://www.kingsfund.org.uk/sites/default/files/field/field_publication_file/polypharmacy-and-medicines-optimisation-kingsfund-nov13.pdf

3 Steel N, et al. A review of clinical practice guidelines found that they were often based on evidence of uncertain relevance to primary care patients. *Journal of Clinical Epidemiology* 2014;67(11):1251–1257.

4 Hoffmann TC, Del Mar C. Clinicians' expectations of the benefits and harms of treatments, screening, and tests: A systematic review. *JAMA Internal Medicine* 2017;177(3):407–419.

5 Joseph RM, et al. Frequency and impact of medication reviews for people aged 65 years or above in UK primary care: An observational study using electronic health records. *BMC Geriatrics* 2023;23:435.

6 Pollock L. *The book about Getting Older*. Penguin Random House, UK, 2021. ISBN: 978-1-405-94443-4

7 Avery AJ, et al. Investigating the prevalence and causes of prescribing errors in English general practice: The PRACtICe study. *InnovAIT: Education and Inspiration for General Practice* 2013 August;6:477.

8   Osanlou R, et al. *BMJ Open* 2022;12:e055551. https://bmjopen.bmj.com/content/bmjopen/12/7/e055551.full.pdf

9   Elliott RA, et al. Economic analysis of the prevalence and clinical and economic burden of medication error in England. *BMJ Quality & Safety* 2021;30:96–105. https://qualitysafety.bmj.com/content/30/2/96

10 York Health Economics Consortium and School of Pharmacy, University of London. Evaluation of the scale, causes and costs of waste medicines, 2010. https://discovery.ucl.ac.uk/id/eprint/1350234/1/Evaluation_of_NHS_Medicines_Waste__web_publication_version.pdf

11 NHS England. Delivering a 'Net Zero' National Health Service, 2022. https://www.england.nhs.uk/greenernhs/publication/delivering-a-net-zero-national-health-service/

12 Greenhouse Gas Equivalencies Calculator. https://www.epa.gov/energy/greenhouse-gas-equivalencies-calculator#results

13 Greener NHS. https://www.england.nhs.uk/greenernhs/

14 OpenPrescribing: Prescribing measures for Greener NHS. https://openprescribing.net/measure/?tags=greenernhs

15 Chart obtained from: https://openprescribing.net/measure/carbon_salbutamol/sicbl/09D/

16 AMR local indicators – produced by the UKHSA. https://fingertips.phe.org.uk/profile/amr-local-indicators

17 NICE's strategy on sustainability: Current progress and next steps. https://www.nice.org.uk/news/blog/current-progress-and-next-steps-on-sustainability

18 Department of Health and Social Care. Chief Medical Officer's annual report 2023: Health in an ageing society. https://www.gov.uk/government/publications/chief-medical-officers-annual-report-2023-health-in-an-ageing-society

19 NICE. Multimorbidity: Clinical assessment and management. NICE guideline [NG56] https://www.nice.org.uk/guidance/ng56

20 Choosing Wisely UK. *Shared Decision Making Resources*. https://choosingwisely.co.uk/shared-decision-making-resources/

21 GP Evidence. Available at: https://gpevidence.org/

22 NHS Scotland. Polypharmacy: Manage Medicines. Efficacy (NNT). https://www.polypharmacy.scot.nhs.uk/for-healthcare-professionals/efficacy-nnt/

23 Electronic Medicines Compendium. https://www.medicines.org.uk/emc#gref

24 British Geriatrics Society. End of life care in frailty: Delirium, 2020. https://www.bgs.org.uk/resources/end-of-life-care-in-frailty-delirium

25 Lewis T, Using the NO TEARS tool for medication review. *BMJ* 2004; 329:434. https://www.bmj.com/content/bmj/329/7463/434.full.pdf

26 NHS Scotland. The 7-steps medication review. https://managemeds.scot.nhs.uk/for-healthcare-professionals/principles/the-7-steps-medication-review

27 NICE. Managing chronic primary pain. In: *Chronic Pain (Primary and Secondary) in Over 16s: Assessment of All Chronic Pain and Management of Chronic Primary Pain. NICE Guideline [NG193]*. https://www.nice.org.uk/guidance/ng193/chapter/Recommendations#managing-chronic-primary-pain

28 Faculty of Pain Medicine. Opioids Aware. https://www.fpm.ac.uk/opioids-aware

29 NHS England. Optimising personalised care for adults prescribed medicines associated with dependence or withdrawal symptoms: Framework for action for integrated care boards and primary care, 2023. https://www.england.nhs.uk/long-read/optimising-personalised-care-for-adults-prescribed-medicines-associated-with-dependence-or-withdrawal-symptoms/

30 Live Well with Pain. *Ten Footsteps Programme.* https://livewellwithpain.co.uk/ten-footsteps-programme/

31 Hahn J, et al. Risk of major adverse events associated with gabapentinoid and opioid combination therapy: A systematic review and meta-analysis. *Frontiers in Pharmacology* 2022 Oct 11;13:1009950. doi: 10.3389/fphar.2022.1009950. PMID: 36304170; PMCID: PMC9593000.

32 ACB Calculator. Available at: https://www.acbcalc.com/

33 Health Innovation Network. *Polypharmacy.* https://thehealthinnovationnetwork.co.uk/programmes/medicines/polypharmacy/

34 Avery AJ, et al. A pharmacist-led information technology intervention for medication errors (PINCER): a multicentre, cluster randomised, controlled trial and cost-effectiveness analysis. *The Lancet* 2012; 379(9823): 1310–1319. doi:10.1016/S0140-6736(11)61817-5

35 Osanlou R, Walker L, Hughes DA et al. Adverse drug reactions, multimorbidity and polypharmacy: A prospective analysis of 1 month of medical admissions. *BMJ Open* 2022;12:e055551. doi:10.1136/bmjopen-2021-055551 https://bmjopen.bmj.com/content/bmjopen/12/7/e055551.full.pdf

36 Think Kidneys. "Sick day" guidance in patients at risk of acute kidney injury: A position statement from the think kidneys board, 2018. https://www.thinkkidneys.nhs.uk/aki/wp-content/uploads/sites/2/2018/01/Think-Kidneys-Sick-Day-Guidance-2018.pdf

37 NICE. *Dementia.* https://bnf.nice.org.uk/treatment-summaries/dementia/

38 Bell B, Avery A. Identifying anticholinergic burden in clinical practice. *Prescriber* 2021;32(3):20–23. https://wchh.onlinelibrary.wiley.com/doi/full/10.1002/psb.1901

39 Medicines associated with dependence or withdrawal symptoms: safe prescribing and withdrawal management for adults. NICE guideline [NG215]. https://www.nice.org.uk/guidance/ng215

40 Jung, YS, et al. Medications influencing the risk of fall-related injuries in older adults: case–control and case-crossover design studies. *BMC Geriatrics* 2023;23:452. https://doi.org/10.1186/s12877-023-04138-z

41 Lee J, et al. Deprescribing fall-risk increasing drugs (FRIDs) for the prevention of falls and fall-related complications: A systematic review and meta-analysis. *BMJ Open* 2021;11:e035978. doi: 10.1136/bmjopen-2019-035978

42 Gompertz D. BGS green issues: Show me your meds, please. https://www.bgs.org.uk/bgs-green-issues-show-me-your-meds-please

43 World Health Organisation. Antimicrobial resistance. https://www.who.int/health-topics/antimicrobial-resistance

44 HM Government. *National Risk Register: 2023 Edition.* https://assets.publishing.service.gov.uk/government/uploads/system/uploads/attachment_data/file/1175834/2023_NATIONAL_RISK_REGISTER_NRR.pdf

45 English surveillance programme for antimicrobial utilisation and resistance (ESPAUR). https://assets.publishing.service.gov.uk/media/6555026e544aea000dfb2e19/ESPAUR-report-2022-to-2023.pdf

46 NICE. Antimicrobial stewardship: systems and processes for effective antimicrobial medicine use. NICE guideline [NG15]. https://www.nice.org.uk/guidance/ng15

47 Royal College of General Practitioners. Target antibiotics toolkit hub. https://elearning.rcgp.org.uk/course/view.php?id=553

48 NICE. Sinusitis (acute): Antimicrobial prescribing. NICE guideline [NG79].https://www.nice.org.uk/guidance/ng79/informationforpublic

49 Vestesson, E, et al. Antibiotic prescribing in remote versus face-to-face consultations for acute respiratory infections in primary care in England: An observational study using target maximum likelihood estimation. *eClinical Medicine* 2023;64:102245.

50 NICE. Suspected acute respiratory infection in over 16s: assessment at first presentation and initial management. NICE guideline [NG237]. https://www.nice.org.uk/guidance/ng237

51 Spurling GKP, et al. Immediate versus delayed versus no antibiotics for respiratory infections. *Cochrane Database of Systematic Reviews* 2023;(10):Art. No.: CD004417. doi: 10.1002/14651858. CD004417.pub6

52 https://www.pharmacyregulation.org/sites/default/files/document/gphc-pharmacist-foundation-training-manual-2021-22.pdf

53 https://www.gov.uk/government/publications/hot-weather-and-health-supporting-vulnerable-people/supporting-vulnerable-people-before-and-during-hot-weather-healthcare-professionals

54 https://www.bgs.org.uk/blog/understanding-frailty-a-beginners-guide

55 https://www.emjreviews.com/wp-content/uploads/2023/06/Infographic-Summary-of-the-British-Geriatrics-Societys-Blueprint-for-Preventing-and-Managing-Frailty-in-Older-People.pdf

56 https://pubmed.ncbi.nlm.nih.gov/26504116/

57 https://thehealthinnovationnetwork.co.uk/programmes/medicines/polypharmacy/

58 https://g-care.glos.nhs.uk/uploads/files/DePrescribing%20in%20Frailty.pdf

59 Falagas ME, Kotsantis IK, Vouloumanou EK, Rafailidis PI. Antibiotics versus placebo in the treatment of women with uncomplicated cystitis: a meta-analysis of randomized controlled trials. *J Infect.* 2009 Feb;58(2):91–102. doi: 10.1016/j.jinf.2008.12.009. Epub 2009 Feb 4. PMID: 19195714.

60 NICE guideline 109. Urinary tract infection (lower): antimicrobial prescribing. October 2018. https://www.nice.org.uk/guidance/ng109/resources/urinary-tract-infection-lower-antimicrobial-prescribing-pdf-66141546350533

Resources

Deprescribing in frailty full guide by Ian Donaldson available at https://g-care.glos.nhs.uk/uploads/files/DePrescribing%20in%20Frailty.pdf

National overprescribing review – https://www.gov.uk/government/publications/national-overprescribing-review-report

8

Lifestyle medicine
Lydia Vogelaar-Kelly and Matt Sawyer

Case study – Health screening

Helena, a 63-year-old non-smoker with no comorbidities or regular medications, requested health screening bloods. They showed a slightly raised HbA1c and cholesterol. Her BMI is 33. Evening meals are mainly home-cooked, eating out or having a takeaway once weekly. At work, she snacks on highly processed "junk" foods. She drinks socially on weekends.

She doesn't do any specific physical activity at present but says she used to enjoy Pilates classes and could be keen to start these again.

She works part time for the Civil Service and lives with her husband. She has an active social life. Her stress levels are low most of the time, although, at times, her job can be challenging.

Helena was shocked to be told her results showed "pre-diabetes" and her BMI was in the "obese" range. She was given a clear explanation of the root causes of diabetes.

Things to consider:

- Do patients understand the impact their lifestyle has on the likelihood of developing chronic illnesses?
- Do patients have enough guidance specific to them and their situation to make positive changes?

Actions taken

Helena and the nurse talked through the six pillars of lifestyle medicine using a visual aid. Helena opted to work on nutrition and physical activity to start with. After chatting

DOI: 10.1201/9781003491583-8

through how to make healthy lifestyle habits stick successfully, Helena was encouraged to set her own "lifestyle prescription" for the next four weeks:

1. Stick to snacking on one chocolate bar (80 g max) twice per week.
2. Attend one Pilates class weekly with her friend.
3. Read about Mediterranean diets before next appointment.

Four weeks later at follow-up, Helena explained that after the consultation, she cleared the "snack" cupboard in her kitchen. It was restocked with healthier alternatives, such as nuts and rice cakes. This resulted in losing 2 kg in weight despite holidaying with friends for a week. She was following the Mediterranean diet plan already and had reduced her alcohol consumption by half. She was attending two Pilates classes per week, one with her daughter and one with a friend. Helena was visibly thriving, was thrilled with her progress, and had thoroughly enjoyed the whole process.

Prevention is a core value of sustainable healthcare. This was an opportune time for lifestyle intervention. The benefits of preventing conversion of pre-diabetes to type 2 diabetes include those to the patient, to healthcare (fewer appointments, medication, and blood tests), to the environment (reducing carbon footprint), and to the community (lower costs).

Resources

https://shcoalition.org/wp-content/uploads/2021/02/Type-2-Diabetes-Care-Pathway. pdf

What is lifestyle medicine?

What is health? Is the World Health Organization definition, "a state of complete physical, mental and social well-being and not merely the absence of disease or infirmity", helpful? "Complete mental and social wellbeing" is impossible to achieve throughout most lives. Physical well-being results from a complex web of factors – some of which can be controlled, others influenced, and others need to be accepted.

If the aim is to increase *healthspan* (i.e., length of healthy life) rather than *lifespan* (length of life), then what approaches can patients and individuals take, considering everybody has different rank and power in society? How can primary healthcare, communities and neighbourhoods, and wider society influence these approaches?

Genetics is outside an individual's control. Poverty, inequality, and air pollution are more determined by society than individuals. Environmental factors like the type of diet and amount of exercise taken are determined by a mix of societal pressures, the power and rank of the individual, and personal choice.

A woman of colour or with disabilities living in poor quality privately rented accommodation, working many hours in a poorly paid job which is undervalued has little power, rank, or agency in society. A male white graduate with income and time has disproportionate power through his rank and agency. The "lifestyle" choices these two people make are conditioned by the agency and rank they have.

Research (1) shows the majority of chronic diseases are caused by environmental and lifestyle factors, and a minority is caused by genetics (from 3% of leukaemia, 8% of cancers, to 48% of asthma). In total, the study showed an average of 16% of Western European deaths could be attributed to genetics. Another paper showed that 70%–90% of disease risks were due to differences in environments (2).

If these two ideas are linked – looking to extended healthspan *and* that most chronic diseases are caused by environmental factors – then a framework for approaching and improving outcomes starts to emerge. This is lifestyle medicine.

"*Lifestyle Medicine is an **evidence-based** discipline which aims to support patients to prevent, manage and reverse certain chronic conditions, using supported behaviour change skills and techniques to create, and sustain lifestyle changes*" (3).

Erasmus stated, "Prevention is better than cure". Prevention is also much greener. Western healthcare today lives in a fictional world of limitless resources and negligible or harmless waste. It is contributing to the healthcare crisis of *today*. Just as the economy and fossil fuels need to decouple, healthcare needs to decouple from the hospital bed, pharmacy prescription, and fee-per-item reactive service to a proactive service funded and focused on prevention. Primary care is ideally situated to provide this through its position within the community, its longitudinal relationship with patients, and as a voice trusted by the public.

Julian Tudor Hart's inverse care law states, "*The availability of good medical care tends to vary inversely with the need for it in the population served*". The later important part is usually omitted: "*This inverse care law operates more completely where medical care is most exposed to market forces, and less so where such exposure is reduced*". The story of a population's poor health is as much a lack of attention to public health policy as it is relentless exposure to market forces. E. O. Wilson described the unequal relationship between our health choices and exposure to unhealthy market forces: "*[W]e have palaeolithic emotions, mediaeval institutions and god-like technologies*", going on to compare the unequal balance between our hardwired human needs in an environment of unfettered market forces as strapping a jet engine to a mini.

Given that healthcare itself is a limited resource, there is an obligation to focus on those populations that need it most. This is important for sustainability, as people from lower socio-economic backgrounds will acquire more chronic diseases, be exposed to more environmental pollutants and addictive substances, and present to health services later and in more carbon-intensive settings. Policy, legislation, the built environment, stigmatising language, etc., are all crucial to health and climate policies in this respect – e.g., sugar taxes, minimum alcohol pricing, green spaces, active transport.

Medicine doesn't always have to be a drug or preparation. It could be meditation, spending quality time with loved ones, or going to a yoga class.

Lifestyle, blame, and society. There is a dislike of the term "lifestyle medicine" in some quarters. The core concern is that the word "lifestyle" includes an assumption that a person's lifestyle is their choice. However, no clearly better terminology has been widely adopted. The ease with which a person may change their diet, housing, exercise

FIGURE 8.1 Human ecology model of a settlement (Barton and Grant 2006).

pattern, or other behaviours will always be determined by societal and peer group pressures, their physical environment, and their income, as well as the individual's desire for change. It is normally easier for those who have more wealth to change than those who have the most disadvantages – another example of the inverse care law. Figure 8.1 highlights where lifestyle sits within the pressures of socio-economic deprivation, political, environmental, and cultural forces.

What are the principles behind "lifestyle medicine"? There are several different approaches:

- The British Society for Lifestyle Medicine (BSLM) has six principles for lifestyle medicine: healthy eating, physical activity, healthy relationships, sleep, minimising harmful substances, and mental well-being (3).
- "The four pillars" – food, movement, sleep, and relaxation can be ascertained from eight key contributors to health and well-being, which are exercise, sunlight, stress, genetics, environment, sleep, infection, and diet (5).

- CLANGERS – Connect, Learn, (be) Active, Notice, Give Back, Eat Well, Relax, and Sleep (6).
- Seven healthy activities – being a non-smoker, having a normal body mass index, eating a healthy diet, being physically active, not having diabetes, not having hypertension, or not having high cholesterol (7).
- Blue Zones "Power 9" covering four areas of "right outlook", "eat wisely", "connect", and "move" (22).

All of these overlap and have essential strands of a healthy diet, being (more) active, sleep, and relaxation (while avoiding stress and harmful substances). These ideas are not new. Some date back over 2,000 years to ancient Greeks (9), others a decade or two (e.g., "CLANG" – from 2008 [8]).

The epidemiologist Geoffrey Rose argued that the most effective change is not individual, but that policy should enable healthier populations – i.e., the population distribution is shifted from disease towards health. Pes and Poulain studied the world's longest-living and healthiest populations. More popularly known as Blue Zones (22), their learning is summarised in Figure 8.2. There are challenges to the validity of some Blue Zone research (36). The nine approaches on the outer rim of the diagram are all low-tech yet high-yield interventions. Crucially, they are within the remit of primary care to influence and leverage. Unfortunately, they are all also within the remit of relentless and unimpeded market forces.

Why use lifestyle medicine?

Disease prevention, slows progression, remission.

Lifestyle medicine is personalised and moves away from traditional medical models that are more suitable for acute presentations and encourage a holistic approach. Some people don't want to take medication every day for the rest of their lives and, if enabled, want prevention. Healthcare professionals might assume all patients want the "magic pill" approach. If we uncover an individual's motivation for change and guide them to make achievable health goals with clear, easy steps, we empower them and support disease prevention and patient empowerment.

Patient empowerment. Healthcare is moving away from *"what works best for this disease"* to *"**what works best for this patient**"*. What is accessible, affordable, practical, achievable, and most likely to last in the long term for this patient? As adherence to a diet can be more important than the diet itself, it is paramount to help each patient choose what is best for them based on availability, preference, taste, and kitchen skills, including a compassionate conversation about what works best for their budget, as the UK Eatwell plate is not achievable on universal credit. Patient empowerment means establishing "what matters most to you". What matters most may be the threat of living in debt rather than the clinical conditions prioritised by clinicians. It gives clinicians the opportunity to signpost to support that may be needed to address the social determinants of health (e.g., in the United Kingdom through Making Every Contact Count [37]).

Mental Well-being

Lifestyle medicine teaches proven techniques to reduce stress and help people with relaxation. Practitioners support people to find purpose in life and improve health through connection with nature.

Minimising Harmful Substances

Lifestyle medicine supports people to stop smoking, reduce excessive alcohol consumption, avoid addictive substances and behaviours such as gambling or excessive internet or social media use.

Healthy Relationships

Lifestyle medicine supports people to develop and sustain healthy and meaningful relationships and increase social connection to reduce stress and promote both physical and mental health.

Healthy Eating

Lifestyle medicine supports people to reduce consumption of ultra-processed foods by teaching the knowledge and skills required to follow healthier eating patterns of people's own choosing.

Sleep

Lifestyle medicine supports people to achieve good quality sleep and to avoid behaviours which have the potential to impair sleep quality.

Physical Activity

Lifestyle medicine supports people to choose ways in which they could incorporate more physical activity in their lives, as well as reducing time spent sitting down.

FIGURE 8.2 The six pillars of lifestyle medicine from the BSLM.

(https://bslm.org.uk/).

The mnemonic "BRAIN" is a decision-making tool which is easily applied to treatment, from starting statins to walking outside in nature for ten minutes every morning.

Benefits – What are the expected benefits of the proposed intervention?

Risks – What are the potential risks, and how likely are they to happen?

Alternatives – What are the other treatment options?

Intuition – What are the emotional thoughts about this suggestion?

Nothing – What would happen if the patient didn't change anything and didn't start on any treatment?

This enables the patient to see the full picture of their options so they can make an informed decision.

Lean pathways. Though lifestyle changes are present in many pathways, there can be the temptation to assume that they are too difficult for the patient to act on (or uncomfortable for the clinician to engage with) and so are not addressed.

Case study – Kirkholt Medical Practice Bloomin' Marvellous Gardens (see also Chapter 15)

Tamara, a 52-year-old lady, arrived in the United Kingdom a few years ago as an asylum seeker with her husband and two children. Her husband died soon after they moved, and Tamara subsequently became very lonely, isolated, and depressed. She visited her GP, who referred her to the social prescribing programme. They prompted Tamara to volunteer with a group restoring a community garden – constructing planters, installing a water butt, compost bin, and a pond. The garden became a bustling centre of activity growing herbs, flowers, and vegetables; creating art; and maintaining the green space. Tamara used the garden to rebuild herself, make new friends, and connect with the community. The garden became a life-transforming experience for her. Her daughters also regularly contribute to the community garden upkeep.

Things to consider:

- What caused Tamara's depression? Would a tablet to balance chemicals in the brain fix that?
- Apart from mental health, what other benefits could Tamara gain from being part of this project?
- How can a project like this be funded in your area?

The main cause of Tamara's declining mental health was loneliness and isolation. Having an opportunity to socialise, have a purpose, and work towards something directly helps the root cause.

The experience of being outside, gardening, and manual work can help with physical fitness, weight loss, preserving functionality, and even promote healthier eating behaviours. Poor mental health is closely entwined with increased risk of physical diseases like cardiovascular, diabetes, autoimmune, and others. The multiple interconnections prevent placebo-controlled trials quantifying the wide-ranging benefits of reducing stress, anxiety, and depression though green prescribing.

Bloomin' Marvellous Gardens is a partnership project and part of the NHS Green and Blue Practice Social Prescribing Test and Learn Project, where patients with depression and anxiety were referred through the social prescriber.

The volunteers for this community garden are now so well established they have formed their own group and raised funds to maintain the garden and support other projects. The garden is open to the public, and the volunteers have applied to make the garden accessible in winter.

Six principles of Lifestyle Medicine

Mental well-being. Recognising stresses from life and learning techniques to reduce these through relaxation can help support people in finding their purpose in life and connecting with nature. Acceptance, recognising what is being gained (rather than lost), and "distress tolerance" can help. Acceptance is really important. Cognitive processing speed declines from around age 30, but wisdom, connectedness, and insights may increase. Distress tolerance is recognising the distress but using compassion to decide on the action. For example, rather than fearing physical (or mental) decline, changing the activity (e.g., from meeting a friend in town to meeting them at home) allows the activity to continue – and, importantly, retain the connection as a result.

Practising mindfulness through focussing on, and noticing, the "beauty in the everyday" can help. Consciously feeling grateful for the special meal, the conversation, the walk outside helps us to live in the moment. A short daily gratitude practice for six weeks enhances mental well-being and has sustained effects at six-month follow-up (33).

The *Journal of Hypertension* (15) recommends meditating for around 45 minutes every day to cut stress-related high blood pressure, among other lifestyle strategies. Although sounding impossible to busy people with hectic schedules, or those with racing thoughts, starting with shorter targets, such as five minutes twice a day, still has profound benefits. Meditation apps or free YouTube videos provide further guidance.

Many people find breathwork easier than the stillness of a classical meditation. Consciously slowing our breathing rate helps to regulate the nervous system, activating the parasympathetic state.

"Laughter is the best medicine" – originated from the King James Bible (Proverbs 17:22). Non-drug approaches can be powerful antidotes to poor health, acknowledged by spiritual and medical worlds, and research is recognising the power of laughter for both psychological and physiological benefits (4).

Healthy relationships. Developing and sustaining healthy relationships increases social connection and reduces both physical and mental ill health. Adverse childhood events such as witnessing domestic abuse or childhood neglect have been strongly linked to the development of physical, mental, and social ill health.

Loneliness is said to be as harmful to physical health as smoking 15 cigarettes/day (16), with both causing an increased risk of heart disease, strokes, and dementia.

Healthy eating

Food decisions are the single most important modifiable factor in preventing illness. Poor diet has been estimated to account for about 50% of common diseases.

If everyone ate optimally, we could prevent or delay around half of all incidences of heart disease, arthritis, dementia, cancer, type 2 diabetes, autoimmune diseases and infertility.

Professor Tim Spector, in his book *How We Choose Food*.

Multiple studies (17, 18) have shown the personal and patient benefits of a plant-based diet with reduced diabetes, cardiovascular disease, and cancers.

The EAT-Lancet diet (20) has developed global recommendations, healthy for both people and the planet. A diet to reduce the incidence of dementia has a similar food list – a high intake of fruits and vegetables, fish, fibre-rich wholegrains, low sodium, and low intake of sugar-sweetened beverages (7). Recent research shows the link between meat consumption and higher rates of type 2 diabetes (21).

It's not that a low-carb diet is better than a plant-based diet or a low-calorie diet. All may work for the medical condition in question, but the key is, "*Which works best for the patient?*" including what the patient can afford.

Tips for a healthy diet

- Key foods identified are "legumes, whole grains and nuts, foods with low sugar, mostly vegan, a few weekly servings of fish and excluding red meat" (19, 35).
- Half the daily intake is fruit and veg (60% veg, 40% fruit), around one quarter is whole grain foods, and the final quarter is protein, with the majority being from plants (nuts, pulses, etc.). Animal protein (i.e., meat) and dairy are in small amounts only (20).
- Avoid ultra-processed foods – if it says it's healthy on the packet, it often isn't! – (24 and work by Dr Chris van Tulleken).

- Tips for lowering blood sugar without changing *what* you eat – food ordering, movement after eating (23).
- Timing of eating is important as "time-restricted eating" triggers cellular repair. Aim to eat within a 12-hour window that suits (e.g., 8 a.m. to 8 p.m.).
- "Eat until 80% full" – Japanese proverb (from Okinawa Blue Zones [22]).
- Eat at a table instead of in front of the TV – eat slower and lower quantity, more attune to feeling full.

Top tips

EAT MORE PLANTS!
(Vegetables, fruit, nuts, seeds, legumes, and whole grains) and aim for diversity. "Eat the rainbow".
REDUCE meat, especially RED AND PROCESSED MEAT.
Reduce highly processed food, food high in sugar, salt, and saturated fat.
Reduce food waste (also increases food affordability).
Reduce dairy (where able, replace with calcium-fortified alternatives).
Where possible, eat more locally and seasonally.

Sleep. Good quality sleep has positive effects on inflammation, and sleep deprivation increases inflammation (25, 26). *Why We Sleep* by Matthew Walker offers additional detail on sleep (27).

Ten top sleep tips (adapted from Dr Phil Hammond [6])

1. Try going to bed at the same time and – most importantly – waking at the same time each day, including weekends.
2. Set an alarm (but not on your phone) to tell you when it's time for bed.
3. Come off close-up screens and games 60–90 minutes before bed.
4. Have the right sunlight exposure. Daylight is key to regulating daily sleep patterns. Try to get outside in natural sunlight for at least 30 minutes each day.
5. Enforce a strict "no caffeine after noon" rule.
6. Eat and exercise before 7 p.m. if possible.
7. Relax before bed by reading, listening to music, stroking a pet, etc.
8. If you can't sleep, counting sheep isn't as effective as repeating the same word over and over (the, the, the, the…). If you still can't sleep, get up after 20 mins and do a relaxing activity.
9. If this routine goes wrong, don't beat yourself up.
10. Set your environment – blackout blinds or mask, 17°C room (cooler rather than warmer), and no screens.

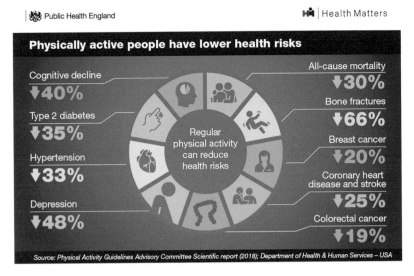

FIGURE 8.3 Physically active people have lower health risks (38).

(Source: Physical Activity Guidelines Advisory Committee Scientific Report (2018); Department of Health & Human Services – USA).

Physical activity. Inactive lifestyles are a proven risk factor for chronic health conditions, including heart attacks, strokes, type 2 diabetes, and depression (34). In the United Kingdom, the highest rates of inactivity are found in those with the least equal access to good health, such as the over 75s, people with disabilities, those with long-term conditions, or those who live in the most deprived areas.

There are multiple health benefits from physical activity (Figure 8.3). They also include the following:

- "Use it or lose it" – deconditioning is caused by inactivity but can be reversed.
- Balance, muscle bulk, and bone density can reduce with age but are not inevitable and can be maintained.
- For every two hours a week a woman spends doing moderate to vigorous activity, the risk of breast cancer falls by 5% (29).
- Physical activity after treatment for cancer can help to reduce the impact of some side effects, anxiety, depression, fatigue, impaired mobility, weight changes.

What are the UK recommendations? Moderate exercise for a minimum of 150 minutes a week or 75 minutes of vigorous exercise for people aged 19 to 64 (38). Any extra minute in movement delivers improvements in healthy lifespan, with the biggest health gains found in those who are the least active.

Quick tests

- Leg strength is particularly essential. An easy test: sit with arms folded and stand up, and then sit down five times. If it's a struggle to complete in under 16 seconds, work on building leg strength.
- "Back scratching test" for shoulder girdle flexibility. See www.topendsports.com/testing/tests/back-scratch.htm for details. If it's a struggle, stretching and flexibility training can help.
- Learn to balance. The ability to stand on one leg for 10 seconds is a predictor of longevity (28).

Consider the aims. Ask patients (or staff) what their aims are. Do they want to improve symptoms, feel fitter, or improve their quality of life? If so, they tend to be more satisfied than if focussing on weight loss.

One in four patients would be more active if advised by a GP or nurse, and very brief advice on physical activity has been shown to be effective.

Top ten tips for physical activity (30)

1. Build activity into the everyday – e.g., get to the bus a stop later or off a stop earlier, park further away, take the stairs, stand rather than sit.
2. Get exercise into your routine.
3. Find something you enjoy – you are more likely to stick to the activity if you do.
4. Track your progress – whether on an app or in a diary.
5. Do it with someone else – an "accountability buddy".
6. Set a reminder (e.g., alarm) to get up and move every hour.
7. Reward yourself when you achieve your goals.
8. Build on your success by doing a bit more each week – e.g., extra 10%.
9. Find a supportive app or programme such as "Active 10" or "Couch to 5K".
10. Do it at home with "home workout videos" from the NHS (31).

Minimising harmful substances. These can include smoking, alcohol, and other addictive substances but also addictive behaviours, such as excessive social media scrolling or internet use.

Drugs and alcohol: Lifestyle changes may allow a reduction in drug and alcohol consumption. This results in a personal health gain but also carbon benefits as whisky (a bottle generates on average 2,745 g CO_2e – or driving 16 km), cocaine (1 kg cocaine releases the same amount of greenhouse gases as driving 2,358 km [10]), or indoor cannabis cultivation (1 kg of dried cannabis has emissions equal to driving 20,000 km) have significant carbon footprints. And that's without the fertilisers used, water needed, land space taken, deforestation, etc.

Electronic devices: "Labour-saving" or "time-wasting" gadgets? Computer and mobile phones have revolutionised the world of work and how free time is spent. Some enable and encourage a more sedentary lifestyle with more time spent scrolling through the latest social media posts or online cat videos.

Synergistic links. An active commute rather than driving may bring not just exercise, lower air pollution for all, and nature connectedness but also interpersonal connection. Actions in one category can have positive benefits on another – physical activity can boost mental well-being and help reduce social isolation (a risk factor for depression), give a sense of purpose and value, provide a better quality of life, improve sleep, and reduce stress. Multiple activities can occur simultaneously. For example, walking for two hours in nature while chatting to a friend offers physical activity, healthy relationships, and mental well-being (through nature connectedness) and may lead to better sleep that evening too!

Inflammatory markers. The rise in inflammatory markers from factors such as poor diet (11), poor sleep, and lack of exercise (12, 13) are linked to many chronic conditions such as bowel disease, heart disease, and diabetes (14). Lifestyle medicine offers additional ways to reduce incidence and improve control of chronic diseases.

How to apply lifestyle medicine in practice?

A number of different opportunities to apply lifestyle medicine exist – whether opportunistic episodes of health promotion pre-diagnosis through to diagnosis (e.g., when providing disease-specific group consultations, such as post–heart attack), treatment, or disease progression. Lifestyle medicine can be seen as both an integral part of delivering good healthcare AND a stand-alone speciality.

How to ask patients about lifestyle issues. Ask about all facets (e.g., the six pillars) and encourage patients to share details. So, move from the following:

- "Do you eat well?" to "What have you eaten over the last 24 hours?"
- "Is your sleep ok?" to "How much sleep have you had in the last 24 or 48 hrs?", "How was the quality of your sleep?", and "Is all your sleep in one block?"
- "Do you ever see your friends?" to "When was the last time you had a conversation with someone? Tell me about it?", "Do you ever feel lonely?", etc.

Food/sleep/symptom diaries are useful tools and save time during consultations.

How to write a lifestyle prescription. What is important to the patient? Ask them to explain in their own words – and don't assume. When trying to improve one aspect of health – e.g., targeting BP with lifestyle intervention, overall health is improved, and risks of a variety of other factors are reduced. Exercise doesn't just improve blood pressure but also lung capacity, balance, mental well-being, and many more. Lifestyle medicine prescriptions enable personalised healthcare and patient empowerment. Use this to set achievable goals and to keep motivated to stay on track.

Remember, the advice is for a change that this person will do for the rest of their life. They have to be bought into the reasons, believe it's possible, and want to change. Some people might not be in the right phase to make the change, but that doesn't mean you can't bring it up. Planting a seed can take them a step closer to being ready for change (see Chapter 17). Asking people how they will sabotage their goals can help them plan how to keep on track.

Group consultations. These can be extremely helpful by showing how other people have risen to the challenge of lifestyle change. For many, talking with expert patients who have been through the same process can be invaluable. There are several key elements to successful lifestyle medicine via a group consultation (32).

Engagement and listening are vital. A common complaint is GP consultations can feel rushed and a patient not listened to – or their ideas are artificially fitted into a medical model of health. Group consultations and support groups outside the one-on-one consultation can allow more opportunities and exploration of individual issues and experiences.

Education is key but can feel like a *one-size-fits-all* approach, whereas a more individualised approach can feel more time-consuming. Group consultations can make more effective use of time for clinicians.

Evolution recognises people are at different points on their journeys. Some are at the entry point trying to undo years of inactivity and poor diet and need a solid foundation building for future endeavours, while others have a good balance of healthy activities and are looking for support with maintenance.

Group lifestyle clinics

A four-session clinic, set up by Dr Hussain Al-Zubaidi in Leamington Spa, covers the following:

1. *Happy, Healthy Me* is a general overview and reflection of what being healthy and happy means to each individual. It explores what areas of wellness they feel they would like to improve. Attendees are asked to complete a food diary.
2. *Behaviour Change and Community* looks at what is behaviour, if we can change it, and what are the barriers? The power of community in adopting new behaviours.
3. *Food and Nutrition* explores what food does for our bodies and what a good diet looks like. Reflections and discussions on how we eat and the food diaries are reviewed.
4. *Physical Activity* examines what has happened to physical activity levels, how much physical activity we should be doing, and what counts. Included are reflections on what physical activity we enjoy/used to enjoy and identifying some barriers to taking part. Looking at where there are opportunities to be physically active within the local community.

Actions. Make a reason or have an event to encourage and enable people to join green spaces. Introduce people to nature "covertly" – e.g., by inviting them on a picnic. Promote green spaces to patients during a consultation and as part of the clinical role. People are more likely to be active if it is seen as "normal" and if their friends and peers are also active. Large, community-wide campaigns have been effective in increasing physical activity but only when supported by local-level community activities.

System changes. The health of individuals is directly linked to the health of society and the policies which enable this. As our environment shapes behaviour, this can be a major factor in discouraging people from being more active. Our homes, workplaces, and local environments have been shaped to make it difficult to be physically active and can be improved to address this. This means becoming involved in street planning, real-locating road space to support walking and cycling, restricting motor vehicle access, etc. The rank and power of individuals will determine how easy it is to change things more widely; system change is easier if individuals are not in debt and under threat. Thus, the inverse care law applies.

Personal actions

- Evidence-based lifestyle input into clinical decision-making tools
- Build a daily routine – rather than fads or short-termism (see "sticky" in Chapter 17)
- Empowerment of patients – giving them agency over what is important to them
- Highlight synergistic effects from multiple actions

Have you ever thought about the opposite of stress? Most people assume calmness, inner peace, quiet, tranquillity, relaxation. In fact, *kindness* produces the opposite physiological reaction in our body to stress. It boosts serotonin, dopamine, and endorphins. This can explain why people get so much out of volunteering. It improves immune function and lowers CVD risk. We can be kind to ourselves, patients, colleagues, friends and family, strangers, and our world – be generous with it! It's also infectious – if you give, receive, or even just observe a kind act, you are more likely to do so again.

Conclusion

Though society is excited by genetic solutions and other high-tech, healthcare inputs, the majority of health outcomes are determined by a mixture of environmental, social, and economic factors. Individuals have different power to address these, largely depending on their rank in society. Lifestyle medicine should be at the heart of any realistic initiative to improve personal and population health, reduce environmental impact of healthcare, and tackle the financial cost of healthcare for individuals and nations. To enable people to make informed decisions on their physical activity and diet choices, we need to work with them to understand and improve the social, environmental, and economic determinants of health. Investment in social and environmental architecture will allow individuals to make the best decisions for their well-being.

Pledges

Pledge – from this chapter, I will pledge to…

1.

2.

3.

Where next?

Chapter 9 to learn about sustainable quality improvement
Chapter 10 for estates and energy
Chapter 11 for travel and transport
Chapter 12 for goods and services
Chapter 17 for behaviour change

Reference and Resources

1 https://www.ncbi.nlm.nih.gov/pmc/articles/PMC4841510/

2 https://www.science.org/doi/10.1126/science.1192603

3 https://bslm.org.uk/lifestyle-medicine/what-is-lifestyle-medicine/

4 https://www.ncbi.nlm.nih.gov/pmc/articles/PMC6125057/

5 https://drchatterjee.com/

6 https://www.drphilhammond.com/blog/2018/09/18/health4all/2593/

7 https://www.researchgate.net/publication/369257012_Abstract_P503_Association_Between_Life's_Simple_7_and_the_Risk_of_Dementia_Among_Women

8 https://neweconomics.org/2008/10/five-ways-to-wellbeing

9 https://www.greece-is.com/the-roots-of-holistic-health/

10 https://www.gpdpd.org/en/drug-policy/drugs-and-the-environment/about-the-life-cycle-assessment-of-illict-drugs-and-why-we-urgently-need-a-green-drug-policy

11 https://www.ncbi.nlm.nih.gov/pmc/articles/PMC4355619/

12 https://www.ncbi.nlm.nih.gov/pmc/articles/PMC3890998/

13 https://www.ncbi.nlm.nih.gov/pmc/articles/PMC6497785/

14 https://www.ncbi.nlm.nih.gov/pmc/articles/PMC3526249/

15 https://journals.lww.com/jhypertension/fulltext/9900/lifestyle_management_of_hypertension_.315.aspx

16 https://extension.unh.edu/blog/2022/05/prolonged-social-isolation-loneliness-are-equivalent-smoking-15-cigarettes-day

17 https://pubmed.ncbi.nlm.nih.gov/26853923/

18 https://www.nature.com/articles/s41598-020-78426-8

19 https://journals.plos.org/plosmedicine/article?id=10.1371/journal.pmed.1003889

20 https://eatforum.org/eat-lancet-commission/the-planetary-health-diet-and-you/

21 https://www.sciencedirect.com/science/article/abs/pii/S0002916523661192

22 https://www.bluezones.com/articles/

23 https://www.glucosegoddess.com/

24 https://www.youtube.com/watch?v=5QOTBreQaIk

25 https://www.ncbi.nlm.nih.gov/pmc/articles/PMC7525126/

26 https://www.tandfonline.com/doi/full/10.2147/NSS.S220436

27 https://www.waterstones.com/book/why-we-sleep/matthew-walker/9780141983769

28 https://bjsm.bmj.com/content/56/17/975

29 https://pubmed.ncbi.nlm.nih.gov/23274845/

30 https://www.nhs.uk/better-health/get-active/how-to-be-more-active/

31 https://www.nhs.uk/better-health/get-active/home-workout-videos/

32 https://www.pulsetoday.co.uk/clinical-feature/clinical-areas/obesity-and-nutrition/lifestyle-medicine-in-primary-care

33 Bohlmeijer, E.T., Kraiss, J.T., Watkins, P. et al. Promoting Gratitude as a Resource for Sustainable Mental Health: Results of a 3-Armed Randomized Controlled Trial up to 6 Months Follow-up. *J Happiness Stud* **22**, 1011–1032 (2021). https://doi.org/10.1007/s10902-020-00261-5

34 https://www.gov.uk/government/publications/health-matters-getting-every-adult-active-every-day/health-matters-getting-every-adult-active-every-day

35 How Not to Die Michael Greger Panmacmillan 2018

36 https://www.biorxiv.org/content/10.1101/704080v1.full#ref-2

37 https://www.meccgateway.co.uk/nenc

38 https://www.gov.uk/government/publications/health-matters-physical-activity/health-matters-physical-activity-prevention-and-management-of-long-term-conditions

Additional Resources

Movingmedicine website – https://movingmedicine.ac.uk/

NHS Choices – videos on movement – https://www.nhs.uk/conditions/nhs-fitness-studio/

Plant-Based Health Professionals – https://plantbasedhealthprofessionals.com/

RCGP Active Practice link https://elearning.rcgp.org.uk/mod/page/view.php?id=12583

Making Every Contact Count – https://www.meccgateway.co.uk/nenc

9

Sustainable Quality Improvement
Alice Clack and Frances Mortimer

Case study – Asthma review

Toby, a 35-year-old project manager, attends for his annual asthma review. He feels his asthma has been getting worse over the last year, and he has more symptoms. He drives to work along congested city streets. He attended Accident and Emergency on one occasion because his inhaler was empty, having forgotten to renew his prescription. He was given steroids and antibiotics for his cough and wheezing. As a result, he missed work for a week and feels he is falling behind on some of his projects. A cough at night is worsening his sleep and impacts his concentration throughout the day. He struggles to manage his inhalers and knows he sometimes forgets to take them.

Things to consider:

- What could be contributing to his worsening control?
- What is the impact of poor control on him?
- What is the impact of poor control on planetary health?

Actions

Using a Sustainable Quality Improvement approach, there are a number of different elements to consider

- Reduce activity (prevention, self-care, lean pathways)
- Reduce carbon intensity of treatments (low-carbon alternatives)

DOI: 10.1201/9781003491583-9

Prevention. His exposure to air pollution on his commute was discussed and led to him cycling down the back streets and across the local park. The time spent commuting was shorter, while he also avoided the worst air pollution and improved his lung function by increasing his physical activity.

Self-care – Toby recognised he needed a better way to make sure he remembered to take his inhalers. He tried several alternatives – starting with placing it in his sock drawer, then near his kettle, before finding placing it next to his toothbrush helped most. An asthma care plan was discussed, and he wrote down what worked best for him.

Lean service deliveries – As part of the review, Toby was set up on the NHS app so he could order his inhalers when needed, access his online records, review his asthma care plan and access online inhaler technique videos.

Low-carbon alternatives – Toby demonstrated that he was better able to use a DPI than his current pMDI, so the inhaler was changed accordingly. He found he managed a MART better, and his control improved.

Resources

https://www.greenerpractice.co.uk/information-and-resources/clinical-considerations/
over-diagnosis-and-person-centred-medicine/
https://www.asthmaandlung.org.uk/symptoms-tests-treatments/treatments/mart

What is Sustainability in Quality Improvement (SusQI)?

Introduction

The Sustainability in Quality Improvement (SusQI) framework is the integration of environmental and social sustainability into Quality Improvement (QI). It is a framework that supports the inclusion of important sustainability considerations within standard QI approaches rather than rewriting QI models.

The framework was proposed by Dr Frances Mortimer (1) and developed by the Centre for Sustainable Healthcare (2). It has been piloted and evaluated in practice through the green ward competition (3), within QI education through the SusQI education programme (4), and has been demonstrated to stimulate interest and enthusiasm for QI, raise awareness of the sustainability agenda, and support the delivery of sustainable transformation in practice.

Fundamental to the SusQI framework is an understanding that *sustainability is a core component of value*. This may represent a re-orientation for industrialised societies whose development is based upon an expectation of continuous resource extraction, but for other cultures, such as indigenous, first world peoples, sustainable value and the reciprocity that results already guides behaviour and cultural norms.

> *In our every deliberation, we must consider the impact of our decisions*
> *on the next seven generations.*
> Iroquois Nation teaching

The First Nation's seventh-generation principle that actions today are judged by their impact on the seven subsequent generations is the perfect illustration of how incorporating sustainability within value supports safeguarding the community, the environment, and planetary resources so that we can continue to thrive – and provide healthcare – in the future. This ethos exists through the Welsh government's ground-breaking Well-Being of Future Generations Act (2015) (5), which places an onus on the Welsh government to consider future generations in all legislation. This illustrates this principle of sustainable value and seeks to place it at the heart of leadership.

Sustainable value as a core component of quality. Providing an episode of quality care, whether to a single individual or a population, has limited value if that care comes at the cost of a stable natural living world and resource degradation, as this undermines the ability to provide care to other populations present and future.

The need for definitions of quality to include characteristics that address equity and sustainability has been recognised by institutions such as the Royal College of Physicians and the Royal College of GP (Figure 9.1). A four-dimensional model of quality has considerations for the future and the current episode of care's impact upon it.

The *sustainable value equation* (Figure 9.2) is not an equation to be solved but a reminder that value (and quality) must consider not only patient and population outcomes (the top line) but also the environmental, social, and financial impacts (the triple bottom line). Importantly, the equation provides a licence, and ideally a requirement, for change makers to broaden outcome measures beyond point-of-care patient metrics and allows sustainability considerations to drive change.

The concept of the triple bottom line, originally introduced as a business concept to challenge and transform capitalism, has been criticised for having become part of

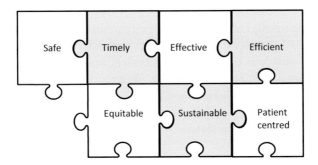

FIGURE 9.1 Domains of quality – interactions and components related to sustainability.

(Based on Dr Donal O'Donoghue, National Clinical Director for Kidney Care, 2007–2013).

$$\text{Sustainable value} = \frac{\text{Outcomes for patients and populations}}{\text{Environmental} + \text{social} + \text{financial impacts}}$$
$$\text{(the 'triple bottom line')}$$

FIGURE 9.2 Sustainable value equation from Centre for Sustainable Healthcare (12).

the "corporate accounting environment" and failed to achieve the intended radical re-orientation (6). Equally, there are concerns the equation suggests a false parity between financial and environmental considerations, thus risking the latter, when the up-front financial costs are too great (see Chapter 1 – updated "nested model of sustainability"). In practice, providing environmentally and socially sustainable healthcare has financial co-benefits, especially when the longer-term impacts of the planetary crisis on health are considered. However, the majority working in higher-income countries operate within a system that prioritises narrow, short-term considerations and live within an extractive cul-ture accustomed to paying no attention to either short- or long-term environmental costs. These criticisms offer a warning to ensure that in the use of the sustainable value equa-tion, it is ensured that not only is the environmental impact prioritised within projects, but importantly, users understand there is no future for human health without planetary health.

The principles of sustainable clinical care are described in Figure 9.3. This holistic guide supports health workers and health policymakers to engage in this and highlights routes to sustainable healthcare transformation. The principles are presented in order of importance, with disease prevention and patient empowerment (through partnership and self-care) recognised as having a greater potential impact on patient out-comes and sustainability than the development of lean pathways and use of low-carbon alternatives, which nonetheless have an important role in transformation efforts.

A later fifth principle – operational resource use – has been added. This relates to estate management decisions, such as energy procurement, recycling, and re-use of

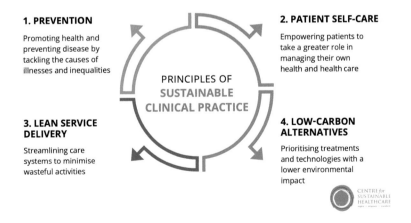

1. PREVENTION

Promoting health and preventing disease by tackling the causes of illnesses and inequalities

2. PATIENT SELF-CARE

Empowering patients to take a greater role in managing their own health and health care

PRINCIPLES OF SUSTAINABLE CLINICAL PRACTICE

3. LEAN SERVICE DELIVERY

Streamlining care systems to minimise wasteful activities

4. LOW-CARBON ALTERNATIVES

Prioritising treatments and technologies with a lower environmental impact

CENTRE for SUSTAINABLE HEALTHCARE

FIGURE 9.3 Principles of sustainable primary care (7).

(Mortimer, F. The Sustainable Physician. *Clin Med* 10(2). April 1, 2010. D110–D111).

waste streams. With at least 35% of primary care emissions being due to non-clinical emissions, it represents an important component and is influenced by owners, managers, and partners.

Why is SusQI important? By 2024, no country met its millennium development goals within recognised planetary boundaries. Many countries, such as those of Western Europe, over-reach Earth's carrying capacity in providing unsustainable care to populations, while others underutilised their "share" of resources and fall short of meeting their populations' basic healthcare needs (13). Although global failure to balance human health and planetary health is disappointing, there are some reasons for optimism. A number of countries and regions, for example, Costa Rica (14) and Kerala (India) (15), have made impressive strides in improving the well-being and health of their populations within the regenerative boundaries of our planet. Moreover, it is evident that *increasing wealth and extraction alone do not lead to improved health outcomes*, and that it is as important how wealth is distributed within society for the benefit of the population's health (16). Addressing the sustainability and organisation of healthcare is therefore a planetary imperative and also an urgent matter of equity and justice which has potential benefits both in financially richer and poorer nations.

QI is embedded within healthcare change management and is often the tool through which health workers are expected to improve care. Within the United Kingdom, it is a core component of undergraduate health professional training and is increasingly a part of postgraduate health education. The majority of UK healthcare trusts and Integrated Care Boards (ICBs) support a QI team and offer QI training packages. Globally, QI is a common improvement tool across especially richer nations in the global north. As a result, ensuring that sustainability is embedded at the core of QI can drive both sustainable clinical transformation and improve health education on the topic of climate and ecological emergency. Engaging health workers in this essential project could empower a generation of health advocates in the crucial project of meeting sustainable development goals within planetary boundaries.

An overview of the SusQI framework. The SusQI framework is not about rewriting QI but about supporting the integration of sustainability within existing QI approaches. To facilitate this process, the framework recognises the four steps common within all QI approaches (Figure 9.4) and provides tools and guidance to apply a sustainability perspective as part of these steps. The framework is not intended to replace the steps or tools already recommended by the QI framework used. It should be considered to offer supplementary tools and an additional perspective rather than a complete QI pathway. The SusQI tools can be downloaded for free from the SusQI website (https://www.susqi.org/templates) and include an overview of the framework and further teaching resources.

FIGURE 9.4 Four-step approach to Sustainable Quality Improvement.

How can I use SusQI in my practice? The four key steps are demonstrated in Figure 9.4.

Step 1 – Setting goals. Within standard QI approaches, health workers are encouraged to set goals based on identified problem areas. Often, problems identified will relate to areas of poor care, complaints, inefficiencies, or staff frustrations. From an environmental sustainability perspective, areas of high environmental or social impact are important problems to be solved and thus become independent reasons to undertake change. Such changes may often also have positive impacts on patient outcomes but can be justified, even if there is no impact, on the basis of their environmental and/or social advantages.

Understanding the areas of high environmental impact can inform goal setting. Educating health workers and other members of the multidisciplinary team about the impacts of healthcare provision on our environment and the key hotspots of environmental harm is an important aspect of integrating sustainability into QI and change management.

As always with QI, spending time to research the work already done in your field of interest is also an important part of the process. This step provides important insights into priority areas and may highlight previous projects undertaken in the area which may be adapted or replicated. Sharing and spreading positive change is always important, but within the context of the planetary crisis, rapidly adopting good practice in this area is a matter of real urgency.

Example. Syed qualified as a GP two years ago. He works as a salaried doctor in the local medical practice. He plans to carry out a SusQI project and reads around the main clinical environmental impacts relevant to primary care. From his reading, he understands that pharmaceuticals are a key hotspot, with propellant (pMDI) inhalers having an especially significant effect. He decides his goal should involve reducing the environmental impacts from propellant inhalers at his practice. He follows the SMART approach to draw up an initial goal. He discusses this with his supervisor, aware that the goal may need to change and develop based upon further discussions with stakeholders, a more thorough assessment of asthma care at the practice and a review of the relevant literature.

Syed's starting aim – Reduce propellant inhaler use (in asthmatics) by 10% at his medical practice over the next 12 months.

Step 2 – Studying the system. Understanding the system that we are considering making changes to is an important step in QI. This ensures that the appropriate stakeholders are involved and supports identification of appropriate and realistic change ideas. Knowledge of the healthcare's key environmental impacts is important to guide goal setting, but once a project area is identified, further assessment and understanding will support development of specific project goals in an iterative fashion.

SusQI tools support inclusion of environmental and social considerations into this step of a QI process. Practical examples of QI project resources include those developed by Greener Practice (8).

A tool commonly used within QI to study the system is the process map. This is a flow chart of the pathway of interest. This may represent a very small part of a larger system or an entire care pathway and can be varied (and repeated) to show as much detail as is useful. Ideally, it will have input from all those who influence the system, as this will maximise the accuracy – and thus usefulness – of the exercise.

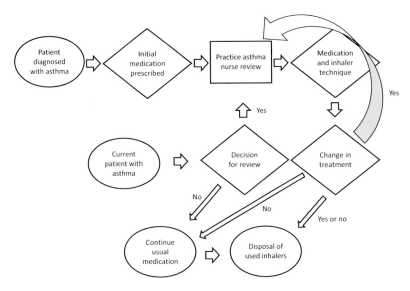

FIGURE 9.5 Syed's process map using SusQI for asthma care in his practice.

(Created by author for this chapter, permission to use given).

Example continued. *Syed works with his colleagues to identify the stakeholders in his project. This includes the practice's respiratory care lead, their pharmacist, asthma specialist nurse, sustainability lead, a receptionist, the practice's social prescriber and one of the patient representatives with asthma. He decides to draw a process map describing the asthma care of an adult asthmatic at the practice and amends this based on input from the team. He realises that including all types of asthma interactions would be incredibly complex, and therefore decides to focus on the diagnosis of asthma and routine asthma review pathways. Figure 9.5 shows the process map drawn.*

Syed then works with his stakeholder team to amend the process map to ensure it correctly reflects the pathway at his practice and to gain greater understanding of what is involved at each step described. He uses tools from the SusQI framework to study this process from a social and environmental perspective.

Resource use table. Creating this table can highlight the categories of environmental resource use. This supports the user to map the environmental and social resources used onto the process map and can be used to identify the carbon hotspots within the process, and the potential steps where these could be addressed.

For example, environmental resources used in the aforementioned process would include the following:

- Medical supplies – metered dose inhalers or alternatives
- Medical equipment – flowmeters
- Travel – patient and staff travel to appointments

- Non-medical supplies – computers, stationery, appointment letters, water, electricity
- Units of healthcare delivery – GP surgery appointment.

Social impacts table. This table helps the team to consider the social impacts of the process on relevant social groups, including the patient, their friends and carers, staff, and different types of vulnerable groups. It reminds the user to consider the social impacts of the changes they are considering and asks how they might measure these impacts in practice.

Considering the social determinants. This is included to support the team to consider the downstream influencers of the pathway under review. It categorises the different social determinants of health – e.g., housing, education, employment – and asks the user to consider how these may be influencing those patients within the clinical pathway. It reminds the team to consider interventions that might prevent or improve asthma care and/or empower patients to partner with health workers in the management of their condition. For example, empowering patients to understand not only their treatment but also the factors which exacerbate and improve their asthma.

Example continued: Syed also studies the asthma toolkit provided on the Greener Practice website (9). This supports him and his colleagues in identifying four broad areas (domains) of potential intervention which he can identify on his process map. These are as follows:

- Diagnosis
- Disease control
- Device
- Disposal

Step 3 – Designing the improvement. Driver diagrams are used within QI to support the categorisation of change types and stimulate ideas for development. The example illustrates how the SusQI framework recommends using the "principles of sustainable clinical practice" within a driver diagram to holistically approach change idea development.

Example continued. Syed decides to use the "principles of sustainable clinical practice" within a driver diagram to help his team develop as many potential change ideas as possible. He refers to the "Greener Practice" website's asthma toolkit, which outlines a number of QI project ideas relating to asthma care. He incorporates his learning into his driver diagram, which is completed with his team (Table 9.1).

It is clear that many of these ideas need to be further developed, as well as adapted to a specific practice context. Existing resources and previous projects should be reviewed during project development. Having other stakeholders on board will support the feasibility of the project and will help identify the most realistic changes within the project time frame and context. Importantly, discussing a breadth of ideas with your team can focus the team's attention on broader changes that might have greater impact and that could potentially be prioritised in the future.

Prioritising improvement ideas encourages users to consider the potential environmental and social impacts, as well as the feasibility of a project, when deciding which projects to pursue.

TABLE 9.1 Using SusQI approach for asthma care

INTENDED OUTCOME	PRIMARY DRIVER – WE NEED TO ENSURE:	SECONDARY DRIVER – WHICH REQUIRES:	ACTIONS – CHANGE IDEAS:
Improve or maintain health outcomes while minimising environmental, social, and financial costs of *routine asthma care*	1. Prevent avoidable disease	Optimise disease control	-Optimise Asthma review consultations -Identifying patients at high risk of poor control
		Smoking cessation	-Asthmatic smoking cessation clinic
		Ensure correct diagnosis	-Improve diagnosis of suspected asthma -Identify patients on salbutamol without a formal diagnosis of asthma
	2. Empower patients to improve disease management	Optimising patient self-management	-Self-management symptom diaries and apps -Patient information platforms and videos
		Social prescribing for asthma care	-Asthma clubs -Community-based groups asthma education -Singing for breathing
		Empower patients to change their risk factors	-Indoor environment -Air pollution
	3. Ensure lean clinical pathways/ systems	Avoid unneeded in-person reviews	Supported self-management apps and remote reviews
		Optimise use of appointments	-Introduce systems of identifying at-risk patients (e.g., high SABA users)
		Avoid duplicate prescribing	-Limit repeat prescribing -Liaise with acute teams to prevent unneeded prescriptions
	4. Switch to lower carbon alternatives	Educate practice staff re lower impact inhalers	Use available toolkits and prescribing protocols
		Swap Ventolin prescription for Salamol	Swap all Ventolin prescriptions to Salamol
		Target patients on highest-impact preventer inhalers	Identify and target patients on highest-impact inhalers first

(Continued)

TABLE 9.1 (Continued) Using SusQI approach for asthma care

INTENDED OUTCOME	PRIMARY DRIVER – WE NEED TO ENSURE:	SECONDARY DRIVER – WHICH REQUIRES:	ACTIONS – CHANGE IDEAS:
	5. Improve operational resource use (e.g., equipment, energy, water)	Education re environmental impacts of improperly disposed inhalers	-Liaise with local pharmacies - Inhaler drop map-Staff and patient education -Education on identifying an empty inhaler
		Recycle inhalers	Recycle inhalers through existing recycling schemes

Step 4 – Measuring the impact. Choosing outcome measures and monitoring impact is a core step in all QI. A core concept of the SusQI framework is ensuring that environmental and social sustainability are reflected within the outcome measures. If environmental sustainability is not part of the project's primary aims, then they should be incorporated as balancing measures. For example, if the aim is to reduce the practice's appointment wait times, then balancing measures might be the carbon footprint of the appointment system (environmental outcome measure) and patient satisfaction (social outcome measure). The important principle here is to ensure that changes are not made that inadvertently have a negative environmental or social impact.

The SusQI framework offers the following tools to support the inclusion of environmental and social sustainability within your outcome measurements.

Environmental outcomes: carbon footprinting for healthcare. This guide (17) provides a beginner's overview of the concepts of carbon footprinting and offers examples of how common carbon footprinting data can be used in practice.

Scanning for social impacts table. This supports the user to consider the social impacts of a change and how these might be measured. When undertaking a QI project, consider how the positive impact of the intervention will be felt and by who. If possible, prioritise actively addressing inequality by benefiting those most in need.

Example continued. *After collaborating with his team, Syed decides to work with the practice's asthma nurse to optimise all asthma reviews and to offer an additional review to all patients at the practice who are using six or more reliever inhalers each year. He knows that other practices have undertaken similar projects and plans to use the resources and experiences of others as much as possible. The team is aware that to succeed in reviewing most of the identified patients, they may need to provide flexible appointment times or even home visits. Having worked through the QI process, Syed develops a new aim, and decides on his outcome measures.*

Project aim: Reduce the number of practice patients needing six or more reliever inhalers per year by 25% in 12 months.

Outcome measures: Number of practice patients needing six or more reliever inhalers over the preceding 12 months

Process measure: Total number of reliever inhalers prescribed to the identified cohort each month

Balancing measures:

- Patient satisfaction questionnaire for selected patient group prior to and following intervention
- Number of acute admissions per month amongst selected patient cohort

Examples of SusQI from primary care. UK medical students, foundation doctors, and GP trainees are required to incorporate environmental sustainability within the QI projects undertaken as part of their training. For example, QI tools for GP registrars reference the triple bottom line. This creates an opportunity to interest the practice teams supporting these projects to sustainably transform the care they provide. Reports of projects undertaken are available (11). The same principles are applicable to optometry, pharmacy, and dentistry. Examples from pharmacy and Sus QI are found in Chapter 5.

SusQI and beyond. SusQI represents an opportunity to motivate and engage students and health workers in sustainability project work as a core part of undergraduate and postgraduate training and within their practice under the umbrella of continuing professional development. Beyond QI, the SusQI framework, its tools, and its core concepts have a role in informing all transformation work and in supporting a re-orientation of clinical priorities towards sustainable transformation which is essential to our continued ability to provide quality care to patients. In this respect, the core principles of SusQI intersect with other concepts such as equity, universal proportionalism, lifestyle medicine, and a generalist approach to care in that they provide a perspective that prioritises long-term health and equity over short-term targets. Importantly, the principles of sustainable clinical practice and the sustainable value equation support an evidence-based approach to public health and primary care, in which primacy is given to the maximisation of health and the prevention of disease through patient empowerment and partnership.

QI is, by its nature, concerned with small changes that can incrementally transform care. SusQI does not therefore offer a framework for achieving the broader public health or political changes needed to achieve a sustainable healthcare system. Importantly, it does encourage participants to consider the broader determinants of health and to understand the fundamental importance of the planetary, environmental, and social factors in health determination. In this respect, as well as supporting change in its own right, it is also a useful framework that encourages health workers to develop, through practice, a perspective that they can carry with them into other fields of work.

Great things are done by a series of small things brought together.

Vincent van Gogh

Conclusion

Sustainable healthcare transformation requires a re-orientation away from a narrow, short-term, and extractive health system to one that appropriately embeds planetary sustainability, equity, and the health of future generations into global healthcare models.

SusQI provides a framework to educate and engage health professionals and models principles that, if applied to healthcare transformation more widely, could support attainment of sustainable development goals within planetary boundaries.

Pledges

Pledge – from this chapter, I will pledge to…

1.

2.

3.

References and resources

1 https://www.rcpjournals.org/content/clinmedicine/10/2/110

2 https://sustainablehealthcare.org.uk/

3 https://www.susqi.org/green-team-competition

4 https://www.susqi.org/susqi-academy

5 https://www.futuregenerations.wales/about-us/future-generations-act/

6 https://hbr.org/2018/06/25-years-ago-i-coined-the-phrase-triple-bottom-line-heres-why-im-giving-up-on-it)

7 https://www.susqi.org/design-improvement

8 https://www.greenerpractice.co.uk/

9 https://www.greenerpractice.co.uk/high-quality-and-low-carbon-asthma-care/

10 https://noharm-europe.org/sites/default/files/documents-files/5372/Guiding_principles_EUKI_pilot_project.pdf

11 https://www.susqi.org/impact-reports

12 https://www.susqi.org/measuring-impact

13 https://eprints.lse.ac.uk/115519/

14 https://www.un.org/sustainabledevelopment/wp-content/uploads/2017/07/Costa_Rica_Partnership.pdf

15 https://english.mathrubhumi.com/news/kerala/kerala-news-1.6408354

16 https://www.commonwealthfund.org/publications/issue-briefs/2023/jan/us-health-care-global-perspective-2022

17 https://www.susqi.org/templates

10

Estates and energy
Ben Holt and Matt Sawyer

Case study – Pain control

Joel, a 40-year-old male fireman, attends his appointment asking for more opiate pain-killers. After six months, he is still recovering from multiple fractures after a building collapsed on him. He had been rescuing people from flooded residential housing and the local pharmacy. He was checking the building when it collapsed on him.

Things to consider:

- Are primary care buildings built on flood plains?
- How effective are opiates in long-term pain control?
- Is this injury caused by planetary change?
- Is it likely that other elements contribute to his persistent pain, such as the impact of multiple fractures on the mood of somebody who previously was very fit, and might this have been a traumatic episode for him?
- Is the fact that he remains off work due to a work-related injury relevant to his speed of recovery?
- What might be the more sustainable ways to enable his mobility and restore fitness?

The precursor to Greener NHS identified that 7.5% of GP surgeries in England were on flood plains (Scotland 7.6%, Wales 18.2%, Northern Ireland 10.5%).

Studies show that opiates offer poor control of patients' chronic pain. Opiates have a high impact on the environment, causing damage to the planet through carbon emissions in manufacture, and opioids are detected downstream of water treatment plants with possible effects on fish behaviour. Research is continuing on other effects on the ecosystem.

DOI: 10.1201/9781003491583-10

The injuries in this case were a result and consequence of flooding/weather change causing mayhem. There are increased flood risks in the United Kingdom due to climate change.

Historically, there has been evidence of work-related injuries persisting with a link to the reality that the compensation schemes for them take so long.

Actions

- Assess for PTSD and other mental health elements which could exacerbate his physical presentation and pain overload.
- Consider benefits and risks of analgesia vs non-medication options for pain.
- Determine if there has been sufficient discussion of activity to aid recovery.
- Learn if there has been a request to the healthcare managers for the surgery to be re-sited.

Introduction

Energy is essential for our current lives so why should we be interested in reducing the energy consumption of our practices? *I'm busy doing other things, I'm stressed so what's in it for me, my patients, my staff, and my practice?*

Energy – what do I need to know?

Energy is vital for delivering high-quality primary healthcare. Energy is also financially costly, may feel wasted, can have a high environmental impact and cost, and can contribute to air pollution. In the United Kingdom, GP and dental practices receive reimbursement of their rates and waste costs but this is not extended to energy costs.

Addressing energy and its use in the workplace can free up the budget for core activities, improving patient care, or improving staff morale through pay rises. There are improved levels of comfort, bringing better productivity and creating a more professional work environment for staff and patients. Passing on learning about energy management to others and the wider benefits of improved energy knowledge is useful to the health community. There are environmental benefits both from reducing energy use and from changing the source of energy to a renewable electricity through lowered greenhouse gas emissions and other air pollutants such as CO_2, NOx, etc. (see Chapter 13).

What uses energy in a practice?

Heating – typically, this is gas or oil.

Electricity for equipment (+/− heating in some cases), including electric vehicles (EVs). Electricity is used for cooling buildings during hot weather/heat waves. In 2022, 20% of hospitals cancelled elective surgery during the summer heat wave due to operating rooms being too hot (1).

Can the practice find out its energy use and energy rating?

Energy use by practices is a significant proportion of non-clinical emissions. It can vary from 10% (typically a practice which has photovoltaic panels) to over 40% if poorly insulated. Energy intensity is measured in energy (kWh) per floor space (m²) per year. A practice can calculate their energy intensity by knowing three figures – total electricity use (kWh), total gas use (kWh), and total floor space (m²). Median energy intensity for health buildings is about 95 kWh/m² for electricity and around 190 kWh/m² for gas (2).

In England, Wales and Northern Ireland, Energy ratings for buildings are assessed by Energy Performance Certificates (EPCs) (3) which must be displayed in public buildings.

The energy hierarchy triangle (4). The energy hierarchy triangle is a diagram showing what we should consider first at the top going down to our last possibility at the bottom. It starts with no- or low- cost/high-gain measures at the top going down to high-cost/low-gain measures at the bottom. This can help a practice develop a prioritised action plan (Figures 10.1 and 10.2).

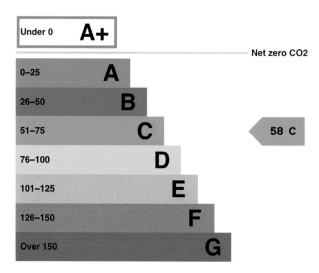

Energy rating and score

This property's energy rating is C.

Under 0	A+
	Net zero CO2
0–25	A
26–50	B
51–75	C	58 C
76–100	D
101–125	E
126–150	F
Over 150	G

FIGURE 10.1 Example of an EPC rating. Details found on government database at https://www.gov.uk/find-energy-certificate.

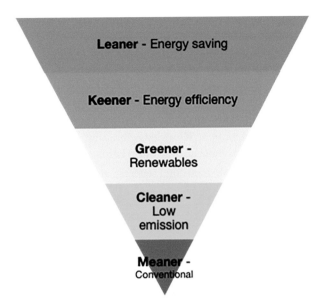

FIGURE 10.2 Energy hierarchy triangle.

There are five steps:

Leaner – The top priority under the energy hierarchy is energy reduction or the prevention of unnecessary use of energy. Make sure every kWh counts. *The cheapest unit of energy is the unit of energy you don't use.*

Keener – The second priority is to ensure the energy that is used *is consumed efficiently.*

Greener – Thirdly, use electricity bought from a *renewable* energy source. This describes naturally occurring, theoretically inexhaustible sources of energy – e.g., "elemental energy" from the sun, wind, wave, tide, or rain (hydropower).

Cleaner – Fourthly, low-impact energy production such as nuclear or fossil fuel with carbon capture and storage (not available at scale currently). This can be self-generated solar or wind.

Meaner – Finally, use energy from unsustainable sources, such as unabated burning of fossil fuels.

Policy context for the NHS. There are several policies which affect healthcare and energy. Three useful (English) documents are the following:

- *NHS and Net Zero – Health and Care Act 2022* www.england.nhs.uk/greenernhs/a-net-zero-nhs
- *NHS Net Zero Building Standard* www.england.nhs.uk/publication/nhs-net-zero-building-standard/
- *Estate "Net Zero" Carbon Delivery Plan* www.jpaget.nhs.uk/media/588250/Estates-Net-Zero-Carbon-Delivery-Plan.pdf

What will be the impact of changing behaviour, and which behaviours are best for my practice and me? Start by "painting the vision" – talk about how your practice, building, or organisation can become a comfortable, low-energy-using entity – but this can only occur when all are involved, and everyone plays their role. The right approach is the one which works best for you and your organisation or situation. Practical actions include:

- Improving staff awareness, enabling and encouraging them to actively partici-pate in energy conservation. Knowledgeable staff can contribute to reducing energy waste with behaviour change often being free or very low cost.
- Better data analysis, sub-metering, energy audits, and regular monitoring. Conducting energy audits to identify high energy usage areas and equipment.
- Demand reduction – make the "green" option the default option.
- Energy efficiency
- "Fabric first" approach
- Decarbonising heat
- On-site renewables

The Estates "Net Zero" Carbon Delivery Plan (5) provides national overarching guidance using two diagrams (Figures 10.3 and 10.4) to explain an approach which could be taken.

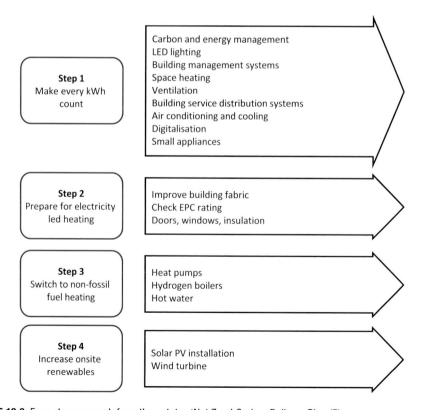

FIGURE 10.3 Four-step approach from the estates 'Net Zero' Carbon Delivery Plan (5).

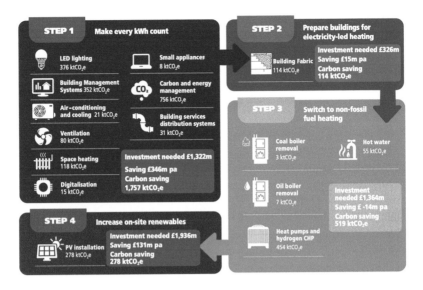

FIGURE 10.4 NHS Estates 'Net Zero' Carbon Delivery Plan (5). **NB** CHP and hydrogen boilers are unlikely to be suitable for primary care as the only potential viable use is large scale.

A step-wise approach to action

Overall priorities. Combining the energy hierarchy triangle and the NHS approach, the priorities develop, though looking at the team's desire for different changes will be important too.

Priority 1 Leaner	Use less energy with behaviour change
Priority 2 Leaner	Using less energy through technology or building modifications
Priority 3 Keener	Use energy efficiently
Priority 4 Greener	Supply electricity efficiently – self-generated
Priority 5 Greener	Supply electricity efficiently – purchased from the grid/energy company
Priority 6 Cleaner	The continued use of (non-sustainable resources) fossil fuels as part of the energy mix but using lower carbon technologies with less emissions
Priority 7 Meaner	Business as usual approach, using fossil fuels as they are now.

Case study – an example from a GP

An area of influence was the GP practice I worked in. I gathered relevant information and spoke to my colleagues about what the problem was, what was happening already and what changes could be made.

We used the "Zero Waste Scotland" small business energy efficiency advice (since replaced by "Business Energy Scotland"). They offered an assessment of the building, its energy use and advice on grants and loans to subsidise this.

With two of us in the practice interested in environmental action, we have done a handful of Green Impact for Health Toolkit actions, but I think it really needs buy-in from more people to be manageable.

My key learning from this work was as follows:

1. I am probably guilty of not giving enough time and acknowledgement to the immediate issues people face before moving on to linking with environmental issues and suggesting change. Indeed, the best successes I have had have come not from talking but from listening and exploring barriers and solutions led by the other party. Much like good General Practice!

2. Unfortunately, even with projected immediate savings, the practice decision was not to make any changes, due to any loan repayments, forecast to be on top of blanket energy tariffs from the health board when they take over the lease. This is a prime example of a lack of joined-up thinking and coordination: the health board and the government are aware of this issue, but it has not yet been resolved.

What would the details of the actions we could take look like?

Heating (and cooling)

Approach – **Behaviour change first**, tech solutions second.

Behaviour change could be changes to staff uniform to include wearing jumpers, closing doors to reduce heat loss, repositioning of desks closer to radiators ("heat the person, not the room"), changes to working patterns to concentrate (e.g., admin) staff in one heated room (rather than separate rooms), turn off heating in rooms not in use. If you have air-conditioning, use it wisely! If it is on, keep doors and windows closed. If it is cooling, check that wall heaters are off and use the thermostat timer setting.

Improving building fabric to reduce energy use is an important early step. New buildings have the advantage of putting low energy demand and renewable energy generation in at the outset, but retrofitting current buildings is appropriate for most practices but may be costly to carry out.

Passivhaus-efficient GP practices are possible, with Foleshill Medical Practice in Coventry (6) being the first constructed. Passivhaus standard for buildings (7) means using the lowest amount of energy through maximising insulation and efficiency. Passivhaus standard consumes an amazingly low 15 kWh/m^2/yr.

Heat can be lost through walls, roofs, floors, and windows/doors but also through "cold bridges" where there is a gap in insulation (8). A "fabric first approach" is taken, as it reduces heating and cooling and improves comfort levels for staff and patients.

Significant reductions in emissions (and energy and bills) can be achieved by upgrading building fabric – effectively investing in tech solutions. Moving from an "average" energy use of around 190 kWh/m²/yr to a retrofitted building which uses 40 kWh/m²/yr reduces energy use by 75%–80%. Some retrofitted properties can achieve 25 kWh/m²/yr (85% reduction in energy use). If summer cooling is needed, then reflective solar film or *brise soleil* for south-facing windows may be helpful.

Improving the efficiency of the heating source is the second step. For heating, the majority of primary care facilities use either main gas boilers which are 80%–95% efficient or electricity. Direct electrical heating (e.g., storage heaters) runs at about 100% efficiency, whereas heat pumps (ASHP – Air Source Heat Pump) work indirectly and achieve about 300% efficiency. All flame-related heaters will also contribute to indoor air pollution.

- Three kilowatt-hours of gas delivers 2.7 kW of heat (if the boiler is 90% efficient).
- One kilowatt-hour of electricity delivers 3 kW heat via an ASHP, as it is 300% efficient.

Table 10.1 shows the amount of energy required (for an average-sized GP practice or primary care facility of about 500 m²) depending on method of heating and the reduction in emissions which can be achieved through various actions.

Investing in technology to reduce heating requirements.

- Examine the current insulation – is it sufficient? The National Insulation Association can help (13).
- Is the thermal efficiency of windows enough? Do they feel cold? Are they double or ideally triple glazed?
- Heating – are there thermostats to control individual room temperatures? There is evidence that multi-zone control can drive higher savings.

Be prepared. Practices have different requirements due to size, location, operating hours, etc. It is worth understanding the options prior to the disaster of a boiler breaking down. Options for space and water heating include heat pumps, electric (and infra-red [11]) heaters, district heating systems, biomass boilers (electric). An ASHP can be cheaper to run – especially when combined with electricity storage battery options. More information is available from the Heat Pump Association (10). Some NHS Trust–owned buildings and health centres may be able to access Salix funding via the Public Sector Decarbonisation Scheme (12).

Heat management. Pre-heating: Where the practice is sufficiently well insulated, it is possible to pre-heat ahead of peak times and access cheaper tariffs (cheaper due to reduced costs associated with producing power off-peak and reducing requirements for network reinforcement to manage peak loads).

TABLE 10.1 Energy use and emissions for different heating types

HEATING	EMISSIONS PER KWH	ENERGY USE (KWH PER M²)	TOTAL ENERGY USED FOR HEATING PRACTICE OF 500 M²	TOTAL EMISSIONS FOR AVERAGE PRACTICE OF 500 M² (KG CO2E)	PERCENTAGE IMPROVEMENT WHEN CHANGING HEATING TO…			
					100% ELECTRIC HEATING (NON-ASHP), AVERAGE GRID ELECTRIC	ASHP + AVERAGE UK GRID ELECTRICITY	ASHP+ 100% RENEWABLE	PRODUCE OWN RENEWABLE ELECTRICITY, ASHP
If Passivhaus standard met		25	12,500					
Produce own renewable electricity with ASHP	0	63	31,500	0	—	—	—	—
ASHP + 100% renewable from energy supplier	0.01769	63	31,500	557.2				100
ASHP + average UK grid electricity	0.21107	63	31500	6,648.7		—	91.6	100
100% electric heating (non-ASHP), average grid electric	0.21107	190	95,000	20,051.7	—	66.9	97.2	100
Gas boiler	0.2111	190	95,000	20,054.5	0	66.9	97.2	100

- Use a simple timer switch to match heating to occupancy.
- Smarter heating management and use: a 3%–6% reduction in heat demand can be achieved through more informed and smarter management of heating practices by Intelligent Building Energy Management, where heating is linked to temperature and weather for even more accuracy.
- Smart meters and real-time displays have been found to result in energy savings of around 3%, driven by associated actions such as turning the thermostat down or reducing the amount of time the heating is on.

Conclusion

Overall, energy for heating can be reduced by up to 87% if Passivhaus standard levels of building efficiency are achieved (compared to current average use) and efficiency of delivering heat increased through installing ASHP which runs off 100% renewable electricity. This will require investment and will reduce energy bills and carbon emissions simultaneously. Behaviour change by staff can significantly reduce bills for very little/no up-front financial investment.

Electricity

Introduction

Electricity is used by kit and equipment throughout primary care. Almost all equipment when plugged in uses electricity. Practice use of electricity varies considerably depending on size, number of staff, services offered, amount of equipment, etc.

Typically, what types of equipment use a lot of electricity?

- Heating equipment (water or space heating)
- Cooling equipment (e.g., air-conditioning, fridges)

What else affects electricity use?

- The amount of equipment and number of computers, monitors, printers, lights, etc., in use.
- How long is it used for? For example, whether for 10 mins or 24 hrs per day.

$$\text{Energy used}(kWh) = \text{power}(kW) * \text{time}(hours) * \text{volume}(\text{number of pieces of equipment})$$

Priority 1 and 2 – Energy saving – electricity

- Gather data
- Prioritise and benchmark
- Plan actions to reduce

Gathering data: an energy audit.

Whether completed by staff, a third party, or by effective sub-metering, gathered data can identify where the energy is being used. Breaking down the proportions of electricity used by different pieces of equipment can help determine the most impactful potential actions. For some practices, computers, monitors, and peripherals use the most significant proportion (ranging between 25% and 50% of all electricity used), lighting is often significant (can be 20%), or refrigeration equipment (1%–10%). As well as consolidating the quantity of equipment (see case study), the audit can also look at how they are controlled – e.g., temps of fridges, putting timers on peripherals to match predicted operating hours, making sure PCs are switched off at night where appropriate (and not left on so they can start up quickly in the morning, etc.).

Example: Current number of fridges = 5 (e.g., if 2 kitchens and 3 drug fridges). Consolidating into one kitchen fridge and one drug fridge (except during flu vaccination season!) would allow the turning off of fridges and reduce the number used.

The most beneficial actions for a practice depend on the amount of equipment turned on, the energy used by each piece per hour, and the number of hours they are used.

Some practices have reported significant (20%+) reductions in the amount of electricity to run their day-to-day operations and deliver healthcare by turning off equipment when not in use, reducing the number of items used, etc. Combining the reduction in the number of items *and* reducing energy use per item is a sensible approach. For example, a practice with 30 staff does not need 30 individual printers, and combining two highly efficient machines in a central location can have a dramatic impact on energy use.

Table 10.2 is an example of how to collect data for an energy audit.

Prioritising and benchmarking. See where the practice/clinic sits in terms of its energy consumption compared to others. Use this process as a tool to identify the specific areas of the practice – e.g., lighting, heating – and assess costs to improve, financial benefits and carbon reduction, time period for payback/return on investment, etc. From Table 10.2, the easiest – and most – gains are made from turning computers off when not being used or having more energy-efficient devices rather than from the photocopier or CCTV system.

The savings that could be made through changing to energy-efficient LED bulbs are demonstrated in Table 10.3. This shows the calculation steps for comparing the current energy use of light bulbs.

In this case, the electricity cost difference is £4,375 vs £150 per year (for 50 bulbs).

Additionally, LED lighting lasts longer. Any "re-lamping" and associated labour costs can be significant on top of the time expense of staff.

TABLE 10.2 Data collection to determine energy use for equipment (completed with example data)

A	B	C	D	E	F	G	H
EQUIPMENT	NUMBER	ENERGY RATING ON APPLIANCE (W)	ENERGY RATING (KW) (C/1000)	NUMBER OF HOURS ON PER DAY (AVERAGE)	TOTAL ENERGY USED (B*D*E) PER DAY	ENERGY USE IF 252 (WORKING) DAYS (F*252)	ENERGY USE IF 365 DAYS (F*365)
Printer (stand by)	20	675	0.675	9	3.24	816	
Printer (on)	20	18	0.018	1	13.5	3,402	
Computer	30	165	0.165	10	49.5	12,474	
Monitor	60	12	0.012	10	7.2	1,814	
Photocopier (stand by)	1	20	0.02	24	0.48		175
CCTV	1	30	0.03	24	0.72		262
Fax machine	0	–	–	–			

TABLE 10.3 Worked example using two bulbs – one halogen 70 W, one energy-efficient LED 2.4 W

	GU10 HALOGEN	GU10 LED 2.4 W
Cost to buy	£7.44	£1.65
Lifespan (hours)	3,000	25,000
Power used (W)	70	2.4
Convert power to kW (/1,000)	0.070	0.0024
Energy use per 1,000 hours (kWh)	0.070*1,000 = 70	0.0024*1,000 = 2.4
If £0.50/kWh	70*0.5 = £35	2.4*0.5= £1.20
Cost to run 2500 hours (1 year @10 hrs/day, 250 days per annum)	£87.50	£3
If practice uses 50 bulbs	£4,375	£150

Baseline – total electricity use – by time of day

Using an electricity smart meter can show the amount of electricity used for different 30-minute segments across the day. This is shown in Figure 10.5 and can be used to understand if equipment is left on when not in use.

The energy use per hour for different days is recorded and can be analysed. For example, total daily electricity use for the Christmas period is shown in Figure 10.6.

This shows the amount of energy used on Xmas Day and Boxing Day when the practice was closed. Could equipment have been turned off and shut down when there were no staff or patients?

Further analysis of the electricity use (Table 10.4) shows 9 hours on Xmas Day from midnight. The number of kWh used per 30 min slot is shown. The practice used more

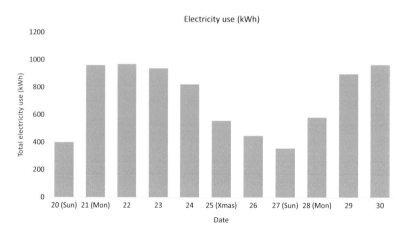

Electricity use (kWh)

FIGURE 10.5 Energy used from midnight to 10 am in one practice (1 March 2020 was a Sunday).

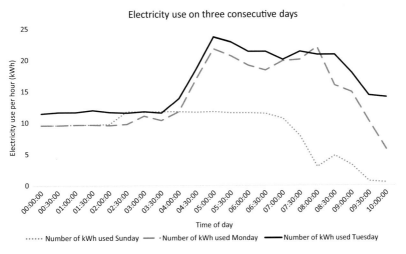

Electricity use on three consecutive days

...... Number of kWh used Sunday — · Number of kWh used Monday ▬▬ Number of kWh used Tuesday

FIGURE 10.6 Electricity use in a practice over the Xmas period.

TABLE 10.4 30-minutely Energy use from midnight on Xmas day (kWh)

TIME	25/12/2020
00:00:00	12.1
00:30:00	12.2
01:00:00	12.1
01:30:00	12.4
02:00:00	12.3
02:30:00	12.6
03:00:00	13.5
03:30:00	13.7
04:00:00	14.3
04:30:00	14.3
05:00:00	14
05:30:00	12.8
06:00:00	13.3
06:30:00	12.9
07:00:00	14.6
07:30:00	17.2
08:00:00	16.9
08:30:00	15.2

electricity between midnight and 9 a.m. on Xmas Day (when closed!) than the whole day on 30 July.

Practices (businesses and homes, etc.) that have smart meters can really (and quickly) see the impact of their behaviour actions and the real results from the changes they make.

What is using the electricity? Some equipment is in use 24 hrs a day – CCTV, fire detection systems, fridges, etc. Others are not needed continually – such as printers, computers, and lighting – and could be turned off.

Reducing demand by turning off equipment. Equipment left on when not being used or left on standby instead of "off" can be responsible for over 5% of the annual practice energy use. This figure will vary by practice and could be higher than 5% when comparing something left on 24/7 and one on 8 hrs/day for 5 days a week. Table 10.5 shows a range of behavioural actions that can be taken by a practice and an estimate of the impact on practice electricity use.

Case study Savings from *properly turning off*

Action. We decided to get everyone to turn off at the wall after their sessions, and a negotiated electrical responsibility plan was rolled out across the practice. GP and nurses' rooms were completely shut down at the wall at the end of each day.

Results. The meter readings show that our consumption has reduced by 37% in October 2021 compared with October 2020.

Conclusion. Modest behavioural changes from our electrical equipment responsibility plan have reduced our electricity consumption and saved about £1,000.

Lighting as an example. "Priority 2 Leaner" – Using less energy through technology or building modifications. Impacts of actions can be seen in Table 10.6. Assessing the starting position, and average wattage of the bulbs in situ can be useful to determine the importance of replacing bulbs. Reducing the number of bulbs used and then improving the energy efficiency of the bulbs that are used is a sensible approach.

Priority 3 – energy efficiency

Reduce energy use by increasing energy efficiency. For example, upgraded lighting and cooling equipment, improved controls and metering.

Short-term investments in technology:

- Use an "on-demand" water heater instead of a kettle for hot water.
- Practices can include measures for water softening. Build-up of limescale in a central heating system due to hard water will reduce the efficiency of heating systems.

TABLE 10.5 Impact of different actions within an example practice on electricity use

	CURRENT % OF PRACTICE'S ELECTRICITY USE	ACTION	REDUCTION IN ELECTRICITY USE	REDUCTION IN TOTAL PRACTICE ELECTRICITY USE
Computer, peripherals, and other office equipment				
IT in use	35%	Reduce number of items by 10%	10%	3.50%
		More efficient IT – reduce energy use per item	20%	7%
IT on standby out of hours	3%	Turning off IT equipment + peripherals out of hours 100%	100%	3%
Monitors	7%	Reduce energy use, brightness – improve efficiency	10%	0.70%
		Turn off (rather than stand by) when not in use	3% of energy use used out of hours	0.21%
		Reduce number used (if 50% of those who have two screens reduce to one)	50%	3.50%
Photocopiers, fax, franking machines, etc.	5%	Reduce number	50%	2.50%
		Reduce amount of time using power	25%	1.25%
Fridges				
Electricity use per fridge (if 400 kWh/year, and average use = 37,000 kWh)	1%	Clean back of fridge – improve efficiency	Up to 10% more efficient	0.30%
Number of fridges = 5 (e.g., if 2 kitchens and 3 drug fridges)	5%	Turn off fridges – reduce number used	100% reduction in use per fridge turned off	1% per fridge

TABLE 10.6 Impact on energy use of changing bulbs

AVERAGE WATTAGE OF BULBS	ENERGY USED FOR 50 BULBS PER YEAR (KWH)	% SAVING IN ENERGY USE				OVERALL PERCENTAGE REDUCTION IN ELECTRICITY USE IF AVERAGE BULB FALLS TO 5 W AND LIGHTING IS RESPONSIBLE FOR 20% OF PRACTICE ELECTRICITY USE
		To...				
		50	25	10	5	
From (average bulb wattage) 75	7,125	33.3	66.7	86.7	93.3	19
50	4,750	–	50.0	80.0	90.0	18
25	2,375		–	60.0	80.0	16
10	950			–	50.0	10
5	475				–	–

Priority 4 – greener energy – self generated electricity

Greener electricity – buy or self-generate?

Self-generation. Solar panels can be a cost-effective way of converting the natural power of sunshine into electricity or heat. Solar PV generates electricity on-site which can be used by the practice, stored for later use, or sold back to the grid. Solar Thermal uses sunlight to heat water and offset heating costs. Many UK solar energy manufacturers, suppliers, and installers are members of the Solar Trade Association (17). Check the position of your mortgage lender, as some have blocked PV installation. Wind turbines, though scientifically logical, are currently unlikely to be granted planning permission.

Priority 5 – greener energy – renewable electricity

Switch to a green tariff. Only those companies that are increasing the amount of green energy provision should be invested in or contracted with. The others are not actually changing the energy mix on the grid. The only truly carbon-reducing tariffs are those that buy renewable energy and the REGOs (renewable energy certificates called Renewable Energy Guarantees of Origin) directly from the companies that generate it. *Greener is not* *more expensive*; most suppliers now absorb the costs of REGOs. According to information from Ofgem and research by Which? (15), the Energy-Saving Trust (16), and Choose (14), the greenest tariffs are available from Good Energy, Green Energy UK, and Ecotricity.

How am I doing? The average total energy use for 80 London practices shows a spread of energy use. For an average-sized GP practice of about 500 m², energy consumption can vary from less than 100 kWh/m² to over 500 kWh/m².

What makes a difference in energy consumption? Size of practice is not the determining factor, but more the building age; building fabric, including insulation levels; double (or triple) glazing, heat loss, and type of heating system; number of staff; practice opening hours; amount of equipment used (and left on); energy efficiency of electrical equipment; amount of self-generated energy; etc.

What can I do? To make changes in behaviour, actions, or purchasing policy, it has to be "sold" on a personal level. It is important to get buy-in from management, partners, etc., and be top-down as well as bottom-up. Ideally, have a senior person responsible in their job description – for example, the finance director, practice manager, or managing partner. Ideally, include energy reduction in people's appraisals and review at each review, provide them with the authority as well as the responsibility to make changes and highlight good practice and performance. Without these processes, energy reduction is reliant on goodwill only. Most people want to help and do the right thing but get frustrated when they aren't able or allowed to. This requires effective people management – allowing people to make decisions, take actions.

Conclusion

Electricity use can be reduced by up to 30% (depending on starting position) through behaviour changes within a practice. Tech changes to more efficient equipment and/or insulation can reduce energy use further. The electricity that is used can be bought from a 100% renewable tariff and/or, ideally, from self-generating solar.

What are the most impactful domestic carbon reduction actions ranked (18)

The same principles and methods can be applied to the work setting.

1. Use renewable electricity **Even if you don't do anything else...**

2. Refurbish, renovate existing premises

3. Heat pump installation

4. Renewable based heating

5. Passivhaus standard buildings

6. Produce renewable electricity

7. Better thermal insulation

8. Smart metering

9. Lower room temperature

10. More efficient appliances

What are the top practical actions I could do this month?

Change energy supplier

- 100% renewable

Simple energy audit

- Identify which equipment are highest users
- Number of pieces of equipment vs high-intensity energy use
- E.g., 20 monitors or 1 heater?

Green team

- Work on reducing energy consumption initially.
- Increase team awareness of the energy hierarchy triangle.
- Identify behaviour changes across the team.
- Reduce energy use.
- Unplug unused phone chargers and other equipment.
- Incorporate a jumper into a staff uniform if your premises are cold. Patients will usually be wearing a coat and in the practice for a shorter time than staff.

Procurement policy

- Most energy-efficient equipment

Prepare for future needs

- E.g., electricity-led heating

Start making a plan as to when you can implement suggestions.

Putting a date to it will help you work out what resources are needed and when. For example,

- set a date to install motion sensor lights for storerooms, toilets, staff rooms etc.;
- look at whether you could fit solar panels;
- install insulation and fit draft excluders where possible;
- ask suppliers to provide information on energy-saving models when buying new electrical goods and optical equipment;
- consider if any freestanding heaters are efficient and environmentally friendly, and make changes where you can; or
- install an energy-efficient water pump/boiler/other eco-friendly plumbing and heating options.

Pledges

Pledge – from this chapter, I will pledge to…

1.
2.
3.

References

1 https://www.birmingham.ac.uk/news/2023/2022-heatwave-struck-off-surgery-in-fifth-of-uk-hospitals
2 https://assets.publishing.service.gov.uk/government/uploads/system/uploads/attachment_data/file/936797/ND-NEED.pdf
3 https://www.gov.uk/find-energy-certificate
4 https://en.wikipedia.org/wiki/Energy_hierarchy
5 www.jpaget.nhs.uk/media/588250/Estates-Net-Zero-Carbon-Delivery-Plan.pdf
6 https://www.passivhaustrust.org.uk/news/detail/?nId=1010
7 https://www.passivhaustrust.org.uk/what_is_passivhaus.php
8 https://www.designingbuildings.co.uk/wiki/Thermal_bridging_in_buildings
9 https://www.passivhaustrust.org.uk/competitions_and_campaigns/passivhaus-retrofit/
10 https://www.heatpumps.org.uk/
11 https://www.homebuilding.co.uk/advice/infrared-heating
12 https://www.salixfinance.co.uk/PSDS
13 https://www.nia-uk.org/
14 https://www.choose.co.uk/energy/guide/green-awards-2022/

15 https://www.which.co.uk/reviews/energy-companies/article/best-and-worst-energy-companies/which-energy-survey-results-ajqM43e6ycY8

16 https://energysavingtrust.org.uk/how-switch-supplier-and-shop-around-save-your-energy-bills/

17 https://solarenergyuk.org/

18 Figure 5 https://iopscience.iop.org/article/10.1088/1748-9326/ab8589

Resources

- *NHS and Net Zero – Health and Care Act 2022* www.england.nhs.uk/greenernhs/a-net-zero-nhs
- *NHS Net Zero Building Standard* www.england.nhs.uk/publication/nhs-net-zero-building-standard/
- *Estate "Net-Zero" Carbon Delivery Plan* www.jpaget.nhs.uk/media/588250/Estates-Net-Zero-Carbon-Delivery-Plan.pdf

11

Travel and transport
Matt Sawyer

Case study

Maria, a 32-year-old pregnant social worker, attends an appointment wanting to understand why her baby has growth restriction. Her midwife said her test for smoking (carbon monoxide) showed a high reading despite having never smoked or lived with a smoker. She's wondering if it could be related to living near one of the busiest roads in town.

Things to consider:

- How common is it for air pollution to be above World Health Organization (WHO) guidelines in UK towns and cities?
- What are the main components of air pollution?
- What other diseases might be linked to air pollution?
- Can you identify which pollutants come from which sources and what needs to be done to prevent the linked problems?

Air quality is determined by the amount of particles and gases in the atmosphere. Small particulate matter less than 2.5 microns (known as PM2.5), as well as particulate matter of other sizes – e.g., 10 microns in size (PM10), nitrous oxides (NOx), sulphur dioxide (SO_2), methane, volatile organic compounds (VOCs) are the commonly identified pollutants in the United Kingdom.

Air pollution is commonly above WHO maximum levels in many cities a lot of the time. Absolute levels have dropped in the United Kingdom from 1990 to 2020 due to improvements in vehicle engines. Since 2013, the biggest source of carbon monoxide has been residential (e.g., from indoor fires) rather than vehicles for most people, but this person lives in an atypical place.

DOI: 10.1201/9781003491583-11

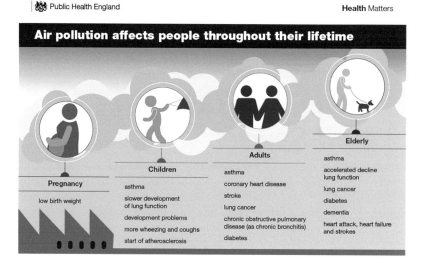

FIGURE 11.1 Impact of air pollution throughout people's lifetime.

Air pollution causes health issues across all age groups and many of the body's systems. In addition to respiratory problems, other impacts include growth retardation before birth, worse educational attainment at school, heart attacks and strokes, early onset dementia, diabetes, and cataracts (Figure 11.1).

Actions

Encourage the patient to reduce their exposure to indoor and outdoor sources of air pollution:

- Walk, cycle, and scoot more, especially using the back streets away from polluting traffic. Walkers and cyclists experience less air pollution on the same journey than conventional car drivers.
- Avoid unnecessary burning at home (e.g., in a stove or fire) unless it's your only source of heat.
- If you rely on wood for your heating, use dry wood or approved manufactured solid fuels), and check that your appliance is eco-design accredited.
- If you have to drive, switch your engine off when you're stationary, and try to choose electric vehicles where you can.
- Reduce exposure by increasing the distance from the pollution source or adding vegetation as a barrier between roads and pedestrians or housing.

Linking with others can help reduce air pollution at the source:

- Talk to your family and friends about what they can do to both minimise their contribution to air pollution and protect themselves from it.

- Tell your local councillor you're worried about air pollution and that you support them taking action to clean up your town/city's air.
- Talk to parents at the school gates about how air pollution in the area could be improved. Ideas might include setting up a walking bus, lift sharing, and suggestions on how to improve walking and cycling routes in the community.
- Ask your boss and/or your human resources manager how they are tackling air pollution in your workplace. From supporting home working, facilitating good travel choices for staff, to improving fleets, there is a great deal that organisations can do to improve air quality.
- Ask companies to sign up to become businesses for clean air and update their transport policies or change suppliers (see "Resources").

Resources

https://www.cleanairhub.org.uk/home
https://www.globalactionplan.org.uk/business-clean-air-taskforce/business-for-clean-air

Introduction

Across England, there are around one million appointments in General Practice each day (336–384 million per year). About 70% were face-to-face in 2023 (1). Additionally, there are about 13 million sight tests per (2), 26 million dental visits (3), and a staggering 438 million pharmacy visits annually. Around 3.5% (9.5 billion miles) of all road travel in England relates to patients, visitors, staff, and suppliers to the NHS. Travel contributes around 14% of the NHS's total emissions.

Impact on patients and community. Some modes of travel carry a high health, social, and environmental cost – and a high carbon cost. Various pollutants – both particulate matter and gases – are generated by petrol and diesel vehicles (collectively known as ICE or "internal combustion engine" vehicles). These contribute to poor brain development and educational achievements in the young, asthma and other respiratory diseases, heart attacks, strokes, diabetes, cataracts, Parkinson's, and dementia in the old (5). Mike Berners-Lee, in his book *There Is No Planet B*, calculated that for each mile travelled by an average diesel vehicle across a town or city, 12 minutes of life is lost from the community. Each 5-mile trip to the GPs, or on the school run, or to the supermarket "costs" the surrounding community one hour of life. In 2021, there were over 12 million diesel cars on the United Kingdom's roads (6).

Additionally, the lack of physical activity due to cars contributes to obesity, diabetes, and heart disease. In contrast, walking, cycling, and being more active will improve health and reduce the risks of developing a host of damaging, lifelong conditions.

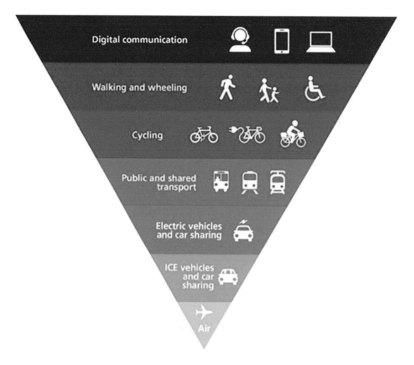

FIGURE 11.2 Travel hierarchy triangle (19).

What is the effect on the planet? In 2022, travel, as the largest emitting sector in the United Kingdom, contributed 34% of all UK greenhouse emissions, with road transport being responsible for the majority (7).

Travel hierarchy. The travel hierarchy triangle (Figure 11.2) classifies various travel options, with the most sustainable at the top. Following the hierarchy approach helps to reduce the environmental impact of the travel to and from the practice.

What will be the impact of changing behaviour, and which behaviours are best for me and my practice? Understanding which actions have the most impact on emissions from primary care is essential to prioritise time and effort. Transport of patients and staff has a substantial emission footprint. ICE transport causes harm directly through air pollution, indirectly through worse physical health and fitness, and it is financially more costly.

Reducing the distance travelled (e.g., home working or consulting people virtually) or less carbon-intensive transport (e.g., hybrid journeys, smaller vehicles, shared vehicles, or electric vehicles) will improve outcomes. Additional benefits of active travel are well documented (8). Changing wholesale from fossil fuel vehicles to electric vehicles is not a panacea. Although in-use emissions and pollution are reduced (9), there are embedded emissions (during the manufacture of the vehicle) and continuing effects, especially on PM2.5 from braking and tyres (10), to consider.

TABLE 11.1 Proportion of staff with different-length daily commutes. Sample size 396. Survey from spring 2023

	PERCENTAGE OF STAFF (%) TRAVELLING DISTANCE			
	LESS THAN A MILE	WITHIN 5 MILES	BETWEEN 5 AND 10 MILES	OVER 10 MILES
Admin	10	49	18	22
Doctor	20	34	22	24
Management	16	20	24	40
Nurse and other clinical roles	5	47	21	26

Understanding current travel patterns. The following data summarises a travel survey of General Practice staff working across the United Kingdom. It also asked, "On a perfect day (sun is shining, no other commitments, etc.), how would you *like* to be able to travel to work?" It illustrates insights, but each organisation will have different potential insights (Table 11.1).

Forty per cent of staff who currently commute less than 1 mile drive on their own (Figure 11.3). This rises to around 75% of those who commute 1–5 miles per day and 80% of those commuting 5–10 miles per day.

When asked about their travel aspirations – commuting on a "perfect day" – the proportion wanting to drive fell substantially, with most wanting to travel more actively – whether walking, cycling, or with others.

Figures 11.3 and 11.4 show the dramatic change in mode of commute for under 1 mile and between 5 and 10 miles per day. The proportion of those wanting to drive almost halves from around 80% currently driving to only 44% having it as their preferred or ideal mode of travel.

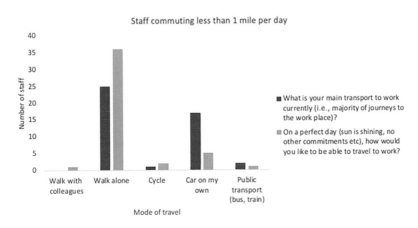

FIGURE 11.3 Staff commuting less than 1 mile per day by current mode of travel (black) and aspirational (grey).

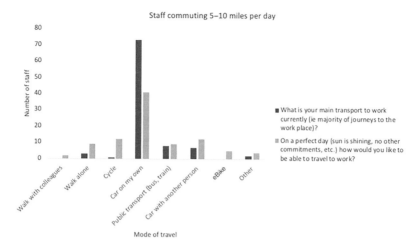

Staff commuting 5–10 miles per day

Legend:
■ What is your main transport to work currently (ie majority of journeys to the work place)?
■ On a perfect day (sun is shining, no other commitments, etc.) how would you like to be able to travel to work?

X-axis (Mode of travel): Walk with colleagues, Walk alone, Cycle, Car on my own, Public transport (bus, train), Car with another person, eBike, Other

Y-axis (Number of staff): 0, 10, 20, 30, 40, 50, 60, 70, 80

FIGURE 11.4 Staff commuting 5–10 miles per day by current mode of travel (black) and aspirational (grey).

Barriers and enablers. If staff want to travel more actively, what is stopping them? Each person from this survey listed different options of what stops them – and what could be done to enable them to change mode of travel. This revealed external, personal, and practice factors.

External factors, such as

- bad weather → **can't** change the weather, but we **can** find protective clothing;
- distance/time to travel → **can't** shorten, but we **can** find routes which are shortest or least hilly; or
- safety on local roads → we **can** find routes which are quietest.

Personal factors, such as

- not having a bike → we **can** explore cycle hire, salary sacrifice scheme;
- not being able to cycle → we **can** signpost cycle lessons;
- not being fit enough → we **can** improve via active practice or park run practice or by considering electric bikes; or
- not being interested → staff who do walk/cycle **can** have an influence.

Practice factors, such as

- lack of cycle racks/secure parking → we **can** discuss with the practice manager/owner regarding installation;
- too much to carry → we **can** discuss alternative carrying options or reducing the amount carried (e.g., shared on-call bag for doctors kept in the practice);
- changing facilities → we **can** discuss installation with the practice manager/owner; or
- need for transport for visits from work base to patients' home/other venues → we **can** alter who does the visits or stagger the input to visits.

What would a travel survey look like in your place of work? Carrying out a travel survey can be very helpful in identifying the (micro-)enablers people need to change their behaviour.

What are the most impactful travel actions? What sort of actions could be taken which had the biggest impact on greenhouse gas emissions (Figure 11.5)?

This research paper suggests "no car" is preferable – what this would mean for delivery of healthcare is addressed in the following section. The second most impactful is changing from a petrol/diesel (ICE) to a battery electric vehicle, followed by using public transport. The reduction in emissions achieved by changing travel – either individually, collectively as staff, or by patient – is shown in Table 11.2. To work out the impact of your action, look in the left-hand column for your current travel and then across the

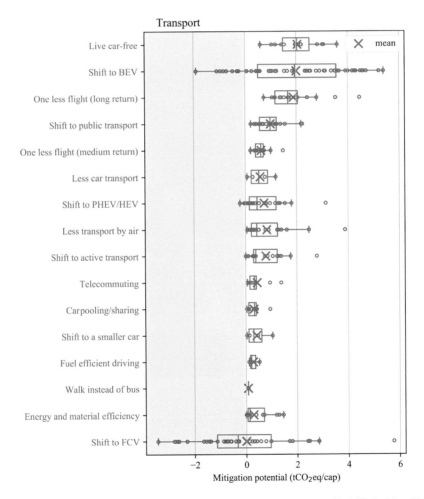

FIGURE 11.5 Priority of travel actions (11). BEV: battery electric vehicle. PHEV: petrol hybrid electric vehicle. HEV: hybrid electric vehicle. FCV: fuel cell vehicle (i.e., hydrogen).

(Diana Ivanova et al. 2020 *Environ. Res. Lett.* 15 093001).

TABLE 11.2 Reduction in emissions associated with travel for different behaviours

	Emissions per mile	SHIFT TO PREFERRED NEW BEHAVIOUR											
		LARGE PETROL	LARGE DIESEL	MED PETROL	MED DIESEL	SMALL PETROL	SMALL DIESEL	PHEV (1)	50% DRIVE: 50% WALK (2)	BUS	CYCLE/ WALK/ ACTIVE TRAVEL	TELE-COMMUTE	BEV
		0.444	0.337	0.296	0.270	0.235	0.225	0.150	0.1375	0.0965	0	0	0
Large petrol	0.444	—	24.1	33.3	39.2	47.1	49.3	66.2	69.0	78.3	100.0	100.0	100.0
Large diesel	0.337	-31.8	—	12.2	19.9	30.3	33.2	55.5	59.2	71.4	100.0	100.0	100.0
Med petrol	0.296	-50.0	-13.9	—	8.8	20.6	24.0	49.3	53.5	67.4	100.0	100.0	100.0
Med diesel	0.270	-64.4	-24.8	-9.6	—	13.0	16.7	44.4	49.1	64.3	100.0	100.0	100.0
Small petrol	0.235	-88.9	-43.4	-26.0	-14.9	—	4.3	36.2	41.5	58.9	100.0	100.0	100.0
Small diesel	0.225	-97.3	-49.8	-31.6	-20.0	-4.4	—	33.3	38.9	57.1	100.0	100.0	100.0
PHEV	0.150	-196.0	-124.7	-97.3	-80.0	-56.7	-50.0	—	8.3	35.7	100.0	100.0	100.0
50% drive:50% walk	0.1375	-222.9	-145.1	-115.3	-96.4	-70.9	-63.6	-9.1	—	29.8	100.0	100.0	100.0
Bus	0.0965	-360.1	-249.2	-206.7	-179.8	-143.5	-133.2	-55.4	-42.5	—	100.0	100.0	100.0

Shift from current behaviour

1. PHEV – plug-in electric hybrid. 2. Average car @0.275kg co2e/mile (2022).

top for your new mode of travel. For example, moving from a large diesel car to a plug-in electric hybrid (PHEV) would reduce emissions by 55.5%. E-bikes were not part of the UK government data set, and so do not feature here, though Mike Berners-Lee suggests that they use less energy than traditional cycling.

No travel option

Can high-quality healthcare be delivered by primary care without patients (or staff) having to travel at all? The most effective way to change travel behaviour was demonstrated during the pandemic – *default telephone appointments and triage assessments*. This appears to work better for follow-up care and reviewing treatment plans and progress than for first contact and diagnosis-making. Dental and optometry are more "hands on" aspects of primary care, and while some remote monitoring of conditions is helpful for patient travel and patient convenience reasons, face-to-face appointments will need to remain a significant part of the picture.

In England, targets to offer telephone appointments in General Practice were introduced post-pandemic, although obviously not at the expense of patient health. NHS England provides updated guidance – for example. An implementation toolkit (12) is available based on NHS England's guiding principles (13).

The COVID-19 pandemic demanded that healthcare professionals rethink how they deliver care in ways that reduce the risk of infection to both the healthcare professional and the patient. Using telemedicine is one approach that kept both patients and healthcare professionals safe. The same standard of care must apply to telemedicine consultations as for face-to-face consultations. Practitioners must ensure they practise in accordance with any applicable laws and regulations around the diagnosis, treatment, and provision of prescriptions to patients. Other options used during the response to COVID-19 included video ward rounds of care homes, remote monitoring of patients' health in virtual COVID wards (14), or using e-consultation tools.

- For staff, offering remote work/working from home where feasible for non-clinical staff and holding staff meetings virtually are options.
- For patients, **combine appointments**. Encourage families to schedule their appointments consecutively on the same day and keep the number of appointments that patients attend to a minimum to avoid duplicated travel.

Case study. The NHS App is helping to reduce travel to GP practices, with an average of 22,000 car journeys saved every month.

How? Using the NHS App to manage appointments and order repeat prescriptions online.

Source: https://digital.nhs.uk/news/2022/nhs-app-saving-around-22000-car-journeys-every-month

Active travel

Staff can be encouraged to decrease their individual (and therefore the practice's collective) carbon footprint with some simple schemes. Walking to work would have the lowest carbon footprint and should be the first port of call for staff and patients where possible. Cycling to work schemes (16) reduce carbon emissions and also lessen the need for a car park. Reviewing your organisation's barriers and enablers (see the aforementioned) to identify the most effective actions is important. Common issues are providing secure bike storage, shower facilities, and an on-site bicycle puncture repair kit and pump helps too!

Priming patients for active travel. For in-person appointments, patients can be primed with active travel information as part of their text booking reminder, including the following:

- Cycle routes
- Walking routes to the surgery
- Bus timetables and location of bus stops, including walking time

Case study – A Scottish GP

I'm not your average climate campaigner. I'm not really a campaigner of any sort. I just fell into this.

I live in Glasgow, and I trained to be a GP there. During my training, I made a commitment to cycle to work every day for a year: essentially, I had expensive hedonistic tendencies that needed to be balanced out. One Christmas Day, after arriving through slush and ice in mud-spattered Lycra, a colleague legitimately asked what was wrong with me.

I explained to her my goal, which she did not understand. I then said that I didn't like driving my electric car because owning one makes you aware of just how much energy it takes to move two tonnes of metal around. Didn't she know that me driving to work was the equivalent of boiling a kettle solidly for two hours? She asked the immortal question: "Are you some kind of eco-warrior or something?"

That was the first time I had equated my actions with being in any way environmental. To me, it just made sense. I cycled because of the fresh air, the buzz as I arrived at work, and the fact I could eat and drink what I wanted. I drove an early electric car because, at the time in Scotland, a charging network meant they were basically free to run, quieter, and a novelty at the time. The betterment of the world was a handy side effect.

Changing behaviour to more active travel and modelling behaviour. Staff are important positive role models for each other and patients. Seeing staff arriving on foot or by bike, or signing up and promoting local activities – e.g., park runs are positive images. The practice can demonstrate its commitment by signing up to the "Active Practice Charter" (17) and improving active travel infrastructure. One in four people say they would be *more active* if it was recommended by a GP or nurse.

Top tip. Start with small, achievable changes – i.e., you don't need to walk or cycle the whole way, and it may be better to cycle part of the journey – e.g., to a bus stop – until you are confident to cycle further.

Communal travel

Where walking or cycling is not an option, encourage shared transport. There are options to increase the number of staff using shared vehicles. For example,

- shared vehicles by practice staff (see the following case study),
- incentivise staff car sharing by reviewing shift times for staff who are geographically close,
- create personalised staff travel plans,
- offer a loan for yearly travel passes at zero interest, or
- facilitate flexible working patterns to fit with public transport timings.

Easy wins include identifying opportunities to incentivise low-carbon travel:

- Publicise the bus routes and bus timetables on the practice website.
- Signpost the path from the surgery to the nearest bus stop.
- Default advice on the bottom of surgery letters to use the bus.

Case study – lift sharing

Action. Staff home postcodes were plotted on a map, and four lived within a couple of streets of each other. All drove separately. When asked, they wished to share lifts but couldn't due to shift patterns and start/finish times differing.

Results. Staff had their shift times coordinated to start and finish at the same time. They started lift sharing.

Conclusion. Four staff started sharing and saved themselves money (quarter of the money spent on fuel), reduced air pollution (reduced cars on the road by 75%), and improved staff morale (saw each other more).

Car use

Single occupancy vehicles create several problems:

- Space used on the road (the United Kingdom has around 250,000 miles of paved road)
- Air pollution from exhaust fumes and gases (diesel, petrol)
- Air pollution from tyre and brake dust (diesel, petrol, AND electric)

Practices can help overcome barriers for staff and patients to "go electric":
- Install practice electric charge points for cars.

What actions could I help my practice take to promote other travel options?

In winter 2023, the NHS Travel and Transport Team published their travel strategy, which includes advice and guidance specifically for primary care and case studies (19) (Table 11.3).

What are the wider barriers? Changing to active travel can be challenging for those whose social status is linked to the vehicle that they drive.

There are well-identified UK issues about the quality and extent of cycle and active travel infrastructure and support which are outside the power of primary care organisations to change. Similarly, current approaches to fuel and vehicle tax do not reflect the health impacts of ICE, and UK air pollution legal levels are dangerously lax compared to WHO recommendations.

Behaviour changes on a wider scale – at system level. Primary care staff are in a special and unique position. Collectively, there is a powerful voice and ability to lobby those in power for a healthier approach. There are many opportunities to get involved in "travel mode shift" (18).

Case study – Modeshift STARS

Primary care will form part of the STARS Healthcare scheme. Modeshift Healthcare STARS recognises healthcare organisations that have shown excellence in supporting cycling, walking, and other forms of sustainable and active travel. The toolkits help create, develop, and implement; monitor; and evaluate a travel plan for practices. This helps promote healthier lifestyles for staff, patients, and communities while also creating safer environments, promoting urban and rural regeneration, and improving air quality. Visit https://modeshiftstars.org/ to understand how your practice can be involved.

TABLE 11.3 Variety of actions for primary care facilities

PROPOSED MEASURE	DESCRIPTION	POTENTIAL LEVEL OF IMPACT	IMPLEMENTATION COST	PATIENTS	STAFF
Staff cycle parking	Provision of long-term secure and covered cycle parking and shower facilities	High	Medium		*
Patient cycle parking	Provision of short-term cycle parking conveniently located and accessible with the potential to secure bikes	High	Medium	*	
Cycle to work scheme	Providing staff with a loan to purchase bicycles at a discounted cost	High	Low		*
Public transport route maps and timetables	Making timetables and route maps for buses and trains available on the organisation's website and providing relevant links	High	Low	*	*
Public transport season ticket loans	Travel loans for interested staff and raising staff awareness of the financial benefits that can be achieved using public transport	High	Low		*
Walking and public transport map	Distribution of tailored maps in order to increase local knowledge of the area and encourage walking and public transport usage while reducing the perceived need to drive	Medium	Low	*	*

(*Continued*)

TABLE 11.3 (Continued) Variety of actions for primary care facilities

PROPOSED MEASURE	DESCRIPTION	POTENTIAL LEVEL OF IMPACT	IMPLEMENTATION COST	PATIENTS	STAFF
Promotion of walking as a healthy way to travel	Raise awareness of the health benefits associated with regular walking and encouraging its uptake	Medium	Low	*	*
Cycle maps	Increase local knowledge of the area encouraging cycling while reducing the perceived need to drive	Medium	Low	*	*
Promotion of cycling as a healthy way to travel	Raise awareness of the health benefits associated with regular cycling and encouraging its uptake	Medium	Low	*	*
Promotion of public transport benefits	Promotion of benefits that can be gained by public transport use	Medium	Low	*	*
Taxi services	Promotion of taxi services for patients when travelling to and from the surgery	Medium	Low	*	
Cycle training	Promotion of cycle training courses through the practice website	Low	Low	*	*
Car sharing scheme	Promotion of car sharing for staff making similar journeys and who are looking to cut the financial cost or environmental impact of car use	Low	Low	*	*
Accessibility to the rail network	Promotion of routes between the surgery and nearby railway stations	Variable by location	Low	*	*

Conclusion

Travel emissions for staff and patients could be substantially reduced by changing transport to more active transport methods. The added financial and health gains of active travel make it a more attractive option than replacing all petrol and diesel cars with electric vehicles.

Reducing overall travel demand

- More compact urban spaces
- Allow flexible working
- Carpooling, car sharing
- Encourage teleconsulting

There is much to be gained for patients, practice staff, and practice finances and planetary health from reducing reliance on motorcars and travelling more actively.

My pledge(s) are

1.
2.
3.

My practice pledge(s) are

1.
2.
3.

Where next?

Chapter 12 for procurement of goods and services
Chapter 17 for behaviour change
Chapter 18 for working with organisations

References

1 https://digital.nhs.uk/data-and-information/publications/statistical/appointments-in-general-practice/may-2023

2 https://www.england.nhs.uk/primary-care/eye-health/

3 https://healthmedia.blog.gov.uk/2023/05/05/nhs-dentists-how-were-helping-more-patients-to-get-appointments/

4 https://digital.nhs.uk/services/podac/pharmacy

5 https://www.gov.uk/government/publications/air-pollution-applying-all-our-health/air-pollution-applying-all-our-health

6 https://www.racfoundation.org/motoring-faqs/environment#a8

7 https://assets.publishing.service.gov.uk/government/uploads/system/uploads/attachment_data/file/1147372/2022_Provisional_emissions_statistics_report.pdf

8 https://www.health.org.uk/evidence-hub/transport/active-travel/health-benefits-of-active-travel-preventable-early-deaths

9 Appendix A2 https://assets.publishing.service.gov.uk/government/uploads/system/uploads/attachment_data/file/1062603/lifecycle-analysis-of-UK-road-vehicles.pdf

10 https://en.wikipedia.org/wiki/Embedded_emissions

11 Figure 3 https://iopscience.iop.org/article/10.1088/1748-9326/ab8589

12 https://www.england.nhs.uk/wp-content/uploads/2020/01/online-consultations-implementation-toolkit-v1.1-updated.pdf

13 https://www.england.nhs.uk/coronavirus/wp-content/uploads/sites/52/2020/03/C0479-principles-of-safe-video-consulting-in-general-practice-updated-29-may.pdf

14 https://www.england.nhs.uk/coronavirus/publication/covid-virtual-ward/

15 https://www.rcgp.org.uk/clinical-and-research/our-programmes/clinical-priorities/physical-activity-and-lifestyle.aspx

16 https://www.sustrans.org.uk/our-blog/get-active/2019/everyday-walking-and-cycling/the-cycle-to-work-scheme-explained

17 https://www.rcgp.org.uk/clinical-and-research/our-programmes/clinical-priorities/physical-activity-and-lifestyle.aspx

18 https://www.health.org.uk/publications/long-reads/how-transport-offers-a-route-to-better-health

19 https://www.england.nhs.uk/wp-content/uploads/2023/10/PRN00712_NHS-Net-Zero-Travel-and-Transport-Strategy.pdf

Resources

Mike Berners-Lee in his book *There Is No Planet B.*

https://www.cleanairhub.org.uk/clean-air-information/air-pollution-health

https://www.cleanairday.org.uk/free-resources/workplace

https://www.globalactionplan.org.uk/business-clean-air-taskforce/business-for-clean-air

https://www.cleanairhub.org.uk/clean-air-information/what-can-i-do/how-can-i-link-with-others-to-create-cleaner-air

12

Procurement of goods and services
Matt Sawyer

Case study

When the COVID-19 pandemic started, like most practices, East Dean adapted to the use of PPE for all clinical encounters. Jenny, a junior partner, was keen for the practice to move to using reusable masks early on in the pandemic and, as the advice changed, to have clear policies to ensure that PPE was used only when there was clear guidance it was necessary. Mark, the practice manager, was very concerned that his practice should be above reproach and encouraged all staff to use only disposable masks and to wear aprons, etc., even when there was no contact with body fluids. The practice meeting became fraught when Jenny asked for a detailed breakdown of the financial and environmental costs of PPE.

Introduction

> *Every time you spend money, you're casting a vote for the kind of world you want.*
>
> **Anna Lappe**

Across healthcare, goods and services are a major financial expense and carry a high environmental impact. Procurement is at least £32 billion in England – or 17% of total NHS spending. It is likely to be an underestimate, as some primary care funding is spent on goods and services. Greenhouse gas emissions for the whole NHS, not just primary care, are shown in Figure 1.7 (Chapter 1). Procurement of medical and non-medical equipment, other procurement, water and waste, and business services are responsible

DOI: 10.1201/9781003491583-12

for just under 50% of total emissions – or around 11 million tonnes CO_2e per annum. Goods which are bought are consumed and then become waste. Procurement and waste are two sides of the same coin.

Scopes Greenhouse gas emissions are divided into three "Scopes". These are used to determine where emissions are coming from and can help identify possibilities for reducing emissions. See Figure 12.1 for details.

- **Scope 1 – direct greenhouse gas release**. Usually, from burning gas on-site (e.g., gas boiler), anaesthetic gas use (e.g., nitrous oxide or f-gases), and using fuel in vehicles on-site.

- **Scope 2 – indirect emissions from purchased electricity**.

- **Scope 3 – emissions from all other aspects**, including purchasing goods and services, staff and visitor (patient/client/customer) travel, including GP visits, distribution of goods, waste disposal, etc.

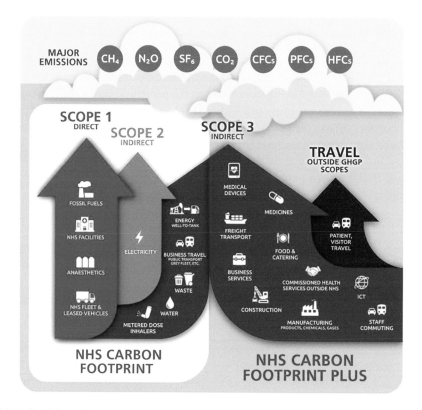

FIGURE 12.1 Breakdown of the NHS carbon footprint.

(https://www.england.nhs.uk/greenernhs/a-net-zero-nhs/)

What happens across healthcare with services, goods, and waste?

Services

Business services cover all the professional services used across primary care, such as telephony, computers and IT, accountancy and finance, and payroll and insurance (see "Resources" at the end of the chapter for a fuller list). Each external service that a practice uses for running their business has a carbon and nature footprint. Part of their footprint forms part of our footprint. We can lower our footprint by influencing those around us, and those whose services we use, to start their own net-zero or decarbonisation and nature-positive journey.

The top actions that can be taken include the following:

- Audit practice outgoings on goods and services.
- Identify your expenditure hotspots.
- Review services and cancel those no longer needed or used.
- For those used, identify any substitutes with lower-carbon alternatives which are less environmentally harmful.
- Work with your suppliers and ask about their plans to tackle their carbon emissions.
- Set deadlines for them to improve.

Goods

The goods that are used to deliver healthcare in the morning often become waste and pollution in the afternoon.

Business as usual? Figure 12.2 shows a traditional, linear approach to goods has been employed of "take – make – waste".

There is no "away" when throwing away. Products, when they are at the end of their useful life are buried in the ground (or at sea) or incinerated or left lying around. There is an alternative, and it's circular.

What is a circular economy? A circular economy (Figure 12.3) keeps materials and goods in use for as long as possible, and through recycling, remanufacturing, refurbishing, and reusing, reduces waste to a minimum.

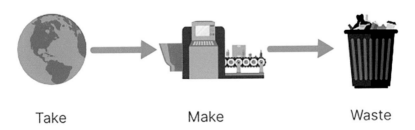

Take   Make   Waste

FIGURE 12.2 Diagram of take-make-waste.

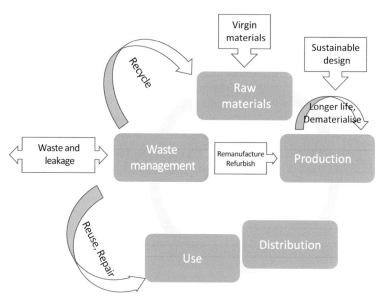

FIGURE 12.3 Diagram of the circular economy.

(Authors own).

A circular approach involves all stages – from better design, low-energy production techniques, reduced resource use – and more sustainable resources, extending life expectancy and repairability of the item – to improved ease of dismantling and recyclability at the end of life.

Improving procurement. The first challenge is to identify whether the product is genuinely needed. The greenest procurement is not purchasing the extra "buy one get one free" printer or another unnecessary item.

How changing product design can help practices. In the product journey, from mineral extraction to clinical usage, all materials used in primary care have an environmental impact. A careful balance is needed between the desired healthcare outcomes and the management of associated environmental impacts. Changing design means products which are better designed and more suited to purpose, constructed from more robust materials for a longer life, and have dismantling at the end of life built in from the outset. This can mean reduced costs in the long run and better quality for the practitioner and patient.

Green procurement plans. Practice *Green Action Plans* can be developed which are focused on your organisation, including the number of employees, key services provided, size, configuration, geography, and any other pertinent background information.

The Green Action Plans normally focus on nine key areas:

- Workforce and system leadership
- Sustainable models of care
- Digital transformation
- Travel and transport
- Estates and facilities
- Medicines
- Supply chain and procurement
- Food and nutrition
- Adaptation

ICS-level green plans and procurement policy. Integrated Care Systems (ICSs) in England have been told to develop a Green Plan which sets out aims and objectives to deliver carbon reduction. Engagement between ICSs and primary care is widely variable. If primary care facilities are not involved in the creation of ICS Green Plans, they are unlikely to feel fully signed up and engaged with the Green Plans. An example of an ICS Green Plan which specifically covers primary care is South East London (SEL ICS) (1). There are opportunities to get engaged with your ICS or the relevant organisation in other countries and their Green Plan and a dedicated Greener Practice network.

Practice-level green plans and procurement policy. Practices can have their own Green Plan covering the key areas mentioned earlier. This book can be used to help provide you with ideas and timescales for the actions required. See Appendix 20.1 for a template and Chapters 10 and 11.

What are the most impactful actions? It can feel difficult to know which actions are most important and will have the most impact. A ranking of action by impact is available for personal actions (2) but what about in the workplace?

Some places start with the easiest (but often smallest and least impactful) actions as a positive example of what can be achieved and then move on to bigger, more complex – and more significant – actions. Other workplaces start by looking to tackle a more significant area first by using the enthusiasm and commitment of the staff. The choice may depend on which gathers the most support in each practice. It can be best to *just get started* and *do something* rather than prevaricate. Some actions are single one-offs, such as changing the bank account provider (which can be very impactful in carbon reduction terms) or electricity provider. Other actions require behaviour change, such as turning off lights and computers when not in use or using active travel to get to the workplace.

Case study evidence from Scotland suggests that the most important factors in making low carbon initiatives successful are *building shared individual and organisational values* through individual and group-based *staff involvement* combined with *senior management commitment*.

Case study

Office furniture. Warp-it (3) helps businesses find, give away, or loan office furniture, equipment, and other resources. They help save money, time, and space.

- Reduce waste disposal and purchasing costs.
- No need to purchase new equipment and resources.
- Find a new owner for your surplus kit in your organisation or beyond.

NHS procurement policy – what is the Greener NHS/NHSE doing to incentivise (or penalise) suppliers? In the United Kingdom in 2023, an Evergreen Sustainable Suppliers Assessment was introduced for the NHS Supply Chain Frameworks and Medicines Framework (4). However, it did not cover other goods and services provided to the NHS and did not mention primary care.

It is not clear how the Evergreen Assessment will impact primary care procurement or care delivery. Understanding the rationale behind the Sustainable Suppliers Assessment may be helpful to practices.

What does this mean to primary care? Currently, it is not anticipated that each primary care organisation will be required to produce its own Carbon Reduction Plan. However, the guidance can support an approach that practices can use when considering their environmental impact in a practice *Green Action Plan*. Some healthcare industries have started to calculate their nature impacts and dependencies both for themselves and their suppliers (8, 9). Whilst the NHS does not currently have nature targets embedded in their procurement frameworks, understanding these will help to harness health's influence for a nature-positive future. Table 12.1 looks at each of the four pillars and how the Sustainable Supplier Assessment could be applied to each.

A practice *Green Action Plan* can help give a desired goal and checklist for the practice, a focus for the minds of the staff and set out the ethos and values of the practice.

Social value. It is important for the NHS to only have reputable suppliers providing goods and services as demonstrated with PPN 06/21. This helps reduce the risk of using child labour, sweatshops, or other heinous social crimes healthcare should not be funding.

Procurement. Developing a sustainability procurement policy covers purchasing, waste reduction, disposal, recycling, social responsibility, energy reduction, and sustainable and ethical supply. Switching suppliers can be a big decision, so start off by simply asking your suppliers for their sustainability policy and research to establish who is greenwashing and who is really moving towards sustainability. A sustainable procurement policy may include the following:

- Gradually move to more sustainable suppliers.
- Talk with your team about ways you can reduce the resources you use.
- Consider energy-efficient options that consume less power when purchasing new equipment.

TABLE 12.1 Evergreen sustainable supplier assessment tool and primary care

CATEGORY	GP	DENTIST	PHARMACY	OPTICIAN
Confirm commitment to achieve net zero by 2045	To confirm within practice *Green Action Plan*			
Provide current emissions for their UK operations at a minimum, for the sources included in Scope 1 and 2 of the Greenhouse Gas Protocol and a defined subset of Scope 3 emission.				
Scope 1 (gas and anaesthetic gases) Scope 2 (electricity)	Gas + electric bill; regas of fridges	Gas + electric bill; regas of fridges; anaesthetic gas	Gas + electric bill; regas of fridges	Gas + electric bill; regas of fridges
Upstream transportation and distribution	Transport of goods bought by the practice			
Waste generated in operations	Waste bill	Waste bill	Waste bill	Waste bill
Business travel	Audit annual business travel (see reference for definitions, etc.); annual accountants submission			
Employee commuting	Annual staff travel survey (How do you travel? How far do you travel?) converted to CO_2e emissions			
Downstream transportation and distribution	Distribution of products sold from the practice and customer			
Suppliers may provide additional categories of Scope 3 emissions if the previous categories are included and clearly identified.	Optional for practices			
Provide emissions reporting in CO_2e (carbon dioxide equivalent) for the seven greenhouse gases covered by the Kyoto Protocol.	Sum together the emissions from the Scope 1, 2, and 3 entries			
Set out the environmental management measures in effect, including certification scheme or specific carbon reduction measures adopted.	To have practice *Green Action Plan* (see Appendix 20.1)			
Be board approved or company director approved if no board is in place.	Signed by senior partner, manager, owner, etc.			
Be clearly signposted and published on the supplier's website.	To publish on practice website			
Be updated at least annually.	To confirm annual review			

- Streamline orders to minimise delivery travel and packaging waste.
- Go paperless for clinical records.
- Go paperless for all accounts and invoicing.
- Go paperless for all communication with patients (who are happy with this)
- Choose items with less packaging.
- Switch to reusable packaging for packed lunches.
- Use refillable water bottles, travel cups, and flasks. Practice branded versions with a logo and team member name encourage feel-good recognition for the staff.

Engaging in product Life Cycle Analysis (LCA). Assess the environmental impact of products throughout their life cycle, including extraction, production, use, and disposal, and opt for products with a lower overall environmental footprint. Healthcarelca.org is a great place to see all the peer-reviewed, healthcare LCAs in one place (7).

Water. Saving water is something we can all do by changing our habits and making a few quick checks. Saving water will cut your bills, too, if you are on a water meter.
  Quick wins include:

- Checking appliances for leaks and getting them fixed. A dripping tap can waste 12 to 20 litres of water a day!
- Putting a reminder in the bathrooms to put the plug in whilst washing hands rather than leaving the tap running.
- Installing water butts to collect rainwater for watering practice plants.
- Add a water bottle to the cistern to reduce water use per flush.

Waste

What is waste? Waste contributes to the overall carbon footprint of primary care. A small minority of waste is potentially hazardous, and if not disposed of correctly, it could result in injury or infection. Managing healthcare waste is essential to ensure primary care reduces the risk.

  All staff are responsible for the safe management and disposal of waste and should understand how waste should be segregated and stored prior to collection or disposal.

  This is driven by the need to reduce environmental impact, reduce costs associated with waste management, and comply with waste regulations and other national guidance. The Health and Social Care Act 2008: Code of Practice has guidance on the prevention and control of infections and related guidance.

  Why address your waste footprint? Following the waste hierarchy (Figure 12.4) is not only the law (6), but it also reduces resource usage, prevents pollution, and reduces

FIGURE 12.4 Waste hierarchy triangle.

the carbon footprint. Legally, the primary care facility, not the waste contractor, must ensure compliance with environmental waste regulations.

What is a waste hierarchy?

Reduce and prevent. The best waste is no waste. The biggest reduction in waste is by preventing its generation in the first place. For example, fewer new products, less packaging, more repairing, and products designed for a longer life.

Reuse. Products and components that are used for the same purpose again – e.g., reusable PPE masks.

Recycle. Waste materials are reprocessed into products and materials that can be used for the same or different purposes.

Recover. Energy is recovered, but the loss of resources occurs – e.g., waste-to-energy incineration plants.

Disposal. A last resort. Either sent to incineration without energy recovery or sent to landfill.

Types of clinical waste

Infectious waste contaminated with body fluids from a patient with a known or suspected infection, with a proven infection risk, or medicines or chemicals present. Examples: contaminated PPE • medicated dressings • contaminated dressings.

Offensive (non-hazardous) waste from patients with no known or suspected infection which may be contaminated with body fluids. Examples: gloves, aprons • dressings (including blood stained) • stoma or catheter bags • cardboard vomit/urine bowls • incontinence pads • female hygiene waste, nappies.

How am I doing? A waste audit can give the answer:

Waste audit

Over a week:

1. Record the number and type of waste bags collected within the practice.
2. Examine the contents of each bag by type (infectious, offensive, recycling, etc.).
3. Separate into categories and weigh the total for each.
   - Plastic
   - Metal
   - Paper/card
   - Mixed/contaminated waste
   - Food waste
4. Return waste to (correct) waste stream.
5. Repeat for other waste streams.
6. Feedback findings to team – e.g., amount disposed of appropriately, amount of avoidable waste.

What can I do? Tackling a "disposable" or "single-use" culture can be difficult. It can feel like this is the only or easiest option. However, simple steps can be completed within a practice.

- Carry out a waste audit.
- Review waste contracts and costs for recycling.
- Identify major sources of waste and examine the procurement of these items.
  - Did they need to be purchased and then used?
  - What are the alternatives?
  - Are there lower packaging alternatives?
- Identify barriers and enablers for staff to reduce waste generated. For example, reuse, refill, and repair are three great ways to minimise the resources used in your practice or business.

Think about how you and your colleagues can

- reuse paper as scrap before shredding (whilst ensuring no risk to confidentiality);
- swap to rechargeable batteries;

- change to refillable ink cartridges/toners (is colour needed on all printers?); or
- reuse boxes, bubble wrap, and jiffy bags or give to others to reuse; lots of online small businesses would welcome free packaging or exchange for charitable donation.

A great idea is to refill packaging where possible – e.g., refill soap and cleaning liquid containers and buy bulk-sized or concentrated tea, coffee, or cleaning products. If an optician, can free or discounted refills of glasses cleaner be offered?

Some moves towards sustainability can require a change in mindset. Starting a conversation at work might include how to

- upcycle, repair, sell, or gift items used in practice;
- buy second-hand items for the business before buying new; or
- use items from charity shops, etc., if you are creating a window display.

The ultimate aim of all these actions is to minimise the waste sent to landfill. Reducing waste can cut waste management charges and material costs too.

Zero-waste strategy. Could the practice develop a strategy to achieve "100% zero waste" or start with a "zero waste to landfill" by a set date? Review all activities to cut the amount of waste the business generates. Look at what DOES not go into the landfill waste bags and consider how each can be addressed. Talk to the local council or waste contractor about how they deal with waste and how to work with them to maximise what is recycled or recovered.

Some things are straightforward to recycle, especially if there are good local schemes. Check whether recycling is happening across the workplace. Consider if paper, plastic, and glass are recycled.

Some things are harder to recycle, so a specialist scheme may be needed. Online are lists of recycling programmes. In the United Kingdom, there are schemes to recycle:

- Ink cartridges and toners
- PPE
- Light bulbs
- Batteries
- Food packaging
- Old spectacles
- Spectacle cases
- Coffee pods
- Pens

The priority should be finding ways to reduce consumption in the first place, saving money, reducing resource use, and reducing waste. Increasing recycling rates for residual waste is second best.

Case study

Green chemistry is the design of chemical products and processes that reduce or eliminate the use or generation of hazardous substances. Green chemistry applies across the life cycle of a chemical product, including its design, manufacture, use, and ultimate disposal. This reduces energy use when making some pharmaceuticals.

Plastics and healthcare. Plastics are incredibly useful – versatile, hygienic, light-weight, flexible, and highly durable. They have changed the way our lives are lived. The ability to be moulded and shaped makes plastic suitable for many applications. Packaging accounts for the largest usage of plastics worldwide. In primary care, they are used as containers, bottles, trays, boxes, cups, and protection packaging (see the following case study).

There is increasing concern about how many plastics are used and their disposal. Generally, they don't fully degrade or corrode, persisting for many hundreds of years before degenerating into microplastics.

Case study

In 2023, Nimbuscare Federation in York successfully funded specialist recycling boxes for empty medicine blister packs for 23 sites for 6 months. Full boxes were sent to a local firm, ReFactory in Hull, where the strips were broken down and made into "storm boards", which went on to become worktops and play equipment, thus closing the loop.

Governance issues in community pharmacies meant the boxes were not allowed there, but the project has been extremely popular with staff and patients in participating surgeries, attracting interest from the rural Highlands down to central London hospitals. So far almost half a tonne of blister packs have been collected, with a saving of approximately 2 tonnes CO_2e.

The payment for recycling came from the health provider, not the manufacturer of the polluting blister packs. This is some distance from the "polluter pays" principle championed by the government.

What types of plastic are there? There are a number of different plastics depending on the characteristics required. These are summarised in Table 12.2.

What is "biodegradable"? Though most plastic is derived from fossil fuels, plastic can be made from bio-based materials (bioplastic). The nature of the material used to make a plastic does not dictate its behaviour at the end of its life. A bioplastic does not necessarily biodegrade.

TABLE 12.2 Different plastics with uses, identifying symbols, and recyclability

NAME	POLYMER NAME	SYMBOL	USES	RECYCLABLE?
PET	Polyethylene terephthalate	1	Bottles, food trays, tops, tote bags, carpets	Yes
PE-HDPE	Polyethylene	2	Milk bottles, bleach and cleaners, toys, shampoo bottles	Yes
PVC	Polyvinyl Chloride	3	Plumbing pipes, tiles, shoes, gutters, window frames	Yes (in some places)
PE-LDPE		4	Carrier bags, food bags, bin liners, packaging films	Harder to do, but "yes" in some places
PP	Polypropylene	5	Margarine tubs, microwaveable tubs, yoghurt pots	Yes
PS	Polystyrene	6	Take out containers, cups, and plates	No
Other		7	CDs, baby bottles, spectacles, exterior light fittings	Not usually

Non-biodegradable

- Lasts for years and can fracture into smaller pieces/microplastics
- Recyclable if collected and sorted into separate material reprocessing streams (see Table 12.1)

Biodegradable

- Material breaks down in a defined period of time
- May be recyclable if separated from non-biodegradable plastic streams and dealt with separately. Cannot be recycled in the same way as non-biodegradable plastic

Compostable

- Material decomposes/biodegrades in industrial (high temperature) composting conditions. Materials that meet appropriate home composting standards can be composted in home composting systems

- Not suitable for recycling with other plastics. Can be separated and sent to industrial composting facilities

Going plastic-free. Recognising the implications of going plastic-free is important. It shouldn't be a "knee-jerk reaction" that *all plastics = bad; all alternatives = good*. Discretion is needed to identify appropriate and inappropriate use, and what single-use plastic can be converted to be refused, reused, or recycled?

Implications and issues. Managing domestic plastic waste by reusing, reducing, and recycling is not easily applied to healthcare. Many of the polymers used are highly cross-linked and processed, which makes breaking them down into constituent raw materials difficult (see blister pack case study). Concerns exist about the risk of contamination or transmission of infection. The complex shape of some of the devices makes them costly and difficult to clean, disinfect and sterilise. Disassembly of devices is difficult when assembled from multiple polymers in multi-layer constructs and glued or welded into complex shapes. These factors combine to make reusing and recycling options tricky.

Overcoming problems. No single action fits all scenarios. It is possible to identify inappropriate plastic through the waste audit and to reduce waste at source:

- Identify and avoid unnecessary plastic (e.g., plastic folders, folder dividers, plastic-coated paper clips). Where these items already exist, use them to the end of their life then don't replace them.
- Create a central supplies library (e.g., for stationery and equipment) with a clear stock management system. Ask staff to check prior to new purchases.
- Use items that expire quickest by rotating to the front of cupboards.
- Check that gloves and PPE are clinically appropriate.
- Use reusable fabric bunting and decorations for practice parties and birthdays. Hire crockery rather than using disposables. Avoid cards and wrapping paper with glitter (a microplastic).
- Provide reusable crockery and cutlery in kitchens/staff rooms – e.g., glass jugs and glasses for water and metal spoons for stirring drinks. Avoid disposable plastic cutlery. Encourage staff and patients to use their own drink containers rather than using paper or plastic single-use cups.
- Replace plastic drink bottles with cans and plastic packaged sweets and crisps with healthy fruit and other alternatives.
- Where possible, purchase products that can be decontaminated and reused rather than single-use items.

Case study

Review what PPE is used for appropriateness. Intact skin acts as an effective barrier to most invasive microorganisms. Any item that contacts intact skin (but not mucous membranes) is considered **low** risk for causing infection. It can be reusable and be disinfected between use when required.

For a practice using 20 rolls of aprons (2 per month) and 100 boxes of gloves per year (2 boxes/week), the greenhouse emissions would be

- 20 rolls of aprons (200 per roll) = 4,000 aprons @ 65g CO_2e/apron = 260 kg
- 100 boxes of gloves (100 per box) = 10,000 gloves @ 26g CO_2e/glove = 260 kg

Correct waste segregation is vital. Putting clear visual signage *with images* on waste bins can be effective.

Environmentally sustainable "green" IT

"Green IT" considers all aspects, from the purchase of new equipment, its software, and energy used through to its disposal at the end of its useful life. "Green IT" reduces the use of hazardous materials, maximises energy efficiency during the product's lifetime, and promotes the biodegradability of unused and outdated products.

Issues include

- Carbon footprint – Dell calculated each desktop computer emitted 720 kg CO_2e over an average lifespan of four years.
- E-waste – The obsolete technology that winds up in landfills and incinerators, often in developing nations – is an increasingly serious global environmental problem, so it is important to maximise the lifespan of IT products.
- Cloud storage – Whilst storing data in the cloud may not seem to have an impact, in reality, data is stored in huge energy-intensive data servers.

Perform an audit of your current IT and electrical systems

The audit can examine the following:

- What is being used and when?
- What is being left on when it is not being used? Can the power management be improved?
- All plugged-in IT equipment, including hard drives, monitors, printers, faxes, and franking machines.
- All consumables, including toners/print cartridges.
- Reuse and recycling options end of life.

Top tips for greener IT

Lifetime of equipment. It can be tempting to purchase new, more efficient computers every couple of years, but the amount of energy and hazardous materials used to produce new equipment can be far more environmentally damaging than the extra electricity consumed by older systems.

Circular procurement. PCs can be leased or rented rather than bought. By considering hardware as a "service", the supplier ensures it is the optimal system and improves longevity through repairing and maintaining rather than replacing.

How much equipment? Recording the amount of IT and peripherals used at different times throughout the week can help practices reduce their purchases. Are there extra monitors, headphones, or toners forgotten in the backs of cupboards?

Do I need more? When making new purchases, look for hardware that can easily be upgraded. Consider sourcing from suppliers that guarantee they will take back and recycle all equipment at the end of its useful life.

Practice website. Use a green web hosting service.

Emails and messages.

- Don't "reply all" – each email comes with a carbon footprint from the energy used to store and send.
- Size matters – small, short emails have a small impact; large documents and files sent have a much larger footprint – especially if sent to 10 or 100 recipients.

My pledges

1.
2.
3.

References

1 https://selondonccg.nhs.uk/covid_19/primary-care-green-plan/
2 https://iopscience.iop.org/article/10.1088/1748-9326/ab8589/pdf
3 www.warp-it.co.uk
4 https://www.england.nhs.uk/nhs-commercial/central-commercial-function-ccf/evergreen/
5 https://bcorporation.net
6 https://www.gov.uk/government/publications/duty-of-care-waste-transfer-note-template

7 Healthcarelca.org

8 https://tnfd.global/

9 http://sciencebasedtargetsnetwork.org/how-it-works/the-first-science-based-targets-for-nature/

Resources

Examples of business services required to run the practice include the following:

- Waste collection, treatment, and disposal services, and materials recovery services
- Buildings and building construction works
- Postal and courier services
- Facilities management/accommodation services
- Telecommunications services, computer programming, information services, IT – communication, website hosting
- Financial services, except insurance and pension funding
- Insurance services
- Legal services
- Accounting, bookkeeping, and auditing activities: tax consultancy
- Services of head offices, management consulting services
- Advertising, market research
- Rental and leasing services
- Employment services – e.g., advertising, pre-employment medicals, Disclosure and Barring Service checks
- Services to buildings and landscape
- Education services
- Services furnished by membership organisations
- Repair services for computers and personal and household goods

13

Air
Sinead Millwood and Malcolm White

Case study

Lissa, a 14-year-old schoolgirl, has poorly controlled asthma. She attends with her dad, and they share concerns that she coughs all the time. The family home is on the main road in town, used by a lot of the commuting traffic each day. In the last six months, her medication history shows she has had eight Ventolin pMDI inhalers and two Clenil pMDI. They're asking for more cough syrup.

Things to consider:

- What is the relevance of living near the main road?
- How could this situation be prevented or the patient's care improved while also improving the health of the planet?
- Should people with asthma cough all the time?
- Is cough syrup effective? What is the relevance of this request to planetary health?
- What do you think about the ratio of Clenil to Salbutamol?
- Is the drug delivery system or the drug the issue here?
- How good is asthma care in the United Kingdom compared to comparable countries?

The United Kingdom has much worse statistics on asthma outcomes than comparable countries (13a) – which is worse for patients and more disruptive for families.

Air pollution exposure can be a trigger for symptoms.

- How could this be reduced? Resources at Action for Clean Air are available. Main roads are likely to have much higher air pollution, both NOx and PM2.5. Roadside vegetation and hedges can reduce the dose of pollutants.

 DOI: 10.1201/9781003491583-13

Cough syrup is non-evidence-based and an example of inappropriate/overprescribing – an example of the healthcare system causing planetary damage through inappropriate actions.

Compared to European neighbours, the United Kingdom has a higher proportion of pMDI prescribing and a higher rate of SABA prescribing, which is worse for the planet.

- The propellant gases from the pMDIs are fluoroalkanes (f-gases). These are potent greenhouse gases contributing to climate change.
- DPIs have a comparatively very small environmental impact through the plastics they are made of.
- Awareness of carrying an inhaler can be off-putting for some teens – partly due to the need to carry a spacer. A DPI doesn't need a spacer.
- Many patients do not use spacers if using pMDIs, and their inhaler technique is commonly more suited to DPIs.
- DPIs are widely prescribed and well used outside the United Kingdom. In Sweden, Denmark, Norway, Netherlands, Austria, and Finland, 80%+ of prescribed inhalers are dry powder versions.
- Since pMDIs tend to have no dose counter, patients don't know when they are empty.
- There are disposal issues, and inhalers, especially pMDIs, should be returned to the pharmacy for disposal. (This is in the UK pharmacy contract.)
- People with asthma should not cough all the time; indeed, treatment should aim to prevent coughing on exertion/after triggers.
- A good ratio of Salbutamol to Clenil would be 0:4. This assumes one dose twice daily of the inhaler, 200 doses per inhaler, and that the patient still has a SABA which is in date from last year.
- The drugs used in asthma do not significantly affect the carbon footprint or environmental consequences; it is the gases in pMDIs which are 1,500 to 3,000 times as powerful as CO_2 which make them such a large determinant of the NHS carbon footprint.

Actions

- To benefit patients and the planet, improving asthma control is vital. Discuss SABA overuse and the need for more regular ICSs to address the cause of their illness – i.e., lung inflammation.
- Consider MART regimes rather than traditional ones.
- Inhaler technique is vital to assess – especially as growing from a child to teen to adult as coordination, muscle inspiratory strength, etc., change.

Resources

- https://www.greenerpractice.co.uk/high-quality-and-low-carbon-asthma-care/
- Greeninhaler.org
- https://www.asthmaandlung.org.uk/living-with/air-pollution
- Action for Clean Air – https://www.actionforcleanair.org.uk/

Reference

13a https://www.rcplondon.ac.uk/projects/national-review-asthma-deaths

Introduction

Air pollution is now recognised as the single biggest environmental threat to human health. Its impact is bigger than that of alcohol but smaller than the impact of cigarettes. In recent years, a growing scientific body of evidence has helped us understand the full extent of its insult upon the human body. What makes it more difficult is that it is mostly invisible, so people are largely unaware of it and the impacts it imposes on our health.

Actions tackling air pollution also work against climate change and are definitely seen as a win–win solution.

What is air pollution? The scientific standards of atmospheric gases in the air around us are mostly nitrogen (~78%), oxygen (~21%), argon (<1%), carbon dioxide (<1%), and water vapour (~1%). However, there are many other gases, tiny suspended solid particles, and droplets of liquids. Of the additional molecules, those that are harmful to human health constitute air pollution.

Air pollution is often grouped into outdoor or indoor sources. Much of the historical research and governmental focus on air pollution has been focused on outdoor air quality, which is also known as "ambient air pollution". Given most people spend most of their time indoors, indoor air pollution is increasingly recognised as a significant contributor to the overall health impacts of air pollution.

Sources of outdoor air pollution. The pollutants with the greatest impacts on human health (in part due to their relative abundance) are nitrogen dioxide and "particulate matter". There are many sources of both types of air pollution, with common sources detailed in Table 13.1.

"Particulate matter" is made up of a mixture of solids and liquids floating in the air.

- The smaller they get, the more dangerous they are, as they're more likely to enter the bloodstream through the lungs, overwhelming or bypassing the body's defences in the respiratory tract.

TABLE 13.1 Common sources of five important constituents of ambient air pollution in the United Kingdom with attributed percentage

POLLUTANT	COMMON SOURCES (% OF TOTAL)
Particulate matter (PM 2.5, 10)	1. Residential/small-scale burning (particularly open fires and solid-fuel stoves) (43.1%) 2. Manufacturing industries and construction (16.1%) 3. Industrial processes (12.9%) 4. Road transport (12.4%)
Nitrogen oxides (NOx)	1. Road transport (33.6%) 2. Energy industry (22.4%) 3. Other transport (16.8%) 4. Manufacturing industries and construction (15.6%) 5. Residential/small-scale burning (10.3%)
Sulphur dioxide	1. Energy industry (37.3%) 2. Residential/small-scale burning (25.5%) 3. Manufacturing industries and construction (21.6%) 4. Non-road transport (8.3%) 5. Industrial processes (4.8)
Ammonia	1. Agriculture (87.6%)
VOCs	1. Industrial processes (54.1%) 2. Fugitive emissions (15.8%) 3. Agriculture (14.4%) 4. Residential/small-scale burning (6.2%)

- The particles are categorised in literature and public health targets by their size: PM10 or PM2.5, meaning less than 10 or 2.5 micrometres in diameter, respectively – both much smaller than the width of a human hair.
- "PM1" is increasingly recognised as a further category for even smaller particles, with worrying evidence that these nanoparticles are particularly harmful to human health.
- The biggest causes of particulate pollution in the United Kingdom are domestic solid-fuel stoves and open fires, although many other sources exist, including vehicle fumes, dust, sand, pollen, rubber from tyres, and metal from brakes.

Nitrogen dioxide (NO_2) is a gas commonly created in combustion processes.

- The biggest source in the United Kingdom is vehicles with fossil fuel–burning engines.

Nitrogen oxide (NO) is produced in a similar manner to NO_2 and is therefore often grouped together as NOx.

Volatile organic compounds (VOCs)

- Volatile organic compounds, or VOCs, are gases that are emitted into the air from products (like paints) or processes (like refrigeration). Some are harmful by themselves, including trichloroethylene and vinyl chloride, which cause cancer.

Ammonia (NH_3)

- Ammonia is a short-lived gas. However, particulate matter can form when ammonia mixes with other gases in the atmosphere, such as nitrogen oxides and sulphur dioxide. These last for several days and have more distant impacts through being transported long distances (13).

Sulphur dioxide (SO_2) (14)

- Sulphur dioxide is an acidic gas mainly created by the burning of coal or oil. It was largely responsible for the deaths in the "Great Smog of London" in 1952. In the 1970s and 1980s, the burning of coal in the United Kingdom was responsible for acid rain affecting forests and waterways in Scandinavia. The gas causes respiratory problems and combines with ammonia to cause particulate matter.

Carbon monoxide (CO) is created during incomplete combustion.

- The biggest outdoor sources are industrial burning and vehicle emissions. Levels have significantly decreased since 1990 – by 79% – largely due to more efficient vehicle engines.
- Indoor burning and poorly installed or maintained gas cookers and heating systems are major sources in the home.
- The effects of carbon monoxide can have both serious short-term and long-term effects that contribute to morbidity and mortality. Once inhaled, CO binds to the body's haemoglobin, making the blood less effective at moving oxygen around the body. A high dose exposure causes headaches, nausea, flushing, dizziness, muscle pains, weakness, and even confusion and personality changes. In serious cases, it can cause death. Long-term low-dose exposure can lead to symptoms similar to flu, which progress over time into memory, vision, and cognition issues that can appear similar to conditions like dementia.

Carbon monoxide can be a killer. For more information, visit https://www.gov.uk/government/publications/carbon-monoxide-properties-incident-management-and-toxicology/carbon-monoxide-general-information.

Indoor air pollution. The profile of indoor air pollutants is different (2). Some gases are from internal combustion (gases from gas cookers and boilers contribute to childhood asthma [3]) or VOCs from paints and carpets, glues, and solvents (some chemicals also

Health Matters

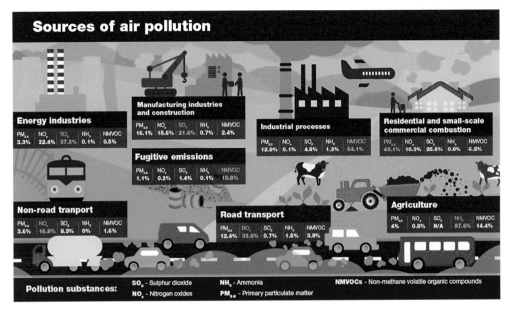

FIGURE 13.1 Common sources of air pollution in the United Kingdom, attributing a percentage of five important types of ambient air pollution.

(*Source:* https://www.gov.uk/government/publications/health-matters-air-pollution/health-matters-air-pollution)

have carcinogenic properties). Particulate matter is emitted by fires and log burners. Some indoor pollution may enter from the outside depending on local levels (Figure 13.1).

Mould grows in damp and unventilated buildings. Inhaling spores can worsen medical conditions such as asthma and contribute to death. In 2022, the death of a 2-year-old boy in Rochdale, England, was formally and officially registered as caused by chronic exposure to mould (4).

Global and UK context

Annual mortality from external air pollution. Globally, the World Health Organization (WHO) has estimated 6.7 million people died in 2019 just from PM 2.5. Funding of investigation and interventions around air pollution is wildly under-resourced compared to other important conditions, despite having significantly greater associated morbidity and mortality. 97% of the urban population of Europe was exposed in 2021 to PM2.5 levels, which are above WHO standards. Rural outdoor air quality is generally better, although it can be poor at certain times of the year – e.g., due to forest or bushfires.

Historically within the United Kingdom, air pollution was terrible. In 1952, the "Great Smog of London" was estimated to have killed 10,000–12,000 people over five days. This improved with the Clean Air Act (1956), updates in 1993, and other measures in the United Kingdom. While this is a story of relative improvement in the United

Kingdom, in many parts of the world, air pollution is a greater threat to human health. This represents a massive global health inequality. Despite significant improvements in the United Kingdom since the introduction of the Clean Air Act, air pollution still causes up to 43,000 premature deaths in the United Kingdom each year and puts an enormous burden on the National Health Service.

WHO guidelines. In 2021, the WHO issued more stringent guidelines on air pollution levels based on the latest evidence, recommending average exposure to PM2.5 be reduced from 10 micrograms per cubic metre of air to 5. Current UK law requires it must not exceed 40 micrograms per cubic metre of air – four times higher than the old WHO guidelines! The UK government is moving to a legally binding limit in England of 10 micrograms per cubic metre of air by 2040.

Many across healthcare are of the opinion that this is not low enough or quick enough, reflecting poor leadership and ambition. Scotland already has an existing target of 10 micrograms per cubic metre of air – much more ambitious than England but still not in line with WHO guidelines. Furthermore, a recent scientific report advises that 10 micrograms per cubic metre of air can realistically be achieved in England by 2030. This target is *the minimum* we should be aiming for.

Clean air has become a significant issue in modern politics. Ambitious policies are rarely set because failing to achieve them reflects badly on the government. Therefore, policies are cautious, judged primarily in the context of what is currently economically comfortable, and poorly reflecting the urgency of the public health emergencies of air pollution and climate change.

How does air pollution affect health? When we breathe polluted air, it inflames the lining of our lungs and can move into our bloodstream, causing diseases in most body organs. Air pollution affects humans from their first breath to their last, and even before. There is growing evidence that air pollution increases the chance of miscarriage, low birth weight, and premature birth. Air pollution affects every part of the body. It causes and worsens high blood pressure, stroke, angina, asthma, COPD, infections related to breathing like pneumonia and COVID-19, diabetes, neurodevelopmental problems, dementia, and lung cancer. Children's health is more susceptible to air pollution because their bodies are still developing. It can affect their lungs and brains, affecting how well they can learn.

Sixty per cent of the pollution that children breathe in each day is taken in during the school run.

Air pollution is a massive social injustice; those who are least well off and already most at risk of these conditions live in the most polluted areas.

In 2013, Ella Kissi Deborah – a 9-year-old girl – died following a severe asthma attack. Ella lived on the South Circular Road in London and was exposed to illegally high levels of nitrogen dioxide and PM2.5. The main source of her exposure was traffic emissions. She was the first person in the world to have air pollution listed as a cause of death on her death certificate. In a report to prevent future deaths, Coroner Philip Barlow said the government should bring existing targets for particulate matter in line with WHO guidelines. As well as reducing deaths, this would reduce years of health lost and the amount of money being spent by the NHS on patients with diseases linked to air pollution.

What is the level of air pollution where I live and work? There are many resources where air quality can be checked, including most weather forecasts. Other resources include the DEFRA pollution forecast https://uk-air.defra.gov.uk/forecasting/, the National Atmospheric Emissions Inventory https://naei.beis.gov.uk/emissionsapp/, the London mayor's new air pollution alert system (Greater London only), and, internationally, Plume Labs (https://plumelabs.com/en/air/) carries live air quality information for cities around the world.

The cost of air pollution. In England, almost 30% of preventable deaths are due to non-communicable diseases specifically attributable to air pollution (6). Between 2017 and 2025, the total cost to the NHS and social care of air pollution in the United Kingdom is estimated to be £1.60 billion for PM2.5 and NOx combined (where there is more robust evidence for an association), increasing to £5.56 billion (if other diseases where there is currently less robust evidence for an association are included) (5). Unless air quality is improved, the health and social care costs of air pollution in England are set to reach £18.6 billion by 2035 (7).

How can primary care reduce air pollution contribution and exposure? The health sector plays a critical role in responding to and educating patients on a multitude of factors that impact health, including smoking, alcohol, exercise, and diet. This is *not* currently the case with air pollution, even though its effect is greater than that of alcohol. Healthcare professionals play a vital role in tackling air pollution as educators, role models, and champions.

- Educators: as trusted messengers in society, healthcare professionals play an important role in informing the public of the health risks and the measures they can take to minimise exposure.
- Role models: showing leadership in the NHS's drive to minimise the air pollution the NHS creates and influences.
- Champions: supporting policy measures at local and national levels that help ensure improvements to air quality.

Health professionals as educators. How can health professionals in primary care advise patients on the impacts of air pollution if training is sparse? The gap in current medical training is demonstrated by the Global Action Plan's (GAP) *Mobilising Health Professionals* project in partnership with the UK Health Alliance on Climate Change (UKHACC) (9). Forty respiratory and paediatric health professionals received training on the impacts of air pollution on patient health and the measures people can take to reduce their exposure. Health professionals reported the following:

- Prior to the training, they were not talking to or advising patients about air pollution.
- Air pollution is not uniformly integrated into healthcare professional training.
- Materials were not readily available for health professionals to share with their patients on air pollution.

Harnessing this insight, GAP worked with the professionals to create materials and resources to educate staff and facilitate sharing their learning with patients. These include educational videos, leaflets, posters, teaching slides, and more. They are freely available on the GAP website. These materials have been adopted by the Royal College of Physicians and the Royal College of General Practitioners and shared with their members.

The main messages to pass on to patients are the following:

- Reduced use of cars. Walk, cycle, and scoot to reduce both exposure to and contribution to air pollution.
- Don't idle. If you drive, turn the engine off when stationary and it is safe to do so.
- When replacing a vehicle, consider switching to all electric. Air quality becomes worse inside the vehicle than outside.
- Use quieter streets and paths to keep away from heavy polluting traffic.
- Use fragrance-free, milder cleaning products, and avoid plug-in fragrances.
- When decorating, choose safer paints and varnishes labelled "low VOC".
- Ask people not to smoke in your home.
- Ventilate your home. Open windows and use extractor fans when cooking or using cleaning products, but close windows near busy roads during rush hours.
- Reduce indoor air pollution exposure – open fires are the worst, followed by unregulated wood-burning stoves, then eco-design stoves.
- Plant hedges if there is space between a building and the road.

Health professionals as role models. Inherently, by delivering healthcare, the NHS creates air pollution. Chief Medical Officer Professor Sir Chris Whitty dedicated his 2022 report to the wider changes in society required to tackle air pollution (10), where the NHS committed to reducing its contributions to air pollution by half within a decade. The majority of UK primary care facilities and hospitals are in areas that breach the recently updated WHO guidance levels for PM2.5 (8, 11), which means that as well as contributing to it, workplaces are also exposing our staff and our patients to danger-ous levels of air pollution.

Health professionals as champions. GAP has helped the NHS reduce air pollution at a regional scale by working in partnership to develop the Integrated Care System (ICS) *Clean Air Framework*. This framework aligns with sustainability requirements in trust/ICS Green Plans and supports the ICS leaders to incorporate air quality improvement measures in all healthcare settings.

- Call on your member of Parliament to support clean air laws to reduce air pol-lution in line with WHO guidelines.
- Support low-traffic neighbourhoods.
- Support clean air zones.
- Engage with local schools to apply for school streets to reduce traffic around schools at drop-off and pick-up times.

GP surgeries, dentists, primary care centres, opticians, and pharmacies should consider the following actions from the ICS Clean Air Framework:

Training

- Sustainability training for all staff to understand the health consequences of exposure to air pollution and how they can reduce their contribution.
- Air pollution training for clinical staff in contact with patients with diseases worsened or caused by air pollution.

Digitalisation

- Increase remote consultations to decrease transport use.

Home working

- Where possible, reduce staff travel emissions.

Active travel

- Carry out travel surveys for staff and patients.
- Improve the awareness of public transport and active travel options.
- Ensure your patients and staff have access to safe bike storage.

Infrastructure

- New buildings must meet WHO indoor air quality targets.
- Reduce carbon footprint and air pollution emissions by switching to a renewable energy tariff.
- Increase electric vehicle charging access for staff and patients and reward by making these the closest parking bays to the practice.
- Place anti-idling signage outside buildings and inside waiting rooms.

Greening the region

- Link with NHS Forest to increase planting – e.g., consider a staff planting away day.
- Green prescribing for patients whose mental or physical health might benefit.

Supply chain

- Transition to sustainable transport like bike couriers for last mile deliveries, laboratory sample deliveries, or medication deliveries to patients.
- Use companies with sustainable delivery policies to have goods delivered.

Not all measures to decrease carbon emissions automatically reduce air pollution. For example, electric vehicles will reduce carbon emissions, as they produce no exhaust gases, but they are heavier, and this will increase the air pollution they cause from tyres and braking. Data from University College London suggests regenerative braking can reduce this pollution by 60%–95%. However, in the last decade, an increasing proportion of internal combustion engine vehicles are bigger and heavier and so cause more air pollution than their predecessors (1).

Indoor air quality. *Primary Care Respiratory Update* wrote an excellent article outlining how to reduce indoor air pollution (12). Some tips from their article:

- Buildings should be well ventilated and have efficient, well-maintained heating systems.
    - Is there a policy on ventilation of rooms?
    - Open windows for ventilation. But if windows face a road, it is important to try to avoid allowing polluted outdoor air to enter the building. Better to open the window at a time of day when road traffic is low.
    - Minimise the amount of vehicle-related pollution near healthcare facilities by operating (and enforcing) a "no-idling" rule in the car park, especially for parking spaces close to the building.
- Buildings in a state of disrepair may be associated with increased levels of small particulate matter and mould spores.
- Air-conditioning systems should be regularly maintained and used appropriately to avoid clogging of filters.
- Surfaces and furnishings should be easy to clean and designed to minimise the accumulation of dust particles.
- The cleaning materials used can have a detrimental impact on indoor air quality, as well as their wider environmental impact. Cleaning materials that are environmentally safe contain minimal fumes, and VOCs should be used where possible.
- Indoor air purifiers may be helpful in clinical areas where asthma reviews are conducted. There is evidence that the use of air purifiers can reduce the medication burden in children with asthma by reducing small particulate matter levels. However, air fresheners should be avoided in healthcare settings, even in the toilets.

Conclusion

Air pollution and its health impacts are one of the biggest problems faced by people today. Akin to other health issues, the knowledge will take some adjusting to in the public consciousness. The smoking-in-public ban was, at the time, controversial, and it took decades to make it happen, but how many lives could have been saved if it had been brought in earlier?

The journey to educate ourselves and act has begun. Even though discussions on air pollution can be hard – and changing our behaviour can feel even harder – starting a conversation can make a difference. Pass on the knowledge gained to patients and colleagues. Reducing personal and workplace contributions to air pollution by all means possible. Use professional status and voices to support local clean air initiatives and lobby for national air pollution laws.

Everyone should have the right to breathe clean air. If we work together, air pollution can be reduced and air quality improved, which protects our patients, our planet, and ourselves.

References

1 https://www.theguardian.com/environment/2023/sep/08/autobesity-on-course-to-worsen-air-pollution-caused-by-motoring
2 https://www.nature.com/articles/d41586-023-00287-8
3 https://www.theguardian.com/environment/2023/nov/08/gas-cookers-pump-out-toxic-particles-linked-to-childhood-asthma-report-finds
4 https://www.theguardian.com/uk-news/2022/nov/15/death-of-two-year-old-awaab-ishak-chronic-mould-in-flat-a-defining-moment-says-coroner
5 Estimation of costs to the NHS and social care due to the health impacts of air pollution: summary report. PHE
6 Longtermplan.nhs.uk
7 Department for Environment Food and Rural Affairs, The Committee on the Medical Effects of Air Pollution, Associations of long-term average concentrations of nitrogen dioxide with mortality, 2018. Available at: https://laqm.defra.gov.uk/air-quality/guidance/publichealth
8 British Lung Foundation (2018) Toxic air at the door of the NHS. Available at: www.blf.org.uk/takeaction/campaign/nhs-toxic-air-report
9 Mobilising Health Professionals project – GAP in partnership with the UK Health Alliance on Climate Change (UKHACC).
10 The Chief Medical Officer (CMO) 2022 Report (Professor Sir Chris Whitty).
11 British Lung Foundation (2018) Toxic air at the door of the NHS. Available at: www.blf.org.uk/takeaction/campaign/nhs-toxic-air-report
12 Reducing indoor and outdoor air pollution in healthcare.
13 https://www.gov.uk/government/statistics/emissions-of-air-pollutants/emissions-of-air-pollutants-in-the-uk-ammonia-nh3
14 https://www.gov.uk/government/statistics/emissions-of-air-pollutants/emissions-of-air-pollutants-in-the-uk-sulphur-dioxide-so2

Resources

World Health Organisation (2021) Ambient (outdoor) air pollution. Available at: www.who.int/news-room/factsheets/detail/ambient-(outdoor)-air-quality-and-health
addresspollution.org
https://plumelabs.com/en/air/
Clean Air Knowledge Hub for the Health Sector
https://www.actionforcleanair.org.uk/health/knowledge-hub-health

https://www.actionforcleanair.org.uk/health/ics-framework

https://selondonccg.nhs.uk/wp-content/uploads/2022/03/Primary-Care-Green-Plan-2022-2025.pdf

https://www.pcrs-uk.org/sites/default/files/pcru/articles/2021-July-Issue-22-AirPollution.pdf

https://www.gov.uk/government/publications/carbon-monoxide-properties-incident-management-and-toxicology/carbon-monoxide-general-information

14

Water
Richard Hixson, Georgie Sowman, and Sharon Pfleger

Case study

Susan – Wild swimming and diarrhoea, a 52-year-old lady, runs a wild swimming group that has been commissioned to deliver sessions to her GP practice's patients as part of a nature-based prescribing scheme. She became unwell last week with diarrhoea and vomiting. Although the vomiting has settled, it is her eighth day of diarrhoea. She has cancelled the swimming groups again this week. When she mentioned her illness on Facebook, a friend contacted her to say she had felt the same way since swimming at the same beach and had seen there was a raw sewage discharge there the day before they fell ill. Susan wonders if she should be tested for "sewage pollution" and what advice she could have in relation to her wild swimming groups in the future.

Things to consider:

- What do you know about sewage discharges in your local area?
- What nature-based prescribing interventions are available to patients locally?
- Where can information be found about bathing waters in your area?
- How does healthcare contribute to water and sewage pollution?

Healthcare's relationship with water, coast, and ocean spans centuries and is complex – both in terms of our threats and our opportunities. This chapter will explore some of our interfaces with water systems, and this encounter with Susan highlights some of the contexts in which we may face challenging conversations in day-to-day primary care. Susan and her wild swimming group have benefited for months from their blue space activity. But pollution in fresh and coastal waters – for example, from sewage overflow and discharges – is a public health threat and risks undermining ecosystems and habitats (1). Sewage pollution also threatens the social and environmental determinants of health

DOI: 10.1201/9781003491583-14

through its impacts on economies that rely on healthy blue spaces, such as tourism and sport. Many of the interventions needed to address these challenges are likely to need a transdisciplinary, global, and whole-systems approach. But as clinicians, we are sometimes the "canaries in the coal mine" in witnessing the impacts of the climate and ecological emergency on our patients and communities. And we may be able to advocate that the oceans, waterways, and nature are not left behind.

Introduction

Human health, nature, water, and climate change are intrinsically linked. This chapter aims to outline the dependencies and impacts of health and healthcare on freshwater, coast, and ocean systems, outline how we can support the recovery and restoration of a thriving aquatic biodiversity, and harness the benefits of oceans to health equitably and sustainably from the perspective of primary care. We may feel miles away from oceans in our day-to-day life, but through the sinks, toilets, and drains in primary care via streams and rivers, we are all linked by one ocean.

The ocean – where are we now? Water systems are amazing. Ninety-seven per cent of the earth's water is found in the ocean. It is Earth's largest interconnected ecosystem, covering 71% of its surface, providing 99% of its living space, and being home to 80% of all living organisms (2). The ocean comprises an astonishing 322 million cubic miles of water and includes not just open ocean but also the areas where humans interface, such as estuaries and coastlines. Marine cyanobacteria produced the first oxygen 2.4 billion years ago, and on a geological timescale, they have produced 87% of the planet's oxygen through photosynthesising CO_2 and have enabled the sequestration of trillions of tonnes of carbon in the deep ocean and sediments. Globally, the ocean and freshwater habitats and species are under threat like never before, with marine ecosystems at risk of collapse from human-derived climate change, biodiversity loss, and pollution. These impacts are greatest in communities with the least equal opportunity for good health. Many local communities and indigenous populations live with nature and the ocean at the centre of their lives, recognising that these natural systems play a vital role in their communities and well-being. As we relearn and reconnect with nature and water systems, learning and listening to indigenous and local community knowledge will be key.

What are healthcare's responsibilities and opportunities? Healthcare organisations are embedded within communities and habitats. As anchor institutions, we can address the social determinants of health through water stewardship, advocating for ocean recovery, and reconnecting communities with ocean and water systems. Healthcare can drive change through its considerable buying power and the health-focussed narratives its actions generate. The NHS has 80,000 suppliers which, through collaboration, can drive change and ensure that they *first do no harm*. This healthcare provider-supplier collaborative approach can be replicated globally, help drive positive actions, improve health and well-being, and reduce the harms from providing human healthcare on the planet.

Opportunities – healthcare/health dependencies on the ocean and freshwater systems. Our health depends on water and the ocean, and it is not possible for healthcare to reach net zero or deliver the United Nations Sustainable Development Goals without thriving ocean and freshwater water systems. The ocean has offered solutions to climate change; it provides every other breath we take, supports weather systems, and provides food, as well as offers spaces to rest and recover, be active, and inspired. Three billion people worldwide depend on marine and coastal biodiversity for their livelihoods (3).

"Blue carbon". Through the ability to absorb heat and CO_2, water systems play a crucial role in climate and weather systems. "Blue carbon" refers to the carbon captured and stored in marine ecosystems, such as sea grass, salt marsh, seaweed, and mangroves. The carbon-storing abilities of this nature are incredible – with blue carbon habitats able to store 50–100 times more carbon in their soils and remove 10–30 times more CO_2 than terrestrial forests. These essential ecosystems also buffer from storms and act as nurseries for fish.

Transportation of healthcare industry supplies. The global healthcare system depends on a fast, reliable, smooth, and affordable maritime shipping sector to deliver the essential goods needed to maintain human health and well-being. The shipping industry is the lifeblood of human healthcare services and is the most cost-effective and environmentally sustainable mode of mass transportation (though with room for improvement). Increasingly frequent extreme weather events may impact our maritime supply chains, which deliver 80% of our healthcare goods in addition to other essentials such as food to billions of people.

Food. Water systems have always been a significant source of food for humans around the world, and it is anticipated that demand will continue to grow. Seafood provides important nutrients, energy, protein, long-chain polyunsaturated fatty acids, and essential micronutrients such as selenium, iron, zinc, protein, iodine, vitamin D, choline, and calcium (4). Land is scarce, but the ocean is not, and some seafood, such as molluscs and seaweed, can help reduce pollution and contribute to decarbonisation. Small-scale fishing remains hugely important culturally to many communities.

Substituting other sources of land-based protein with low trophic level fish can reduce the carbon footprint of food, and thereby help reduce ocean heating and acidification. Small-scale fisheries and fisheries for small pelagic fish have lower environmental footprints than some plant-based foods (5). However, the IPCC reported near-term risks with a high to very high confidence that there will be biodiversity loss in kelp, seagrass, arctic sea ice, and warm-water coral reef ecosystems, all of which contribute to the destruction of species habitat and subsequent reduction in food from salt and freshwater habitats (6).

Currently, there is a trend for declining fish availability, with overfishing, pollution of rivers and the ocean, habitat destruction as well as practices such as bottom dredging being hugely destructive to water species. The greatest impact is felt in communities with the least equal opportunity for good health. However, there are many examples of improved management practices – e.g., imposed fish catch quotas, community-based management for small-scale fisheries, or increased marine protected areas that have resulted in some fisheries rebuilding (7, 8). Tools are being made available to assist with responsible choices of seafood, such as the WWF Seafood Guide, the Marine Stewardship Council's Sustainable Seafood Guide, and the Environmental Defence Fund's Seafood Selector.

Freshwater. Freshwater is crucial to all life on Earth and is home to a wide range of species, including birds, mammals, amphibians, and plants. Three per cent of Earth's water is fresh, with the bulk locked away at the poles, in glaciers, and in groundwater. Only 0.03% of the planet's total water is accessible for human use in the form of ponds, lakes, rivers, and streams (9). Freshwater scarcity affects 40% of the world's population, and as many as 700 million people are at risk of being displaced because of drought by 2030 (10). Conversely, an estimated 1.8 billion people, or 23% of the world population, face significant flood risk.

Despite being a Sustainability Development Goal, over two billion people do not have access to clean, safe drinking water, leading to more than three million deaths per year. Freshwater not only provides hydration but enables the development of fisheries, irrigation of crops, and increased economic activity. With the need to feed an increasing population, the demand for this scarce resource will grow (11). It is essential we secure "credible water stewardship that recognizes and secures the social, cultural, environmental and economic value of freshwater" (12).

New pharmaceuticals. Biodiversity-rich marine areas have led to the production of pharmaceuticals, 23 of which are approved for use to treat cancer, pain, cardiovascular disease, and some viral infections. More marine pharmaceuticals are in clinical trials, and from the 4,000 bioactive marine-derived compounds reported between 1985 and 2012, 56% had activity against cancer cells, whilst 21% worked against bacteria, fungi, or viruses. Horizon scanning for emerging climate-associated disease threats such as antimicrobial-resistant water- and vector-borne diseases is essential to ensure developments can benefit all global citizens. Production, use, and disposal of new (and existing) drugs must, however, consider their impact not just on humans but on the ecosystem. Even when pharmaceuticals are used correctly, their metabolites are transported from toilets to rivers to coasts. There is very little understanding of the ultimate impact of these chemicals in isolation or combination.

Healthy blue spaces. There is increasing evidence of the benefits of time spent in high-quality blue spaces to the physical, mental, and social health of patients and populations (13) (Figure 14.1).

The marine capital of the UK coast has been valued financially at £211 billion (14). The ability for nature to thrive and the benefit the human population gains from this natural capital depend on addressing challenges such as sewage pollution, nitrogen run-off from agriculture, and over-tourism.

Fair access to the health and economic benefits of ocean, coast, and water systems are not shared equally. The UK CMO 2021 *Health in Coastal Communities* report (15) highlighted many of the opportunities and threats that contribute to our unequal coastlines.

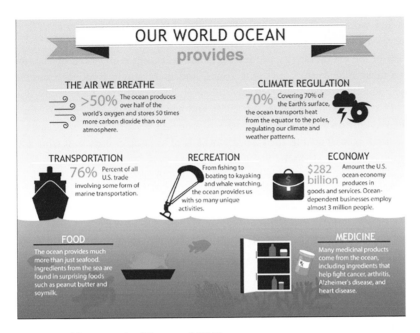

FIGURE 14.1 Why should we care about the ocean? NOAA.

(https://oceanservice.noaa.gov/facts/why-care-about-ocean.html).

Primary care is well placed to identify patient populations who may benefit the most from more targeted healthcare that recognises these differences – e.g., through population health management strategies or for individual patients through specific nature-based prescribing interventions that support nature and people.

Threats: Healthcare/health impacts on the ocean and freshwater systems. Human health is inextricably linked to ocean health, and when the ocean pH and temperature change through greenhouse gas emissions, pollution, and loss of biodiversity, both the planet and human health suffer. All industries, especially healthcare, must first do no harm, minimise their ocean footprint, help restore what has been lost, and include good ocean stewardship in sustainability strategies for the ocean and us, not just for us. Primary care has an important role through strategies such as addressing overprescribing (see Chapter 7), amplifying antibiotic stewardship, advocating for clean blue and green spaces for nature-based prescribing, and contributing to nature recovery (see Chapter 15).

Ocean acidification, climate, and healthcare. Healthcare systems are significant producers of CO_2 (see Chapter 1). The ocean absorbs around 23% of the CO_2 generated by human activity, which acidifies the seawater. That puts marine ecosystems at risk, and the more acidic the ocean becomes, the less CO_2 it can absorb. Healthcare systems have taken steps to address and reduce their carbon footprint and, therefore, their contribution to ocean acidification. Led by Greener NHS, NHS England has made significant progress towards its 2040 and 2045 targets by facilitating the development of green plans and workstreams to deliver change through *delivering a net-zero NHS* (16) – and primary care can be a key actor in this work.

90% of the excess energy producing global warming is absorbed by the ocean, leading to marine heatwaves, hypoxic zones, and increasingly frequent extreme weather events, which threaten supply chains and coastal communities. CO_2 removal is required to successfully reach "net zero" by 2050, and healthy oceans are essential for humanity to thrive. Our present emissions pathway, coupled with the loss of ocean biodiversity and pollution, will lead to the loss of synthesis of organic compounds from CO_2, which fuels the marine food chain.

Representative Concentration Pathways (RCP) are predictions for future climate scenarios based on the rate of fall of CO_2 levels. RCP 2.6 assumes CO_2 will decline from 2020 and reach zero by 2100, estimating a global temp rise of 2 degrees. RCP 8.5 assumes CO_2 will rise throughout the 21st century. Figure 14.2 highlights the reduction in the total weight of sea animals (their biomass) in two different scenarios depending on how quickly the planet collectively reduces emissions.

Biodiversity loss. Biodiversity is the variety and abundance of species within a habitat. Water biodiversity continues to decline both in marine and freshwater ecosystems because of pollution from cities, agriculture, and industries; climate change; overuse of species; by-catch and direct strikes; and the introduction of exotic plants or animals. When these fragile ecosystems are degraded or destroyed, the impacts can be widespread. For instance, when seagrass in coastal ecosystems is degraded, "blue carbon"

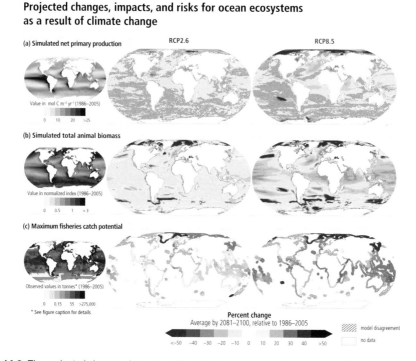

FIGURE 14.2 The projected changes, impacts, and risks for ocean ecosystems as a result of climate change (17).

stored for centuries is released into the atmosphere and oceans, becoming a source of greenhouse gases; we lose nurseries for fish and buffers for the coast from storms. Over 1 billion tonnes of carbon dioxide are estimated to be released annually from degraded coastal ecosystems through processes, which include bottom trawling. This is equivalent to 19% of emissions from tropical deforestation globally.

Healthcare supply chains – marine logistics. The National Health Service in England has committed to reaching net-zero carbon emissions for its supply chain by 2045. Transportation of healthcare goods from manufacturer to user is part of the product's lifecycle, and it is estimated that up to 80% of NHS goods arrive by sea. Although container shipping is the most economical and sustainable global mass transportation, there are still environmental impacts, including emissions (1 billion tonnes of CO_2/year), transfer of non-indigenous species, underwater radiated noise, and marine mammal collisions. NHS England's total supply chain emissions represent 62% of its overall greenhouse gas footprint (much of which in part or totally comes from abroad), so decarbonisation of the maritime shipping sector is essential to achieve the NHS's net-zero goals. Many of NHS England's suppliers deliver goods to industries beyond healthcare, and changes implemented through their relationship with human health can be amplified across multiple sectors, accelerating change.

Pollution. Pollution and contamination in water systems impact health, increase inequities, reduce quality of life, and affect natural habitats and ecosystems (2). Land-derived pollutants such as persistent organic pollutants (forever chemicals), pesticides, pharmaceuticals, antibiotics, heavy metals, macro- and microplastics, and excessive nutrients such as nitrogen and phosphorus enter freshwater and marine systems – mostly from urban, agricultural, and industrial (including the healthcare industry) runoffs and discharges.

The impacts of pollution on living organisms are broad, from the individual level to population and whole ecosystems. Many of the impacts on health are unknown – those understood currently include chronic stress to marine organisms, reduced photosynthetic efficiency, causation of some cancers, inhibition of reproduction and birth defects, and antimicrobial resistance (18). Impacts on ecosystem and human health can occur at the site of discharge in freshwater and marine ecosystems but also at every stage in the pollutant's life cycle, often directly impacting the most vulnerable communities globally, such as from the production of neoprene, pharmaceuticals, or healthcare derived PVC (19).

Pollution with plastic or sewage or by causing algal blooms affects recreation, fishing, and tourism for the three billion people worldwide who depend on marine and coastal biodiversity for their livelihoods or through their need for blue spaces.

Pharmaceutical pollution. The largest carbon footprint in primary care is from pharmaceuticals, and it is likely that this will be our largest water footprint too. Pharmaceutical chemicals are vital components of modern healthcare, but the Ridge review suggests that 10% of the current quantity prescribed in the United Kingdom could be avoided. Even when pharmaceuticals are used correctly, their metabolites find their way to our rivers, coasts, and oceans through toilets and wastewater. Pharmaceutical pollution has now been identified in river and coastal systems globally. Active pharmaceutical ingredients (APIs) are bioactive substances, and this contamination of global water-ways is threatening environmental and human health, contributing to biodiversity loss, driving antimicrobial resistance, and jeopardising progress towards Sustainable Development Goals. Water from many rivers is full of medications, and antibiotics are found in these. This is a global problem. In the United Kingdom, Glasgow had the river with the highest cumulative concentration (20). Only two rivers in the world had none (21)! Any unused or expired medication that is not disposed of via pharmacies (which in the United Kingdom have an obligation to accept them) and incinerated will add to these "pharmaceuticals in the environment" (PIE). These drug residues are not removed by wastewater treatment plants and have known antimicrobial resistance (AMR) and possibly other unknown environmental impacts.

The most common medications found in rivers are paracetamol and caffeine. Then neurological medications (carbamazepine, citalopram, gabapentin, temazepam, venlafaxine), antihistamines (cetirizine, fexofenadine), diabetic medication (metformin, sitagliptin), pain killers (naproxen), and antimicrobials (trimethoprim), beta-blockers (atenolol), and anaesthetics (lidocaine).

How do medicines get into the environment?

- Ninety per cent from patient use (they are excreted with minimal changes)
- Five per cent from flushing unused medications down the toilet
- Five per cent from pharmaceutical production
- Thirty per cent to 100% of the medicines we take are excreted in urine or faeces
- Wasted medications end up being flushed or sent to landfills

Wastewater treatment plants have generally not been designed to break down waste medicines, and their efficiency varies. The sludge from them (containing intact pharmaceuticals is used on crops as a fertiliser and transferred into the food chain; Figure 14.3).

FIGURE 14.3 Number of pharmaceuticals detected in surface, ground, and drinking water.

https://www.researchgate.net/publication/330934183_Pharmaceuticals_in_the_environment_Global_occurrence_and_potential_cooperative_action_under_the_Strategic_Approach_to_International_Chemicals_Management_SAICM

Over 600 medicines have been found in sewage or sludge around the world. Sampling of rivers found >25% of sites had at least one API at levels considered unsafe for aquatic wildlife. There is good evidence of freshwater molluscs not adhering properly because of medication in water and of fish changing sex due to hormones from the contraceptive pill in UK waters.

Addressing pharmaceutical pollution is complex and will not be the work of any one actor, with a whole-systems approach involving multiple stakeholders being key.

Actions

- Awareness of inappropriate prescribing – reduce where possible (see Chapter 7).
- Discuss medicine return to pharmacies to prevent "leakage" into the water supply.
- NEVER put medication "down the toilet or sink" – inform patients of this.

Antimicrobial resistance (AMR). The World Health Organization has declared AMR to be one of the top ten global public health threats facing humanity. Misuse and overuse of antimicrobials are the main drivers in the development of drug-resistant pathogens. Lack of clean water and sanitation and inadequate infection prevention and control promote the spread of microbes, some of which can be resistant to antimicrobial treatment. Recent evidence has shown that there is an identifiable human exposure risk of exposure to AMR bacteria for coastal water users, which varies with the type of water sport undertaken (22). Understanding the impact on aquatic ecosystems amplifies the need to continue to resource and prioritise these strategies.

Plastic pollution. Plastic has supported advances in human civilisation and healthcare (see Chapter 12). In 2019, the NHS in England produced 624,000 tonnes of waste. Plastic comprised 23%, almost 50% of which was packaging. Whilst macroplastic, healthcare–associated pollution can be seen and sorted, it is essential not to forget sources of equally important microplastics: 9.5 billion miles a year – 3.5% of all road travel in England is linked to NHS activity (23), which generates significant amounts of microplastics through tyre and brake pad wear. These particles first contribute to particulate air pollution and then are washed into storm drains, rivers, and, thereafter, the ocean (24). Both macro- and microplastics can harm fragile ecosystems, and there is increasing evidence that the production, shipping, use, and disposal of plastics can cause disease, disability, and death, especially in the most vulnerable communities (19).

Despite most plastic being used by secondary care, there is still a burden arising from community healthcare from medical devices, blister packs, and packaging, much of which ends up in landfills, slowly leaching into the environment. Different waste disposal legislation means there is scope to change how waste is managed and may help speed adoption of new technologies like home-compostable casings and packaging for community-used medical devices. See Chapter 12 for more information.

Case study: displacing medical plastics with seaweed!

Sixty million inhalers are distributed across the United Kingdom each year, of which only 0.5% ever get recycled. The rest go to incineration or landfills, from where toxic compounds can enter the environment, causing harm to both the planet and people. SymbioTex provides an alternative to the current shortfall of other bioplastics – its material does not compete with land used for crops, is fully home compostable, and uses a 100% renewable feedstock – seaweed. They aim to provide the NHS and healthcare manufacturers with an affordable solution which does not compromise its existing waste management infrastructure. The current manufacturers will produce the same medical devices, but instead of using plastic, they will use seaweed along with natural plasticisers to produce products which are home compostable – the ultimate circular solution for a plant-based product.

Nature recovery. As well as recognising healthcare's dependencies and impacts on nature and oceans, healthcare systems can contribute to nature recovery. Nature recovery is the restoration of habitats and wildlife and the protection of species (24). Nature recovery depends on policy and community action at every level, and there are opportunities for healthcare to play a role. The post-2020 global biodiversity framework agreed upon at COP 15 in Montreal 2022 included a target to ensure that at least 30% globally of land and sea areas, especially areas of particular importance for biodiversity and its contributions to people, are conserved.

There are significant co-benefits to population health from advocating for place-based marine, freshwater, and coastal nature-based solutions. The IUCN Nature-Based Solutions (NBS) standards define NBS as actions to protect, conserve, restore, or sustainably use and manage natural or modified terrestrial, freshwater coastal, and marine ecosystems which address the social, economic, and environmental challenges effectively and adaptively, whilst simultaneously providing human well-being, ecosystem services, resilience, and biodiversity benefits.

Nature connection. For many, water systems are huge sources of joy, creativity, and inspiration. Population health recognises the influence of the social determinants of health on well-being and health outcomes. Spending time in nature, including in coastal or freshwater environments, has been found to have positive impacts on health outcomes through mechanisms such as increased rates of physical activity, connection with nature, improved sleep, and mental health outcomes. These benefits are not shared equally, and in particular, the UK coastal strip has a consistent pattern of unequal access to good health compared to their inland neighbours (25).

Healthcare is unique in its opportunities to identify patients and populations who may benefit most from connection to nature or increased access to nature through mechanisms such as population health management, advocating for improved blue and green infrastructure in areas of inequalities, or interventions such as nature-based prescribing (26).

There is evidence that the nature connection (28 and see Chapter 15) from these place-based approaches can be key in enabling increased stewardship and marine citizenship, and strategies that optimise listening to local knowledge are vital in increasing a participatory approach and a just transition.

Further actions. Many industries have started to address their impacts and dependencies on water and oceanic systems through frameworks such as the Taskforce on Nature-Related Financial Disclosures and the science-based targets for nature (27). These ask organisations to examine their interfaces and relationships with nature and start to disclose and quantify their risks and opportunities in nature.

In smaller organisations, a similar approach can be undertaken to ensure an ocean- and water-friendly approach by considering three domains:

Ocean and water footprint

- Water stewardship. Engage the whole practice team to review water usage and check what is being disposed of through water systems.
- Consider the Green Impact for Health Toolkit to record actions relating to water.
- Encourage quality improvement projects that address overprescribing (see Chapter 9).
- Review current practice estate management and challenge herbicide and pesticide usage.
- Use water pollution alert systems to report illness from time in blue spaces and check for sewage discharges for water users (28).

Ocean and water recovery

- GP practice and floodplain risk. Discuss adaptation strategies at practice meetings, prioritising NBS, such as collaborating with regional nature recovery strategies.
- Explore ways to connect with local recovery partnerships or species and biodiversity plans (29).

Ocean and water connection

- Connect with your local social prescribing link worker to map local opportunities in blue prescribing or social prescribing in blue spaces.
- Consider staff well-being activities involving being in or around water.

References

1 https://pubmed.ncbi.nlm.nih.gov/35409855/
2 Fleming Lora et al. (ed.), *Oceans and Human Health. Opportunities and Impacts.* 2nd Edition, Elsevier. July 14, 2023.
3 https://www.un.org/en/conf/ocean/background.shtml
4 https://ods.od.nih.gov/factsheets/list-all/
5 J. Gephart et al., 2021; OurWorldinData.org
6 https://www.ipcc.ch/srocc/chapter/chapter-5/
7 M. Melnychuk et al., 2021) (see Chapter 2). https://www.nature.com/articles/s41893-020-00668-1
8 B. Halpern et al., 2022. https://www.nature.com/articles/s41893-022-00965-x
9 https://education.nationalgeographic.org/resource/freshwater-resources/
10 https://www.who.int/health-topics/drought#tab=tab_1
11 https://www.oecd.org/agriculture/topics/water-and-agriculture/

12 https://a4ws.org/about/

13 https://oceanservice.noaa.gov/facts/why-care-about-ocean.html

14 https://www.ons.gov.uk/economy/environmentalaccounts/bulletins/marineaccountsnaturalcapitaluk/2021

15 https://www.gov.uk/government/publications/chief-medical-officers-nnual-report-2021-health-in-coastal-communities

16 https://www.england.nhs.uk/greenernhs/a-net-zero-nhs/

17 https://www.ipcc.ch/srocc/chapter/summary-for-policymakers/

18 Mezzelani M, Gorbi S, Regoli F, Pharmaceuticals in the aquatic environments: Evidence of emerged threat and future challenges for marine organisms. *Mar. Environ. Res.*, 2018 Sep;140:41–60. doi: 10.1016/j.marenvres.2018.05.001. Epub 2018 May 14. PMID: 29859717.

19 https://www.minderoo.org/plastic-waste-makers-index

20 Der Beek Aus et al., Pharmaceuticals in the environment – Global occurrences and perspectives. *Environ. Toxicol. Chem.*, 2015;35. doi: 10.1002/etc.3339

21 Wilkinson Boxall et al., Pharmaceutical pollution of the world's rivers, 2022 February. https://www.pnas.org/doi/10.1073/pnas.2113947119

22 https://www.umweltbundesamt.de/en/database-pharmaceuticals-in-the-environment-figures-0

23 National Health Service (UK), https://www.england.nhs.uk/greenernhs/wp-content/uploads/sites/51/2020/10/delivering-a-net-zero-national-health-service.pdf 2022.

24 https://assets.publishing.service.gov.uk/media/5ab3a67840f0b65bb584297e/25-year-environment-plan.pdf

25 https://assets.publishing.service.gov.uk/media/60f98750e90e0703bbd94a41/cmo-annual_report-2021-health-in-coastal-communities-accessible.pdf

26 https://www.ecehh.org/research/nature-prescription-handbook/

27 Taskforce on nature-related financial disclosures and the science-based targets for nature.

28 https://www.sas.org.uk/water-quality/sewage-pollution-alerts/

29 https://www.gov.uk/government/publications/map-of-local-nature-partnerships/locations-and-key-contacts

Resources

Book – Oceans and Human Health, Opportunities and Impacts

Water stewardship https://a4ws.org/about/

Pharma pollution hub – https://www.pharmapollutionhub.org/

Nature on prescription https://www.ecehh.org/research/nature-prescription-handbook/

Sewage pollution alerts – https://www.sas.org.uk/water-quality/sewage-pollution-alerts/

Land
Angela Wilson

Case study

Alan is a 35-year-old auctioneer who has worried about bowel cancer ever since he had some beetroot and noticed the toilet bowl was red the following day. He has no other symptoms. He eats lots of meat, including a sausage and bacon bun for breakfast most days, and a beef burger for his lunch.

Things to consider:

- Does a high-meat diet cause personal health problems?
- Does a high-meat diet cause planetary health problems?
- What other impacts does diet have?
- Are low-meat diets affordable?

There is considerable evidence linking red meat to cancer, especially colonic and rectal. Red meat is also positively correlated with higher lung, renal, endometrial, and breast cancer rates.

High-meat diets have planetary impacts – from high greenhouse gas emissions to water pollution and changes to land use (e.g., from rainforest to pastureland).

There are major reductions in greenhouse gas emissions as we reduce red meat consumption.

Making food affordable to all people is at least partly political but also intensely personal, as diet may be linked to status and identity. The cost of food is affected by the agricultural subsidies that governments have in place, as well as the raw costs – i.e., supermarket prices are the prices after subsidies have been used.

DOI: 10.1201/9781003491583-15

Can people afford a low-meat diet? Various studies have shown that vegetarian and vegan diets are cheaper; however, there are multiple barriers:

- Uneven access to fruits and vegetables, favouring the rich
- Ability to prepare new foods and knowledge of how to cook vegetarian meals
- Access to affordable cooking equipment
- Worries about wasting food/money if the new meals are disliked

Actions

Introduce the concept of a planetary health diet – which is better for the person and planet simultaneously.

Moving to a "flexitarian" diet with – e.g., only one portion of red meat per week could reduce food system-related greenhouse gas emissions by up to 80% while reducing premature mortality by 20%.

Remember that you will get health benefits (and planetary health benefits) from eating foods which are vegetarian for just a day (Meat-Free Monday!); you DON'T have to be vegetarian or be vegan.

Resources

https://www.greenerpractice.co.uk/information-and-resources/clinical-considerations/promoting-healthy-living/

https://www.ox.ac.uk/news/2021-11-11-sustainable-eating-cheaper-and-healthier-oxford-study

https://theecologist.org/2022/sep/01/vegan-cost-living-crisis

https://bjgplife.com/why-family-doctors-should-support-patients-to-remove-red-meat-from-the-diet

Introduction

No one will protect what they don't care about:
and no one will care about what they have never experienced.

David Attenborough

Our species is dependent on land-based plants, minerals, and animals. How we manage the resources of the land influences human health. To create a healthier world means seeing ourselves as part of nature rather than separate from it.

There are important links between our health and agricultural systems, as well as direct and indirect co-dependencies between human health, healthcare systems, and land health. Work has already been done by some healthcare systems to restore nature.

Through green social prescribing, clinicians can help patients connect with nature to improve health outcomes.

Primary care can help catalyse changes in how we live to improve the well-being of patients and communities while at the same time reducing the harms done to land and soil. If this work is done through a lens of social justice, we can also ensure that health inequalities are reduced.

Land use has undergone significant transformations throughout history. Human settlement and cultivation commenced approximately 12,000 years ago, with an acceleration in changes since the Industrial Revolution of the 1760s. Seventy-one per cent of land can be described as habitable – i.e., neither barren nor covered in glaciers. One thousand years ago, only 4% of the habitable land was used for farming, but by 2019, this had risen to 46% (1). Of the remaining land, 38% is forest, 11% grass and shrubland, 1% is freshwater, and only 1% is built on (i.e., buildings) and transport infrastructure. The World Economic Forum estimated that in 2020, the collective weight of man-made objects surpassed the total dry weight of all terrestrial plants and animal matter on the planet for the first time (2).

The European Environment Agency notes that Europe is one of the most intensively developed continents in the world, with land under pressure from economic activities, agriculture, increased mobility, and expanding transport systems (3).

In the United Kingdom, land has been very intensively 'developed' with 9% of land built on. The UK government describes the remaining 91% as "non-developed", but this is misleading. Agriculture covers 63.1% of UK land, forestry open land and water 20.1%, and residential gardens 4.9% (4) (Figure 15.1).

The distribution of UK land ownership reflects massive inequality. Research in 2019 calculated that half of UK land was owned by only 1% of the population (5). In England, the Right to Roam movement calculated that only 8% of land and 3% of freshwater is accessible. The Right to Grow food exists in law, but it has proven difficult to implement, with over 150,000 people on allotment waiting lists.

Global patterns of inequality in land access and usage echo the United Kingdom's pattern (6). Colonialism significantly contributed to this disparity, involving the acquisition or control of vast tracts of land well beyond the norm of local land ownership. A 2017 Oxfam report highlights that, in developing countries, an area equivalent to Western Europe has been either leased or purchased by international companies since 2001 (7). Inequality in land control or ownership continues to expand. This inequality has far-reaching consequences on local economies, environments, social well-being, and human rights.

Healthy agriculture? Agriculture has had the greatest impact on land-based ecosystems and could be a key solution to the challenges posed by climate change and the ongoing nature crises. Analysing it also helps clinicians understand the increasingly international diet and its health problems.

The combustion engine changed the way pasture and arable land were managed as ploughing became mechanised. It also accelerated deforestation. After World War II, companies that had produced explosives shifted to production of pesticides and fertilisers. For several decades, crop yields increased, but this was at the expense of soil and water health. Driven by market pressures, many farmers had to adopt these methods to

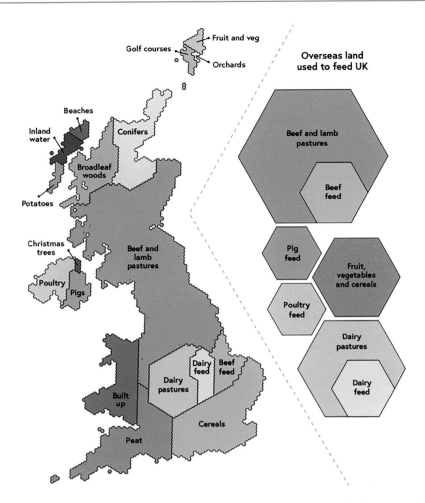

FIGURE 15.1 UK land area divided up by purpose. The right-hand side of the chart, using the same scale, shows how much land is used overseas to produce food for the United Kingdom. About half of the total land use takes place overseas. The combined land area for rearing beef and lamb for UK consumption is larger than the United Kingdom itself (p. 90 4).

make a livelihood. Several studies of crops grown for human consumption show that nutrient density in these foods is declining alongside the health of the land (8). At the same time as obesity is approaching 75% in the United States, studies suggest the population has increased micronutrient deficiencies (9).

The adoption of 'Western' agricultural practices has led to fewer crop varieties being grown globally. Just six crops – rice, wheat, maize (or corn), potato, soybeans, and sugarcane – account for more than three-quarters of total plant-derived energy intake globally – with three – rice, wheat, and maize accounting for half of all food energy (10). Agrochemical companies have designed and sold seeds that are promoted as resilient to some diseases or that will resist the herbicides they sell. This industrialised food system requires more food miles for packaging, processing, and delivery to consumers.

Industrial food production has led to less varied diets globally, with increased consumption of ultra-processed foods which are linked to physical and mental health issues (9). The COVID-19 pandemic and the Ukraine war have highlighted the reduced resilience of the food system, as we rely on the continuous flow of food products into markets rather than have local storage.

Globally, waste has surged, with an estimated 17% of production lost annually. Two-thirds of this loss occurs within households, while the remaining third is attributed to the food industry itself (10).

Over the past 50 years, global meat consumption has sharply risen, reaching 367 million tonnes in 2013, with expectations of further increases in the future. Nearly half of Earth's land is agricultural, of which 77% is used for raising livestock, which only contributes 18% of calories and 37% of protein supply globally (1). The cultivation of soy for animal feed is linked to deforestation in various parts of the world. Increased meat consumption has involved factory farms with poor animal welfare practices and cramped conditions, risking the transmission of zoonotic diseases. Livestock raising accounts for approximately two-thirds of all antibiotics used globally, posing risks of antimicrobial resistance as they enter soil, water, and food (11).

Animal agriculture is the leading cause of species extinction, ocean dead zones, water pollution, and habitat destruction. It is responsible for 18% of greenhouse gas emissions. Livestock and their by-products account for at least 32,000 million tonnes of carbon dioxide per year, or 51% of all worldwide greenhouse gas emissions. Livestock is responsible for 65% of all human-related emissions of NOx. Emissions for agriculture are projected to increase 80% by 2050. The NHS produces 140 million in-patient meals a year, and both primary and secondary care can adopt a predominantly plant-based diet and promote it to other staff and patients (see Chapter 8).

Action: All NHS providers and at all corporate events could offer plant-only menus.

Numerous initiatives are being trialled to produce food more sustainably. By bringing food growing closer to the projected 80% of the world's population that will live in urban areas, there is a potential to improve the connection between people and the food they eat (12). Rooftop and underground growing spaces are being developed, and disused buildings, such as car parks and factories, are being used for aquaponic horticulture. Some believe that precision fermentation can be used to produce protein to decrease the meat industry's impact on the environment (13). Others argue that animals continue to be needed for the benefits of their manure and the action their grazing has on soil health (8).

Biofuels. One of the most perverse changes is the conversion of land from a space for growing food to producing crops for burning. Annually, 10% of grain worldwide and 40% of corn in the United States is now turned into biofuel. Biofuels from previously cultivated land can exhibit lower emissions than fossil fuels; however, they come at the expense of diminishing food availability. When deforestation and other alterations in land use are involved in cultivating these crops, the environmental impact can be significantly worse.

Whatever form of food production is considered, it is vital to involve local and indigenous people in decision-making. Allowing people more access to land can help people become custodians, reconnecting for the benefit of people and wildlife.

Actions

- Adopt and enable others to adopt a more varied plant-based diet.
- Avoid ultra-processed foods (see Chapter 8).
- Engage with growing food, whether on a windowsill or in a garden.
- Understand "use by" and "best before" dates, as confusion contributes to food waste.
- Support enterprises which work to reduce food waste and improve food availability for all.
- Support nature-positive businesses, community-supported agriculture, and regenerative agriculture (which focuses on increasing biodiversity, enhancing health and vitality of topsoil, and improving the water cycle, etc.).

Soil and health. Soil is a complex, living ecosystem, teeming with a kaleidoscope of life: 90% of land-based organisms live in soil (8). How we treat soil impacts the nutritional value of food and can influence the climate (14).

The area around the roots of plants is vitally important for plant life to grow and thrive. Inspection of roots shows fine fungal filaments in a symbiotic relationship with plants (8). This mycorrhizal network shifts energy between plants to support them, meshes soil together, prevents erosion, and locks up water and carbon. Plants in turn release complex chemicals into the soil that are necessary for the fungi to grow. Bacteria, fungi, and other microbes change nitrogen, minerals, and organic matter into forms which plants can absorb. This cooperative process not only aids in nutrient absorption but also triggers the plant's immune system and shields them with antibacterials, acting as a defence against harmful soil pathogens.

Carbon is stored in soil in vast quantities. Glomalin is a sticky carbon rich protein found in the rhizosphere, entrapped for millions of years and accounting for one-third of the world's carbon, more than all plant and animal life combined (15).

Life above and below ground level is under threat from human action. Pollution (including pharmaceutical and plastic), lack of organic matter in the soil, heavy ploughing, pesticides, fertilisers, erosion from flooding, construction, and wind have all reduced the quality and quantity of soil. This damage to soil is linked to reduced biodiversity above ground level with losses to the bird and insect populations (16).

Soils in some places are so degraded and lacking microbial life that they no longer cycle water, carbon, and nutrients effectively. Plants here can grow only when supported by heavy applications of chemical fertilisers and pesticides like Glyphosate due to being less resilient. This is expensive, pollutes water and land, and can be harmful to human health. Glyphosate has been classified as a class 2A carcinogen by WHO IARC (17). Heavy metals from industry, building work, or roads can remain in soil for decades. Lead and microplastics from cars and arsenic from technology are all potential contaminants. Poor soil health is a factor limiting crop yield (8).

Healthy soil provides "ecosystem services" worth trillions of dollars: climate regulation, drought and flood mitigation, soil erosion prevention, carbon storage, and water purification. Looking after the ecosystem under our feet could be one of the biggest leverage points for a sustainable and healthy future.

Healthy soils may be achieved by regenerative and organic agriculture, permaculture, reducing the use of agrochemicals, and drastically reducing ploughing. These techniques improve soil quality, storage of carbon, as well as the levels of micronutrients and phytochemicals in food (8). By learning how best to store and cook food, we can further increase its nutritional content (18).

There are parallels between maintaining a healthy soil (avoid too much fertiliser/pesticides/herbicides, variety of crops, avoid ploughing) and maintaining a healthy gut microbiome (helped by variety of food and avoidance of antibiotics) or skin biome (avoid lots of washing/cleaning and avoid antibiotics). All involve starting to understand that we are working with complex systems with feedback loops. Nature is a system, not something we can do stuff to.

Action: Protect the soil biome through supporting regenerative food production, growing your own/taking part in community growing of veg, and eating a variety of seasonal and local fresh fruits and veg (see Case Study, "Kirkholt Practice Bloomin' Marvellous Gardens", in Chapter 8).

Healthcare dependencies. All healthcare facilities have a footprint on land: from the materials and energy involved in construction to the land site they occupy. The operation of providing healthcare has an impact (Chapters 10–12). The land "lens" prompts awareness that food and medicines, as well as buildings are all derived from land. Primary care exerts diverse impacts on the land, and this intricate relationship becomes apparent when examining the life cycle of various objects. Building materials and healthcare equipment involves resource extraction (with implications for local communities and ecosystems), processing, transportation, packaging, utilisation, and eventual disposal.

Action: Follow the waste hierarchy in Chapter 12 to reduce reuse, repair, and recycle equipment.

Humanity has harnessed the medicinal properties of plants for thousands of years. Otzi the Iceman, found in the Tyrol in 1991, was carrying mushrooms with known anthelminthic properties. Opium (poppy), aspirin (willow bark), and St John's wort are older, nature-derived pharmacotherapies. Atorvastatin (fungal) and streptomycin (soil bacteria) are modern and nature derived (19, 20).

Most drugs were originally naturally derived or are synthetic mimics of a natural molecule, including over 65% of cancer drugs (21). Many indigenous communities still employ plant-based remedies—Ayurvedic medicine in the Indian subcontinent and traditional Chinese medicine coexisting with modern approaches. This intertwining may be rooted in cultural values, or it's a practical choice driven by affordability and accessibility.

The climate and ecological emergency causes biodiversity loss and ecosystem damage. Reduced species diversity (including fungi and bacteria) has multiple implications, including fewer drug precursors.

Action: Consider recommending self-care using natural remedies where appropriate. For example, lavender for relaxation and peppermint tea to aid digestion.

Healthcare impacts on land. The impact of healthcare, especially pharmaceuticals and plastics, on nature has been well documented in the water chapter. Land, too, can be polluted via the spread of manure containing veterinary drugs, landfill, discharges from pharmaceutical factories, and improper disposal of medication (22). In India, a local vulture population became extinct from renal failure after they fed off cattle that had been treated with diclofenac. Soil type, organic material content, and other factors determine how long drug residues stay in soil. Pharmaceuticals in soil can enter plants, affecting growth and accumulating in food (23). Further studies are needed to clarify the impacts on human and planetary health of pharmaceutical pollution on land.

Nature restoration in healthcare settings. There has recently been a concerted effort to use the NHS estate to restore nature. Hospital sites have undertaken both small-scale development of greenspaces and large-scale tree planting. NHS Forest, a partner with the Centre for Sustainable Healthcare, has provided a wealth of knowledge and skills to sites (24). Nature rangers work on some hospital sites to coordinate this and other nature-based work.

Tree planting is especially important in urban areas to provide shade, reduce air pollution, and improve well-being (25). Trees take several years to establish successfully. Extremes of heat and drought, followed by flooding, is making that harder. After ten years, their growth counts towards carbon capture calculations and offsets emissions. It takes many more years for trees to become ecosystems rich in biodiversity. It is *really* important to keep mature trees growing where and whenever possible.

Primary care has also been involved with nature restoration – e.g., Oxfordshire practices starting a "Bee Healthy" pollinator-friendly planting scheme (28). Practices from Cornwall to Scotland have mini gardens and allotments for staff, patients, and green social prescribing ventures. Every effort, no matter how small, can benefit biodiversity and people.

Biodiversity Net Gain targets are legally required in England: for every new construction project, there must be a 10% increase in biodiversity (29). This can be on-site so locals can benefit, but where infeasible, the building must invest in projects elsewhere.

Nature-based solutions (NBS) involve the sustainable management and use of natural features and processes to tackle socio-environmental issues (30). Examples include natural flood alleviation plans, swale planting, natural flood management, installing green roofs, and large-scale planting of urban trees. Primary healthcare providers can implement these approaches when managing infrastructure and estates. NBSs can go some way to helping manage the climate and ecological emergency but are not a solo solution.

Action: Look for inspiration for a nature-based action or activity, such as producing planters to make a mini allotment at work or home.

Nature connection. Humans evolved in rural environments. Humans prefer landscapes that are complex, more natural, and navigable. Places that provide our needs for shelter, water, and food. We also have other basic requirements to belong, to feel valued, and to be safe.

A 2023 report from Create Streets (32) measured the value of living near a green space or small park. These included a positive impact value of £6,495 per person living within 500 metres of the green space. This includes a combination of lower depression (£750), higher cognitive development (£150), reduced mortality (£2,999), reduced crime and a higher house price (£3,375).

Nature connectedness

More nature connections = better health = more active

Less green space = increased loneliness, increased death rate, less social support

Plant more = make more contacts and connections

Less aggression, less anger, better mood, more pro-social behaviour

More feelings of connectedness

The "3-30-300 rule": suggests that for health, everyone should have sight of three trees, every neighbourhood should have 30% tree canopy cover, and everyone should live within 300 metres of a park or green space (32).

The evidence. There are multiple beneficial mental and physical health effects of being in nature (33–35). The evidence base for this is rapidly expanding. The senses can all be engaged when in nature. For example, looking at fractals or repeated patterns (seen, for example, in trees, ripples in water, the unfolding of a fern) sets off alpha waves in our brain, producing a relaxed but still alert state. The parasympathetic (or soothing) nervous system is activated by nature sounds. Birdsong played to those under anaesthesia lowers blood pressure. Phytocines are chemicals released by some trees such as Cypress, cedar, oak, birch, beech, and hazel, which are associated with the smells of the forest and boost the immune system through increased natural killer cell activity.

If we stop and contemplate nature, we can experience awe – even at micro levels, such as when looking at a raindrop on a leaf. As a result, markers of a stress reaction decrease, and happiness improves. We are more kind, ethical, and generous, and we show less self-interest and introspection. Complex environments help develop neuroplasticity. Through exposure to micro stressors like adapting to weather, to uneven paths, and to contact with other animals including humans, we learn to adapt and become more resilient.

Contact with soil may also have some benefits to health

Over the last decade, the benefits of bacteria in our intestines and bowels have become more apparent. The human skin and gut microbiomes have been changed by the impact of urbanisation, reduced connection to the natural living world, a cleaning obsession to remove dirt and microbes, reduced animal contact, changing use of antibiotics, a processed diet, reduced rates of breastfeeding, and many more. The importance of soil microbes on our gut microbiome is not fully understood. However, babies left to their own devices will eat soil, and other animals do the same. A study in Finland added biodiverse soil from forests to nurseries and measured the response from the immune system (36). After play, analysis showed altered skin and gut microbiomes leading to better-functioning cytokine messengers and a higher proportion of regulatory T-cells, both of which are associated with improved immune modulation activities.

Although high-quality studies on the impact access to nature has on surgical recovery times aren't yet available, small observational studies report benefits. For example, less analgesia, shorter stays, and better-reported well-being if the patient has a view of a natural scene through a window rather than a brick wall (27).

Green horticultural therapies can improve behaviour in children who have a diagnosis of attention deficit hyperactivity disorder and autism spectrum disorder. Reduced rates of offending have been demonstrated in prisoners who have access to nature-based interventions. Nature can restore our attention – e.g., office workers who took micro breaks looking out over green roofs made fewer errors and achieved better results.

Meta-analyses show that overall exposure to green spaces resulted in a statistically significant reduction in diastolic blood pressure, salivary cortisol, and heart rate. There was a decreased incidence of diabetes mellitus, all-cause mortality, and cardiovascular disease (35).

Nature, urban spaces, and inequalities

Urban effects can be buffered to an extent through the amygdala being activated by green spaces, where relaxing alpha waves are activated. Access to trees increases sociability and reduces criminality.

Deep inequality in access to nature remains and is a social justice issue. Those oldest, poorest, and most deprived, as well as ethnic minorities, all face additional barriers to accessing nature.

However, being rural does not necessarily mean being connected to nature. The wealthiest have 80% more footpath access paths than the most deprived, and where health is worse, the number of paths is lowest (37).

Reassuringly, income related inequalities in health are less where there are green spaces (40) – indicating that modification is possible – to improve nature and health outcomes for those who need it most.

Shifting baseline syndrome. The lack of time in natural spaces and reduced biodiversity is producing children who are used to nature-depleted spaces; their assumptions have changed, and they have a "shifting baseline" (31). The RSPB reported 80% of children do not have adequate connection with the outside world. Children under the age of 7 spend twice as much time looking at screens as playing outside, and in the United Kingdom, many spend less time outside than prisoners – described as "the extinction of experience" by Robert Pyle (38). There are huge inequalities here too – children in deprived areas have nine times less access to green spaces than children in affluent areas. The quality of green space is more important than its quantity. Creative play needs varied areas to get into a flow, and more nature contact in childhood leads to less depression in adults (Figure 15.2).

FIGURE 15.2 Shifting baseline syndrome. Also known as generational amnesia or ecological amnesia.

(Created by Cameron Shepherd. Used with kind permission).

Statistics for adults show only 1%–5% of time spent outdoors. The health benefits of natural spaces can be reduced by personal insecurity, reduced biodiversity, and pollution of air and land. Most people have lost access to nature's rhythms – whether our circadian rhythm (melatonin appears to prevent damage to cells, as there is a 40% increase in breast cancer in night shift workers) or seasonal rhythms of the natural living world.

Richard Louv called this *nature deficit disorder*: the impact of a lack of nature connection on people's health. "It describes the human costs of alienation from nature, among them: diminished use of the senses, attention difficulties, higher rates of physical and emotional illnesses".

Other terms have become more common with increasing awareness of the ecological crises. Eco-empathy and eco-distress have become more widely used (see Chapter 19): *solastalgia* – a combination of nostalgia and the powerlessness of watching a place that previously brought solace being destroyed, and *species loneliness* – the collective sorrow and anxiety from our disconnection from other species. Some may identify more with the experience of *Biophilia* as described by E. O. Wilson: an innate or genetically determined affinity with the natural world (397).

How and where? Nature connection can occur in everyday life as we walk home under a canopy of street trees, pass a neighbour's garden, or look out of the bus at a green space. Activities can take place in natural spaces: a run in the park, a walk in a local wood, a holiday spent beside the seaside, or an hour in an allotment. Some activities involve a direct observation of nature – mindfulness, silent spaces, and art horticultural therapies. Others form a deeper connection – both spiritually and culturally.

How we connect may vary depending on emotional, mental, or physical health; time; available resources; preferences and abilities; and geography. Introverts may connect with nature more without direct facial contact and extroverts in company. Five ways to deeper nature connection have been identified: through increased *contact* using all senses, identifying any *emotion* present during the contact, appreciating and reflecting on the *beauty* of nature, and its *meaning* to the individual or group, and then recognising any *compassion* felt towards the natural world which may lead to making pro-environmental choices in life (33) (Figure 15.3).

Green social prescribing is supporting people to engage in nature-based interventions and activities to improve their mental and physical health (40). The number of green social prescribing projects has been increasing. Some are organised through national organisations, such as Ramblers or Right to Roam, others are local, such as Sheffield Environmental Movement. Websites such as Gardening 4 Health (41) have over 1,000 projects on their interactive map of the United Kingdom, and in Scotland, there is Trellis. For some, green gyms or community gardens, care farms, or forest schools will be suitable. The RSPB's Nature Prescription and Dose of Nature provide ideas for observations on and activities in local seasonal nature that people can do. In some areas, Nature Recovery Networks and Local Nature Partnerships are becoming increasingly active (42).

Case study

Green Social Prescribing (GSP) is an underutilised but valuable tool for primary care to improve patient outcomes. Frequently, lack of knowledge or awareness and signposting are identified as barriers to referring to it.

Methods: Members of staff at one GP practice were surveyed prior to a short educational intervention on their understanding, knowledge, confidence, and perceptions surrounding GSP. The intervention was a ten-minute presentation, informing staff about the benefits of GSP for patients, the community, the environment, and the healthcare service. Staff were informed how to signpost patients to the available GSP services. Staff were re-surveyed following the presentation, and results were analysed to determine the impact of the intervention.

Key results: The short educational intervention increased understanding and knowledge of GSP by 45% and 59%, respectively. Confidence in explaining and signposting GSP to a patient also increased by 44% and 37%, respectively.

Discussion: The quality improvement (QI) project shows promising benefits of a short educational intervention in breaking down barriers to utilising GSP.

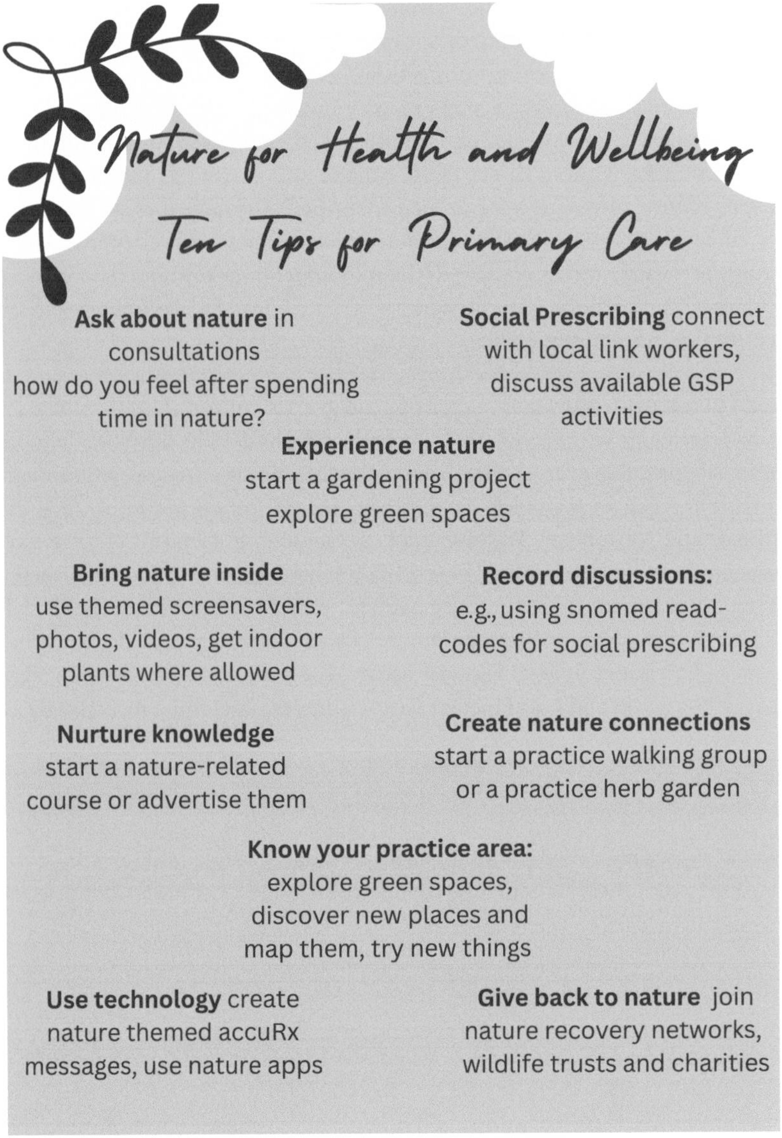

Nature for Health and Wellbeing
Ten Tips for Primary Care

Ask about nature in consultations how do you feel after spending time in nature?

Social Prescribing connect with local link workers, discuss available GSP activities

Experience nature start a gardening project explore green spaces

Bring nature inside use themed screensavers, photos, videos, get indoor plants where allowed

Record discussions: e.g., using snomed read-codes for social prescribing

Nurture knowledge start a nature-related course or advertise them

Create nature connections start a practice walking group or a practice herb garden

Know your practice area: explore green spaces, discover new places and map them, try new things

Use technology create nature themed accuRx messages, use nature apps

Give back to nature join nature recovery networks, wildlife trusts and charities

FIGURE 15.3 Ten ways to nature connection.

(Adapted by Angela Wilson, Duncan Still, and Alan Kellas with permission from Marion Steiner).

Risks and considerations

We need to appreciate that there are some potential risks involved in taking part in nature-based activities – e.g., injuries, stings, allergic reactions. Some people may have some hesitation entering green spaces due to lack of experience in accessing them, feeling inadequately equipped, or due to past adverse events that took place in a similar environment. There are toolkits available to help those setting up a GSP project. It is important to ensure that nature connection projects that are good for us and our patients are not harming the planet and are equitable in terms of access. Linking patients up to organisations involved in nature recovery work, nature-based charities, and trusts helps ensure there is enough capacity and there is mutual benefit to nature. Good quality studies will also be needed to analyse the longer-term benefits of nature-based interventions. Initial studies have been very positive.

Funding

Most of these projects need funding – Mind used a £7.4 million ecotherapy fund to develop and run nature-based therapies. The results showed participants had reduced depression and stress and boosted self-esteem. Fellow healthcare workers, managers, and commissioners may need persuading that nature deserves promotion as a therapy. There is now significant evidence that this is cost-effective and well-liked by those who partake (43, 44).

Funding has been obtained for additional roles reimbursement scheme (ARRS) roles in one primary care network (PCN) for horticultural therapists who engage referred patients in gardening activities. Volunteers, patient participation groups (PPGs), and local charities have helped projects to take off and then flourish. In the United Kingdom, the Green Infrastructure Framework was launched in 2023. The aim is for the public to have quality green space accessible within 15 minutes of where they live. This has released funding in some areas of the United Kingdom where councils are working with nature recovery partnerships and health services to provide safe, accessible nature-based activities.

Conclusion

GPs and primary healthcare teams are in a position to reduce the impacts of healthcare on biodiversity through choices made at work and in their personal life. Through projects that connect humans to nature, biodiversity can be restored, and we can move towards every member of society appreciating the links between land, well-being, and human health.

References

1 https://ourworldindata.org/land-use
2 https://www.weforum.org/agenda/2021/12/weight-accumulation-human-made-mass-earth/

3   https://www.eea.europa.eu/en/topics/in-depth/land-use

4   The National Food Strategy, Part II. https://www.nationalfoodstrategy.org/

5   Who Owns England?: How We Lost Our Land and How to Take It Back. How We Lost Our Land and How to Take It Back. Guy Shrubsole.

6   https://www.tandfonline.com/doi/full/10.1080/03066150.2012.691879

7   https://oi-files-d8-prod.s3.eu-west-2.amazonaws.com/s3fs-public/file_attachments/bp151-land-power-rights-acquisitions-220911-en_4.pdf

8   https://www.dig2grow.com/sources

9   https://www.ncbi.nlm.nih.gov/pmc/articles/PMC4517043/

10 https://idrc-crdi.ca/en/research-in-action/facts-figures-food-and-biodiversity

11 https://www.nature.com/articles/d41586-023-00284-x

12 https://pacecircular.org/sites/default/files/2019-03/Cities-and-Circular-Economy-for-Food.pdf

13 https://rethinkx.medium.com/precision-fermentation-what-exactly-is-it-7004eeaa798e

14 https://drawdown.org/solutions/regenerative-annual-cropping

15 https://e360.yale.edu/features/soil_as_carbon_storehouse_new_weapon_in_climate_fight

16 https://www.sciencedirect.com/science/article/pii/S016788091730525X

17 https://www.iarc.who.int/featured-news/media-centre-iarc-news-glyphosate/

18 https://eatwild.com/eating_on_the_wild_side.html

19 https://www.ncbi.nlm.nih.gov/pmc/articles/PMC3901206/

20 https://www.ncbi.nlm.nih.gov/pmc/articles/PMC6273146/

21 https://pubs.acs.org/doi/10.1021/acs.jnatprod.9b01285

22 https://www.ncbi.nlm.nih.gov/pmc/articles/PMC4213584/

23 https://link.springer.com/article/10.1007/s11270-020-04954-8

24 https://nhsforest.org/

25 https://link.springer.com/article/10.1007/s00468-023-02389-2

26 https://sustainablehealthcare.org.uk/sites/default/files/bee_healthy_project_guide_report.pdf

27 https://www.gov.uk/guidance/understanding-biodiversity-net-gain

28 https://designatedsites.naturalengland.org.uk/GreenInfrastructure/WhatIsGreenInfrastructure.aspx

29 https://esajournals.onlinelibrary.wiley.com/doi/10.1002/fee.1794

30 https://www.createstreets.com/greeningup/

31 https://www.ncbi.nlm.nih.gov/pmc/articles/PMC5580568/

32 https://www.thelancet.com/journals/lanplh/article/PIIS2542-5196(23)00212-7/fulltext

33 https://www.sciencedirect.com/science/article/pii/S0013935118303323

34 https://www.helsinki.fi/en/faculty-biological-and-environmental-sciences/news/forest-based-yard-improved-immune-system-daycare-children-only-month

35 https://www.ramblers.org.uk/who-has-access-our-paths

36 https://esajournals.onlinelibrary.wiley.com/doi/abs/10.1002/fee.1225

37 https://www.britannica.com/science/biophilia-hypothesis

38 https://socialprescribingacademy.org.uk/what-is-social-prescribing/natural-environment-and-social-prescribing/green-toolkit/

39 https://gardening4health.co.uk/

40 https://www.gov.uk/government/publications/nature-recovery-network/nature-recovery-network

41 https://www.mind.org.uk/information-support/your-stories/ecotherapy-works/

42 https://socialprescribingacademy.org.uk/media/3ozd3tv2/nhs-green-social-prescribing-toolkit.pdf

Resources

https://consciousplanet.org/en/save-soil/soil-policy/global-policy-draft

https://www.ramblers.org.uk

Right to roam https://www.righttoroam.org.uk.

Sheffield Environmental Movement https://www.semcharity.org.uk/.

Gardening 4 health https://gardening4health.co.uk/

Trellis (Scotland) https://www.trellisscotland.org.uk/

https://www.parkrx.org/parkrx-toolkit

https://findingnatureblog.files.wordpress.com/2022/04/the-nature-connection-handbook.pdf

https://www.derby.ac.uk/short-courses-cpd/online/free-courses/nature-connectedness-relationship-with-nature/

https://www.rspb.org.uk/about-us/annual-report/nature-boosts-health-and-wellbeing

https://www.doseofnature.org.uk/

https://www.greenerpractice.co.uk/information-and-resources/clinical-considerations/nature-and-health/

https://issuu.com/healthierwithnature/docs/wenp_booklet_web#:~:text=This%20directory%20provides%20information%20about,therapies%2C%20all%20rooted%20in%20communities" https://issuu.com/healthierwithnature/docs/wenp_booklet_web#:~:text=This%20directory%20provides%20information%20about,therapies%2C%20all%20rooted%20in%20communities

https://bnssg.icb.nhs.uk/health-and-care/healthier-with-nature/

Finance
Spencer Casey and Denise Smith

Case study

A hypothetical conversation between a visitor from a neighbouring practice and a keen practice manager

Visitor	I know you're keen, but I am just not sure we should be doing the "green stuff" in the practice. You can do all those actions when you're at home. I mean, what has environmental sustainability ever done for your practice?
PM	Well, we reduced our printer numbers, and look at our energy bills and the reduction in reduce energy we used; changed bank accounts so that it gave us more income and less expenditure; and we got money from the local green incentive schemes all of which helped our financial stability last year
Visitor	Yes, but apart from financial stability, what has environmental sustainability done for your practice?
PM	Well, we did look at travel and helped more staff walk, cycle, and lift share so that they had more money in their pockets and were fitter and more active. As well as freeing up car park spaces for other things, which has reduced practice parking complaints from patients.
Visitor	Yes, but apart from financial stability, and healthier staff and reduced complaints, what has environmental sustainability done for your practice?
PM	We also created the surgery community garden, which gives the staff a connection with nature and improves their well-being and mental health and involves a group of patients who are taking fewer antidepressants as a result.
Visitor	Yes, but apart from financial stability, physically, and mentally healthier staff, patients taking fewer antidepressants and improved green spaces, what has environmental sustainability done for your practice?
PM	Well, we also helped patient health by reviewing their asthma inhalers and prescribing less SABA and more treatment inhalers, checking inhaler technique,

DOI: 10.1201/9781003491583-16

moving appropriate people to DPIs rather than MDIs and worked with the couch-to-5k and park run, and put in cycle racks and walking schemes for patients which also improved air quality and has reduced the number of patients attending with respiratory exacerbations and improved our work load.

Visitor   Yes, but apart from improving practice finances, improving staff well-being and morale, and improving patient care and your community's health, what has environmental sustainability ever done for your practice?

PM   We also found it easier to recruit staff because of our green credentials, and we were nominated for – and won – a green practice award meaning we have been able to spread our influence of providing high-quality care with less environmental harm to a wider audience.

Visitor   Okay, I see that by delivering environmentally sustainable healthcare, you have more money and financial stability as a practice, more staff who are physically and mentally fitter, and more health being created for patients, and you have been able to use your positive influence across our community to improve care and outcomes for patients. Just one question though – why hasn't our practice started doing all this already?

Introduction

Primary care has a variety of approaches to generate income to pay for staff, buildings, and delivery of healthcare to patients.

In the United Kingdom, General Practice is funded via a "global sum" – or set amount of money per patient on the practice books – for providing care through a contract with the NHS. There is no limit on the number of appointments for patients – so one "global sum" covers whether there are zero appointments or 100 per patient per year.

"Quality Outcome Framework (QOF) payments" are a second stream of income. The QOF is paid on a graduated scale for practices reaching certain thresholds of patient monitoring or treatment. For example, checking if diabetics had an annual review or if patients with high blood pressure had it successfully controlled. There are some items which are reimbursed (e.g., rates), and there are some areas in which primary care is paid for hitting targets (e.g., childhood vaccination). There are other smaller pots of ad hoc money (Local Enhanced Schemes, Direct Enhanced Schemes, local incentive schemes, etc.) which are often short lasting for a year or two and targeted to local healthcare demands. These schemes may be used to incentivise environmental actions which benefit patient outcomes and planetary health. Practices also earn money from the completion of non-NHS required reports, providing travel vaccinations for their own patients, and offering private treatment to other patients. Things like teaching medical students or training the future generation of primary care staff will also be additional sources of income (and of work!) General Practice has a more guaranteed income stream but may have fewer options for managing rising costs than most businesses. Dentists, opticians, and pharmacies can all have NHS contracts – to provide dental care, dispense prescriptions, carry out eye tests, etc., following particular NHS expectations. Whereas General Practices generate most of their income via their NHS contract, this is not the case for the other pillars of primary care. Some dentists only provide private dental care – i.e.,

100% private; some opticians and pharmacies will generate the majority of their income through sales of other items.

All businesses need to balance the books, ensuring money generation is greater than money spent – but options are (relatively) limited in General Practice (compared to other healthcare businesses). This makes cost reduction – for example, through environmentally sustainable actions – an even greater imperative. Lessons from GP can often be applied in the other pillars.

The biggest challenge? Sustainability projects are often shelved or dismissed because of the perceived upfront costs; the time they will take to set up, implement, and generate savings; and the lack of immediate benefit they may bring.

Public awareness of the environmental problems we are encountering has improved, but this has not translated into financial help for public-sector businesses wanting to make organisational changes. Practices are afraid of government or local authority policy changes, market fluctuations, and technological obsolescence.

Be smart with the direction of your green strategy. Ensuring the practice's initial green projects provide "wins" means the cost reductions in energy savings and consumables can be enough to offset the upfront costs of more costly projects. Becoming completely environmentally sustainable is difficult, as businesses in the healthcare system consume too much in an unsustainable manner. The barriers can be grouped as social (people, patients, staff, manager, etc. – see Chapter 17), economic (including finances, upfront costs, external funding, etc.), and environmental (knowledge, legislation, supply chain, etc. – see Chapter 12 and Appendix 16.1).

Demonstrating that "green actions" will fit the business case of your organisation and that you are able to measure the impact you are having on those key stakeholders

The practice demonstrated that it is possible for a GP practice to invest in sustainability *and* be financially better off than those that do not. Employees and patients became happier and more committed to becoming sustainable. Simple green activities like creating a green communal staff garden yielded improved staff morale and improvements in work output.

Business and healthcare decision-making does not fully capture the value of sustainability-related investments, so the practice had to ensure that its initial initiatives made tangible rewards and had a short-term impact on the practice's bottom line. It was essential that the initial sustainability investments did not exceed the acceptable payback period of the partners to gain their approval and enable engagement in future initiatives.

A GP practice manager making a difference. To gain the engagement of the GP Partners and their manager in a practice green action plan, it is vital to demonstrate that it is possible to make significant financial savings by thinking in an *environmentally* sustainable manner to show that the practice wouldn't be losing money by being a greener business and that it would improve the profits.

Being bold

At our practice, *we made a bold change that would net us quick returns as a business.* We decided to remove all the free printers we were provided with by the NHS and replace them with the greenest and most sustainable printer alternative that was available. Why would you replace free printers with printers you had to lease? The answer was simple. The free printers had created an illusion that this was the best financially viable printer option. This wasn't the case – it was a complete false economy.

The new energy-efficient printers were using 90% less energy than was required previously. They were more efficient for the user as printing took 5 seconds instead of 21 seconds. The biggest savings were the consumable costs. Toners, drums, and imaging units are expensive, inefficient, and, in most cases, not recyclable. The new printers just used a simple reusable ink bag. This was both a fraction of the cost and also drastically increased by up to four times the amount of prints. We went from 10,000 prints for each consumable to 40,000 prints overnight.

The result? We saved over £55k over three years on printer consumables and also made significant energy savings. This was the sort of big impact that we needed as our first sustainability project. It gave us the financial savings to reinvest, and, most importantly, it gained the trust of the key stakeholders within the business to do more.

Being a leader is never easy. The practice stuck its head above the parapet, and its leaders were exposed to criticism internally and externally. But as this first initiative demonstrated, it can come with great rewards too.

Reinvesting. The practice *reinvested some of these savings* into solar energy. The energy crisis and rising prices have put pressure on all businesses and homes from 2020. Using solar energy would reduce energy bills, but the initial investment prohibited the change. By not having to purchase energy from the grid, the practice would potentially be able to save significant money in the long run. Is investing in solar worth it for a GP practice or a business in the United Kingdom?

The practice saved 64% on our electricity bills by going solar. The large upfront cost would have been unachievable without the initial savings. The benefits from this investment were huge, but the practice wanted to go further. How close could the practice get to becoming totally self-sufficient? Could it generate income by creating a surplus of energy that we could resell back to the grid?

General considerations. Climate change risks can affect financial statements in various ways: through physical impacts (e.g., extreme weather events), transition risks (e.g., carbon pricing), and liability risks (e.g., environmental lawsuits).

Financial statements should reflect the potential financial impact of these risks. This includes considering the following:

- Direct costs: Costs associated with adapting to climate change, such as investing in renewable energy or resilient infrastructure
- Indirect costs: Potential losses or costs from disruptions to operations, supply chains, and demand
- Financial opportunities: Potential benefits from investing in climate-friendly solutions or adapting to changing markets
- Judgements, assumptions, and estimates are crucial: Due to the inherent uncertainty of climate change, significant judgements will be required in assessing its financial impact; transparency and clear disclosure of these judgements are essential

The energy trilemma. All organisations face a growing challenge to balance their energy priorities. Conflicting but equally important priorities pull on limited resources, time, and infrastructure. The World Energy Council refers to this challenge as the energy trilemma and their framework aims to balance energy security, provide access to affordable and reliable energy, and reduce environmental impact (1).

1. A GP practice requires a reliable, uninterrupted energy supply and an emergency backup to provide safe care to its patients.
2. Energy needs to be affordable. The cost of energy is in sharper focus because of the dramatic increases in price and because of its volatility. For any NHS organisation or business with a finely balanced budget, achieving stable and affordable energy prices is essential.
3. The final element of the energy trilemma is sustainability. UK carbon reduction goals for the NHS are to reduce direct emissions by 80% by 2028–2032 and achieve net zero by 2040. Alongside the ongoing decarbonisation of the National Grid supply, this means significant changes for all NHS healthcare organisations to electrify and decarbonise.

We decided to install a Battery Energy Storage System (BESS). This has reduced our unused self-generated electricity by as much as 97%. This created a dramatic further reduction in energy costs and was also a major boost to our sustainability. Battery storage has ensured the maximum use of on-site generation from our solar energy. The power generated, particularly on a weekend when the facility is not in use, is now stored for use later. It can be sold back to the national grid when it is surplus to the requirements of our practice, though this is less financially useful.

Battery storage has also allowed us to reduce our electricity costs by storing energy purchased at times of lower cost for use at peak times. It has also reduced the maximum power demand needed by our site by buffering large peak loads.

Start with the first step. The energy savings in our pop-out practice example wouldn't have been achieved if the practice had attempted the smaller printer project first. The initial calculations were that it would take 12–14 years to break even. This is unlikely to be acceptable in businesses where the balancing of the books is more of a challenge than ever. However, making a saving through "green" changes elsewhere provided the initial solar investment. The savings and reduction in energy consumption at the practice are significant. They have also allowed the practice to focus on other projects which are not necessarily about saving or making money for the business.

The practice has invested heavily in energy-saving technology for its websites and invested in Search Engine Optimisation (SEO), which was a direct benefit to the patients' energy use rather than that of the business. The amount of electricity used to store the internet's data is large and growing as people continue to use more data. This huge power consumption has an enormous carbon footprint, and by investing in SEO, the practice began to address its part of this and support its patients too.

Investing in green projects can be a smart financial decision. The practice challenged the preconceived idea that the costs outweigh the benefits and that a sustainability strategy is not good business.

A practice which offers attractive financial returns whilst helping to create a more sustainable future is playing a huge part in the welfare and healing of the planet whilst continuing to be financially viable.

Offsetting. A business should work towards reducing their emissions by 80%–90% before they consider offsetting the remaining few percentages. Offsetting credits can be bought to neutralise any residual emissions. It is not considered good practice (and should be considered "greenwashing") if offsetting was the first thought. It may be impossible to avoid all greenhouse gas emissions, but these schemes, when run well, compensate for an organisation's emissions by funding equivalent carbon dioxide savings elsewhere or investing in forestry projects or schemes to develop sustainable energy. Carbon offsetting is only the final part of the solution and *must* be used in combination with reducing your carbon footprint. There are significant concerns about offsetting companies and verification.

What is the BIGGEST action our practice could take today?

Bank accounts and why they are important. Our financial decisions have real consequences: when we save at a bank, we endorse that bank's lending policies; when we invest in companies, we create demand for their shares and lower their cost of bonds, making it easier to do business.

For most organisations, there are opportunities to significantly reduce their finance-linked emissions – the emissions attributable to the investments they are making (or enabling their employees to make) and those attributable to the funds they have deposited or saved with banks. As funds are shifted away from certain high-emitting businesses, these businesses are unable to expand their operations or grow profitably. At the same time, these funds can be shifted towards greener solutions, providing much-needed capital to fund the energy and other transitions required.

Some emissions – from materials (such as steel production) and utilities (focused on the businesses required to reach net zero and decarbonise our economy) – are an important part of a climate-aligned pensions portfolio. There are many options to cut industries such as oil and gas, tobacco, certain heavy industries, and weapons out of the portfolio entirely. And the impact is not limited to carbon emissions – for instance, many of the largest fund providers in the world have no or insufficient publicly disclosed policies on deforestation, meaning many people's pensions could be funding biodiversity loss. The same is true for other environmental topics, such as use of chemicals, circularity, and water preservation.

Similarly, most organisations keep their deposits with banks that continue to lend to and generate bonds for fossil fuel companies. Although some banks are beginning to reduce their exposure to carbon-intensive businesses, many organisations have a significant opportunity to reduce their carbon footprint by switching banks. As Mike Berners-Lee notes, "[E]very time we invest or allow a bank or pension scheme to do so on our behalf, we are pushing for one kind of future or another". And some of the greenest banks are putting their clients' money to good use – funding critical activity for the net-zero transition, like renewable energy projects or green homes.

The outcome? The carbon footprint of an organisation can be several times higher once financed emissions are considered. For Google, who keep over $130 billion in the bank, their reported carbon footprint, including their supply chain, doubles when the financial footprint from the bank is included. For the average UK company (ten employees), it's a similar story: the overall footprint (including the supply chain) is roughly the same as the footprint from the company's banking carbon footprint.

Removing the practice's business (and saying why it's doing this) will make the bank's borrowing more expensive and reduce its stock market value if carried out widely. The process of changing banks is more complex for practices than individuals. There are companies set up to facilitate this, like Mothertree, and advice on the most ethical banks from places like Ethical Consumer.

We fund the future we want.

Conclusion

Financial sustainability for all healthcare businesses is essential. It is clear that achieving this is not at odds with environmental sustainability. Investing in the staff, patients, customers, and practice can lead to patient and planetary health gains and financial savings. Understanding the co-benefits to finances and environment of business continuity planning through, e.g., installing battery storage is important.

Whilst each business is set up differently, there are some common factors which can be tackled easily and quickly and have a large impact. The biggest two are changing the banking provider and the energy supplier.

Pledges

Pledge – from this chapter, I will pledge to…

1.
2.
3.

Appendix 16.1 Example of barriers broken down into social, economic, and environmental areas (Source Dr Matt Sawyer)

Social							
Owner	Characteristic	Responsibility to local community	Time	Personal values	Scepticism "burden of environmentalism"	Knowledge	Risk-averse nature
Staff	Time	Eco-literacy/ knowledge	Training	Skills – e.g., recycling knowledge	Motivation/ enthusiasm to be a "green champion"		
Customers/ patients	Knowledge	Awareness	Cycle of demand	Other priorities – e.g., health vs wealth	Amount where action follows ideology		
Society	Size of network	Willingness to share information	Government direction and leadership	Government legislation, uniformity/ standardisation	Support, funding, training opportunities	Digital technology	
Economic							
Internal	Savings/budget	Cost of efficient measure		Ranking of investment strategy vs sustainability	Rating of sustainable products/services	Expectations of return on investment	Cost of measure vs benefits
External	Knowledge of funding	Available funding	Institutional flexibility	Admin burden	Taxes or subsidies		
Strategy	Resistance to change	Familiarity of practices		Market vs entrepreneur orientation	Non-monetary benefits – e.g., business/brand image	Lack of available services[a]	Degree of management support

Environmental

Knowledge	Knowing the definition	Opportunity for greenwashing	Awareness of impact business has	Availability of sector-specific information in usable form		"Greenness of suppliers"
Supply chain	Degree of support	Technical barriers	Circular ready options	Marketplace limitations	Distance product travels	Number of parties in supply chain
Size	Understands impact of business	Feelings of impotence to make change happen		Type of tenancy agreement	Size of premises for recycling options	
Legislation	Understanding of regulatory bodies	Degree of legal requirements				

[a] E.g., packaging return scheme, electric vehicle charging points.

References

1. https://www.worldenergy.org/news-views/entry/blog-the-global-energy-challenge-balancing-the-world-energy-trilemma

Resources

Mothertree – https://www.mymothertree.com/business and https://www.mymothertree.com/bank-league-table

Greening the business case https://www.england.nhs.uk/long-read/greening-the-business-case/

17

Behaviour change
Manda Brookman and Denise Smith

Case study – Improving physical activity

Freya, a 38-year-old healthcare assistant, was worried about gradually gaining weight. She was feeling more sluggish, as she didn't feel able to go to the gym for exercise. She has been wanting to go on a health kick for months, but somehow it has never quite started.

Things to consider:

- What barriers might there be to changing personal behaviour – and what could enable the change?
- What internal and external motivations or incentives could help?

Actions

Her workplace set up a step count challenge competition between several practices. The aim was to increase the average number of steps walked by staff, with a small prize for the winning surgery and for the individual who achieved the most steps. Her practice decided to use this to work towards attaining Royal College of General Practitioners (RCGP) Active Practice accreditation (1).

Over the four weeks of the challenge, Freya's competitive spirit manifested in walking at every available opportunity. She stopped using her car, opting for an active commute instead. She walked every lunch break at work, taking colleagues with her when

DOI: 10.1201/9781003491583-17

possible. Staff set up a practice WhatsApp group to encourage and motivate each other. Freya even placed her phlebotomy equipment on the other side of the room to encourage herself to get up throughout her day, adding to her step count. She even achieved her personal goal of walking 500,000 steps over the month. Freya won the £50 competition prize voucher, which she spent on a smartwatch to help monitor her health.

After the challenge finished, she continued her commitment to an active healthy lifestyle. Two months later, Freya received a Gold Award from her slimming club for maintaining 150 minutes of exercise per week for 8 weeks. She completed her first 10k run. She continues to inspire both colleagues and patients alike.

Social connection – the competition in the workplace brought colleagues together, boosting staff morale. The WhatsApp allowed participants to share their favourite walks, encourage each other, and celebrate successes. People felt accountable for keeping up their steps, as everyone shared their step count at the end of each week. Fostering a culture of health in the workplace positively influences the personal physical health of staff and gives them the confidence to encourage patients to do the same.

Physical activity – Participants were more active both in and outside of work, breaking up long periods of sitting to regularly walk over 10,000 steps a day. This competition was an opportunity to highlight the recommended UK physical activity guidelines (a survey in 2022 showed only 35% of GPs were familiar with these [2]). When healthcare professionals are more physically active themselves, they are more likely to recommend it to patients. Patients expect their healthcare provider to be a healthy role model and are more confident in advice received from someone they perceive to be healthy.

Introduction

Most of this book is written in the third person, "he", "she", and "they", etc. This chapter is deliberately written about us, as behaviour change is so personal and an area almost all of us need to develop.

Personal actions or system change? We need both. Chapter 18 covers system change through working with organisations; this chapter looks at personal actions and behaviour change in the people we work with and look after.

The behaviour shift thing. *How to Talk About Climate Change* by Rebecca Huntly gives a useful rule of thumb when discussing climate issues: to use a ratio of *three parts positive* to *one part negative* when communicating environmental issues. While establishing a shared awareness of climate issues, negativity, fearmongering, and doomsaying can be overwhelming for anyone, and how many of us have spare capacity for extra problems on top of our own?

Many of us are in a rush to tackle the environment because we are human. Few of us are logical automatons that act only based on evidence and rationale; rather, we are complex and emotional beings, much less in control of what we do than we would like to think. Humans get hooked on positives, opportunities, altruism, and ambition.

Hope is the most effective motivator, so talk about real and active hope: an evidence-based vision for a better future where people are healthier, the environment is considered in all that we do, and we have better productivity and happier lives.

The people thing. The thing about people is we're proper odd when it comes to what we do and don't do. Most think we do what we do (or don't) because of logic and reason. Actually, it's much more to do with who we know, what our "worldview" is (spoiler alert – not all people think the same), and, crucially, what other people we trust are doing. There are many interesting phrases that describe our behaviours and habits, and a couple mentioned here that might be useful in understanding how to help each other take positive action.

Why our actions are super important. The reason it's so important to enable people to take action and continue behaviours which reduce climate risk and ecological damage and *not* rely on technology or on rich guys to throw money to sort it out is simple.

1. We have loads of tech already, and it's not necessarily managing to sort it out – because we have not decided to direct all our tech power in the right direction, and a lot of it is still causing the problem. Some of the people with the most tech oomph are using it for space tourism. So, *it comes back to us making the right decisions*.

2. Relying on tech is a poor idea, as it puts all our eggs in one basket. To decide that we can continue to emit carbon and damage our eco-systems and wait for tech to clear it all up afterwards is like having a party and expecting the Clean-Up Fairies to tidy up. Only this time, the fairies are the tech "solutions" that no one has invented yet and so we're heaving all this responsibility onto our kids' shoulders. Not fair. Not likely, either. So, *it comes back to us taking responsibility*.

3. We know people behaving differently is a massive part of the solution. The Intergovernmental Panel for Climate Change (IPCC) and the UK Climate Change Committee (advising the UK government) both agree that actively changing how we behave (and not relying on tech or a few rich guys) could help us deliver up to two-thirds of emissions reductions (3). That's a lot. *It comes back to us making change contagious*.

How to make the good stuff happen? Let's have a quick skip through some of the odd ways our minds work.

1. Why people do and don't

   Most of us behave in a particular way because of how other people are behaving. It's called responding to the "social norm", and that's why acting together is so important. We are social beings and like to behave as a group. It feels safer, we feel more confident, and it means we're not the odd one out (which feels bad, so we tend not to do it unless we're a positive deviant – see number 5). The crucial thing for making lots of good change happen is helping people feel they are taking part in something positive, that there are loads of people doing it and it's the normal thing to do, and that this positive thing is bigger than them with lots of good potential for impact.

2. The thing about denial and disengagement

   You've probably met people who just don't want to talk or think about it. That's understandable. It's a tricky thing; it feels too big, and it might make us feel bad, or guilty, or fearful, or that we have to put in effort to change. So, we decide to pretend it's not happening. It's a form of denial. It feels safer. This is why it's all about making the action each of us takes feel positive, feel normal, and feel better than not acting. Keep that in mind when you're planning your route forward. Make taking climate action sexier than not!

3. The thing about the words we use – activism, carbon footprint, net zero, etc.

   There are loads of words used – some help, some confuse. Just use the minimum and use words the people you are talking with use. See the glossary regarding carbon footprint, net zero, and offsetting.

4. Why we DO get involved

   We get involved in things that make us feel welcome, that feel like a big positive tribe, and that make us feel safe, useful, valued, and able to participate. It's almost as simple as that. That's the *creating a social norm* thing. Get as many people involved as you can – and ideally join something that already exists – that's half the work done!

5. There are also other people who might be called "**positive deviants**"

   These are people who take positive action even though no one else is. We tend to love them as they point us in the right direction. You'll know some. They're people like Greta Thunberg, Rosa Parkes, Chris Packham, Gandhi, and Martin Luther King. They break the social rules and just crack on anyway. You may know one, admire one, or even be one. They tend to be brave and compassionate and take action on principle, not because they want to be a leader. But they often end up leading. Have a look around – they can be our superpower!

Individual responsibility. According to *Oxfam*, the richest 10% are responsible for 50% of "consumption emissions", which in turn are about two-thirds of total global emissions. How rich do you need to be to be in the top 10%? Do only millionaires need to worry? Various reports (4) state that a net worth of around £85,000 puts you in the top 10% of wealthiest people in the world. The average global income in 2021 was around £16,700.

Mike Berners-Lee would argue that you should put more of your efforts into influencing wider change, such as in your workplace, your professional body, and how you vote. But as many of us are wealthy individuals (at least on a global scale), it would be remiss not to mention our individual responsibility and, indeed, the opportunity to influence those around us.

Spheres of influence. As healthcare staff, where is our "sphere of influence"? Should we expect to influence policy and wider behavioural change, or that the focus of our sphere of influence should be closer to home?

Speaking at a 2022 conference, Dr Bansal described what General Practice is to her, how sustainability is "the golden thread" weaving through all issues, and how we need to "join the dots" between the cost of healthcare, environmental impact, and health inequalities – a recognition that these are not competing issues but problems with common solutions and where opportunities are found. As the health of our patients and population is interconnected to many different aspects of planetary health and wider health inequalities, we *should* aim to influence all the "spheres" we possibly can. Different people may be more effective in different arenas.

Importantly, individual shaming is likely to cause defensiveness, division, and defiance, as well as a lack of engagement. Far more effective is to discuss *collective* guilt – i.e., "*we* can do better; *we* all need to act". Much like in clinical practice, the act of freeing from guilt and blame can be useful for messaging – showing understanding of how we have come to less environmentally friendly lifestyles, removing blame, and looking forwards without judgement. Evidence shows it is vital to focus on short-term, local, tangible examples and to emphasise opportunities and benefits rather than only discuss negativity.

But it's just me ...

Some people may say, "What can I do? It's so huge!" It can definitely feel huge. But if some*thing* is threatening someone you love, you don't tend to make a decision based on how huge the *thing* is. You decide on how much you love the some*one*. That's why so many people are taking positive action now. It's really important to remember the only reason people in charge change is when enough people make it impossible for them not to. That has always been the case. The fossil fuel companies and the political and financial structures that support them are clearly at the root of the problem, but they won't change unless we make it so. Your part is every bit as crucial as everyone else's.

Are you an activist?

What comes to mind when you think of activists? You may not think of yourself as one, but I think that you are. You see, activism doesn't just involve gluing yourself to structures or protesting in the streets. If you believe passionately that something can be better and you take action to improve it to benefit your community, then you *are* an activist.

Every letter you write, every challenging conversation you have, every time you refuse to walk past something that clashes with your values and decide to do something about it,.... well, that's activism and its leadership.

"But I'm really tired," I hear you say. "I'm not as much of an activist as some people; I don't deserve that title".

If we all wait to be the perfect activist, to have the energy to take on the world and make it a better place, nothing will get done, and nothing will improve.

Changing behaviours or habits

"Easy and sticky"

Habits are "sticky", whether good (regular exercise) or bad (smoking and drinking), and they remove much of our daily decision-making. We tend to stick to the same coffee, the same breakfast routine, the same parking space at work, the same chair for lunch, etc.

Can habits be changed if we recognise they are causing planetary harm? Recognising our sticky behaviours is the first step. People who plan their future actions around their behaviour change goals are more likely to be effective in those goals. Like all animals, we want to conserve our energy, so we will take easy actions where possible.

"Grease vs grit"

Sometimes determination, resilience, or "grit" to overcome struggles is vital for succeeding with – e.g., weight loss or getting fitter.

When it comes to making collective behaviours "easy and sticky", the amount of "grit" needed – factors making the action difficult or uncomfortable to others – is important. The converse is "grease" – a lubricant to make the action easy to achieve for others.

"Grease" includes putting in a cycle lane to make cycling more attractive, an electronic bus time display at the bus stop, or displaying the least environmentally impactful purchase as the default. Conversely, making cycling harder by creating cycle routes further, uphill, and out the way adds "grit" to the actions.

More grit = more effort.

When planning behaviour change, making the preferred actions easy and well-greased makes them more likely to become sticky.

So how do we get cracking? Good news! There are a million ways of doing something about this:

1. Getting people's attention and building momentum

   This isn't just about carbon. It's about building a social movement – in fact getting active and social engagement and linking up with the much bigger social movements that are already there. That's when the magic happens.

THE WHAT	THE HOW	THE WHY
Green team, network, or community	Start by finding out what interests people via a short survey, poster, or inviting people for a coffee at lunch or a walk or drink in the evening.	People need to believe that they're joining something positive and they're not the only ones.
Call yourself something	Decide amongst yourselves what your name is – ideally not "the green team", as that sounds a bit worthy and boring. Choose something interesting!	To get people involved, you have to throw a better "party"!
Join a bigger green team	Remind people there are people like them everywhere, and they have already started – talk about who else is doing it and how.	People feel disheartened if the action seems small in relation to the size of the problem. Knowing we're joining something even bigger inspires and motivates.

(Continued)

THE WHAT	THE HOW	THE WHY
Pick perhaps *two* people to run the team for the first three months	Choose two people to be the primary "activators" at the first meeting.	No one wants to be the one making everything happen; two people are better, and if people take it in turns, say for three months at a time, it makes it manageable.

2. Decide on specific actions

It's much more important to start with actions that are important to people than actions that might be great at saving carbon or improving the environment but bore your team.

Make a plan	Decide on your top five (or so) priorities for the next six months (say) according to the passion of your members (rather than having to know the carbon value of everything).	People bring energy to what's important to them. Good examples could be creating a habitat outside the practice, getting some bike racks in place, deciding to focus on locally grown and unpackaged food, or having an energy audit done for the whole practice to see hot (or cold!) spots.
Get inspired	Check out who else is doing what – there are examples via the Greener Practice Network (5), the Cornwall website of ideas.	We all know there's nothing more energising than seeing something you think you can create face-to-face, in a book, or online. See who else is doing something, bring examples, even organise a trip out to see a community garden. You'll be amazed how much people's imaginations will be set alight.
Make a goal	Decide what you have to have achieved by a certain month. Make a plan in stages (with milestones) if that helps.	It helps focus the mind and helps you backcast to see what you need to do first. Once you have achieved something, it makes even the bigger stuff much more digestible.

Some start with small steps and grow. Recognising having multiple steps of continuous improvement is vital. We can't stop with one action and assume it's "job done".

Some actions are one-offs (such as changing electricity supplier or bank), and other actions require ongoing commitment (for example, cycling or walking to work or turning lights and computers off).

3. "Comms" versus actual communication

"Comms" is mostly about transmitting: social media posts, press releases, newsletters – really important but only half the story. Getting real communication going is how the magic happens. It's a two-way collaboration, with ideas flowing and people feeling invested.

Join the dots!	Make it a campaign – give it a name – and have consistent messaging: a logo, a character, a font that brings it all together. It can be a fab thing to do first as a group – *Our People, Planet and Place Plan*, or our *Big Green Adventure*, or *Happy Planet = Happy People* – whatever is catchy and works for the group and your audiences.	Single actions feel like single actions. If you show people you're working on a whole campaign, with half a dozen things they can join in with, they feel they're joining something bigger that makes sense and sounds fun, and this also helps them see the connection between cycling and eating a plant-based diet and switching off lights and reducing single-use plastics.
Talk about it – everywhere	Communication and inspiration don't happen with a press release or a poster. Use all your means: staff room, toilet door, waiting room, website, Facebook, newsletters, walls, meeting agenda, T-shirts, partner meetings. Use pictures of what you're doing and real comments from staff and patients who love what you're doing. Use humour and images, not just words.	We probably need to hear something up to ten times before it logs itself in our memory. So, sharing the message (e.g., we're raising funds for a bike rack) in the staff meeting, WhatsApp group, PCN meeting, waiting room, partner meeting, PPG meeting. Make it a collaboration and ask everyone how they can help.
Get feedback	Ask people face-to-face at reception as they walk past, in surveys, how they feel about the actions you're taking.	It makes *such* a difference to know that other staff, and patients, think what you're doing is ace. And they will. So ask.
Get it *on the agenda*	Add the issue (and the campaign and the specific action) to meetings – regular, ordinary meetings – as a standard.	People (staff and patients) will not take the issue seriously if all they see is one poster and no other indication that the practice is taking action in any way. If the ask is to switch things off *as part of a fab green campaign that the practice is working to achieve in every context*, more people are likely to want to help.

4. Measure the magic

What we measure is actually incredibly important, as that sets the target. If it's the wrong target, we then have a problem, as all the energy and effort is invested in the wrong thing. Measuring the amount of paper a school could recycle resulted in pupils raiding the stationery cupboard for clean paper to add to the recycling bin. We need to really think about what we want to achieve and set a target that will get us there. Beware the tyranny of the (wrong) target!

Remember, taking action on climate and nature breakdown has multiple benefits. A reusable sanitary products project achieves many things: it reduces waste from single-use products; it reduces the carbon emissions from the production line; it avoids plastic (sanitary products are 90% plastic); it also faces straight into health inequalities and climate injustice by doing something regarding the unfairness of young girls unable to afford sanitary protection also then unable to go to school and access education.

Or, getting involved in developing a community garden benefits patients, staff, and pollinators; increases carbon "sequestration" (absorption) into the soil; provides a community space; reduces loneliness; and even grows food.

Identify how projects can deliver multiple co-benefits – and shout about it!

Decide what you want to achieve and how you will know you have succeeded.	Say you want to create a small garden in the practice. Then give yourself a goal.	We need to know we're enroute to achieving something specific, or we tend to give up.
Then think in systems – and in the measures different people have!	Think of all the very different ways you can measure the impact!	There are multiple co-benefits of many of these actions – identify them and then use them to engage more people.

Examples to highlight the co-benefits (Table 17.1):

Bikes: Enabling a practice manager to secure a grant to invest in an e-bike for clinical visits and a bike rack

- reduces carbon emissions,
- reduces costs from buying fuel,
- improves air quality,
- reduces congestion,
- improves the health of the clinician using it,
- enables the practice manager to feel great about being able to offer something exciting and positive to stressed colleagues,
- shows patients the practice is taking its own advice about active travel and the environment seriously, and
- offers patients a bike rack to get active.

Community gardens: Whether with a planter outside the reception area or a full-blown community garden developed in partnership with a community organisation, getting involved in growing spaces is welcomed by

- staff who have a "peace space" for breaks,
- patients who can set up their own "Garden Group",
- community members who can create a beautiful space to use,

TABLE 17.1 Adapted from Cornwall Health and Climate Resilience Network

NAME OF INITIATIVE	STAFF MEMBERS INVOLVED	DATE			
What is the impact of the project on:			Poor/ worse	Neutral	Good/ better
Patient health	Patient emotional health Patient physical health Patient mental health				
Practice benefit (staff)	Sense of satisfaction, purpose, and results Staff morale Staff collaboration				
Practice benefit (financial)	Economic savings from unnecessary future care Economic savings from unnecessary meds				
Community benefit	Greater collaboration between staff and patients Patient contribution to community initiatives				
System benefit	Reduction of workload on future staff				
Planetary benefit	Lower carbon pathway chosen Positive ecological benefit Development of lower carbon habits (e.g., walking)				

Source: https://www.healthandclimateresilience.net/

- lonely members of the community or those without access to green spaces who can rediscover "purpose" and friendship,
- pollinators, and
- community members who will be triggered to have conversations about food, health, diet, and climate.

Energy audits: Practices getting involved in implementing advice from their energy audits are discovering they can

- save money,
- save carbon,
- make the practice cooler in the summer and warmer in the winter, and
- put money into other areas such as energy self-generation (e.g., solar).

All these projects can improve staff morale – because people want to get involved in something positive and relatable. Once we feel we are part of the "doing something about it" tribe, the "it" seems much more doable – and we tend to start imagining more things we can do something about.

A practice in Cornwall developed *A Beautiful Day Out Map* for its lobby to encourage staff and patients to walk, cycle, and take public transport, and is now planning an event for all staff and community members to think more about how it can connect with its local community for human and planetary health.

A practice which developed reusable sanitary products is working with local colleges to secure funding for their students to access these; a practice which ran a pilot food box prescription programme and saw great results in Hba1C levels is now working in partnership with a local community food enterprise and bringing social prescribing thinking into its clinical consultations rather than being something completely separate.

When it comes to engaging partners or owners, this may be the thing that gets us to the "tipping point". Reducing waste saves money, as the practice would be paying to have it taken away even to recycle; reducing energy will save money; working on "health creation" (creating the conditions for good health, not sickness) will pay dividends in money and time and stress, and patient well-being. Sometimes it just takes one of those positive deviants to say "what if", "imagine different", and "dream big".

Pledges

Pledge – from this chapter, I will pledge to…

1.
2.
3.

References

1 https://elearning.rcgp.org.uk/mod/page/view.php?id=12583
2 https://bjgpopen.org/content/6/3/BJGPO.2021.0227
3 https://lordslibrary.parliament.uk/behaviour-change-and-reaching-net-zero/
4 https://www.credit-suisse.com/about-us/en/reports-research/global-wealth-report.html
5 Greener Practice greenerpractice.co.uk

18

Working across organisations
Helen Kingston and Emma Radcliffe

Sustainable healthcare is integrated: building the ARC

The ARC Healthy Living Centre (www.archlc.com) is a community-led health and well-being charity based in Sally's Wood Estate, Irvinestown, County Fermanagh. In 2001, four derelict social houses were renovated into a community centre in an area which, at that time, had some of the highest levels of poor health, unemployment, and crime in the county.

Understanding that poverty was making people sick and good employment with an adequate income enabled people to have more control over their lives and health, it became obvious that addressing health inequalities via interventions which emphasised individual lifestyle change alone was impossible. To increase effectiveness, ARC advocated for broader social reform. Early participatory research showed a need for child-based services, support for residents struggling with addiction, and more opportunities to access advice and work. Residents were dissatisfied with the condition of their homes and the level of crime and fear of crime they faced. ARC responded with practical actions and services. Platforms were established, allowing local people to engage with and influence those who were tasked with delivering services.

As the services developed, ARC worked closely with the six policy objectives in the Marmot Review (2010) to address health inequalities:

1. **Give every child the best start in life**. ARC is the accountable body for Cherish Sure Start, delivering in 13 wards.
2. **Enable all children, young people, and adults to maximise their capabilities and have control over their lives**. ARC runs a summer scheme catering for up to 250 young people, a childcare centre, and a child contact centre.

DOI: 10.1201/9781003491583-18

3. **Create fair employment and good work for all**. Additional psychological support has been contracted for staff.

4. **Ensure healthy standards of living for all**. ARC has set up a community food initiative, delivers a low-threshold addiction service, and has incorporated other support and well-being services, including financial advice and foodbank provision.

5. **Create and develop healthy and sustainable places and communities**. There are bimonthly community information exchange forms with residents and quarterly interagency meetings.

6. **Strengthen the role and impact of ill-health prevention**. The community is empowered through access to a range of early intervention services, such as hypertension checks, fall prevention courses, and fuel poverty support.

Over two decades, ARC has led to multiple positive outcomes in the local area: decreased antisocial behaviour and reported crime, increased breastfeeding rates, and reduced numbers of void dwellings, with Northern Ireland (NI) Housing Executive noting increased tenant satisfaction and housing retention, and a high uptake of Sure Start services – consistently within the highest in Northern Ireland.

The ARC story suggests that a community-embedded, preventative approach to addressing health inequalities can be effective and sustainable over time. It provides transferable ideas for policymakers and communities attempting to tackle similar challenges elsewhere. However, providing job security to those employed by the ARC centre is an ongoing challenge, as most services do not receive core funding.

Introduction

Will a few enthusiasts be sufficient to make the required changes for a sustainable healthcare system? Not when working alone, but encouraging research suggests collectively an impact occurs when 3.5% of the population are engaged in demanding change, and this can drive wider action (1).

Where is the balance between personal actions, practice change, or system change? We need all three of these to happen at scale simultaneously. Different people and different teams will feel comfortable working at different levels. Enabling and supporting each other to work in all these ways is key. Chapter 17 examined personal behaviour change actions; this chapter looks at the effect "the system" has and how to act to influence the wider community and health sector. By looking to influence at a larger scale, opportunities can be identified which increase our impact.

Facilitating a small shift in behaviour at scale – for example, a 1% average shift in the right direction for a population of a small market town of 30,000 residents – will be far more impactful than a much larger shift by one individual in isolation (Figure 18.1).

Our individual actions are not negated and *do* matter. The choices each individual makes personally and professionally have a direct impact on the resources used. Actions

The Bell-Curve Shift in Populations

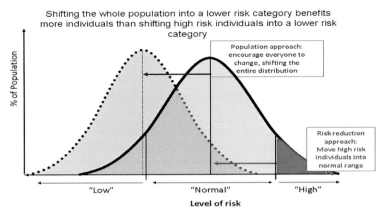

FIGURE 18.1 The bell-curve shift in populations (2).

as individuals influence those around us to raise awareness, shift the culture of what is "normal", and support others to act and make changes themselves.

Individuals have influence across networks of friends, family, and neighbours and the potential of influence to enable wider system change

- across the community,
- across primary care networks,
- across integrated care systems, and
- across the United Kingdom at the political level through local medical committees, the British Medical Association, and the Royal College of General Practitioners and working with the Department of Health or similar at the national government level (see Chapter 3).

The cumulative impact of multiple individuals has measurable impacts on carbon emissions and together can build momentum and incentivise system change. Consumer buying power can help steer a capitalist-oriented economy towards enabling environmentally sustainable choices. For example, the cost of solar PV modules has dropped by 92% since 1998 due to improved technology and efficiency and as more people have installed them. Individuals have power but a greater influence when engaging in shaping systems and processes.

Long-term thinking. People can be more powerful collaboratively if focussing on long-term thinking.

- Set a clear vision.
- Establish a long-term goal.
- Sense-check that day-to-day decision-making aligns with this long-term aim.

What is your long-term vision?

Ask, "Is what is happening today aiding or hindering that long-term goal?" Being clear about the values and communicating this can help the decision-making process.

Case study: Frome Medical Practice

Sustainability is one of three core values set by the practice. The practice declared a climate emergency. Having this vision has enabled the practice to become one of the greenest in the United Kingdom, hosting sustainability conferences and achieving gold in the Green Impact for Health Toolkit.

Capacity and pushing for change and seizing opportunity. Being involved creates opportunities to negotiate *your* agenda. What would enable other people's wider engagement? What will help people be able to say "yes"? Avoid pushing people into saying "no", as it can be harder to ask them to back down later.

If there is time pressure, what might need to stop to be able to give time to this?

Could getting involved be within the current job plan? Are there paid roles to get involved in the larger scale that might help the sustainability agenda such as a paid role within the Integrated Care System (ICS)?

People don't need to have an official "net zero" or "sustainability role" to influence others. For example, a good position within a General Practice is the prescribing lead or respiratory lead who works towards greater use of sustainable dry powder inhalers.

Playing a role within an ICS prescribing and medicines management committee could help advocate for greater prominence of dry powder inhalers within the formulary and help ensure that sustainability and patient outcomes, in addition to cost, are considered in the first and second choices of inhalers throughout the ICS.

Key pointers:

- Recognise that the individual and the problem are separate.
- Try to understand different perspectives.
- Understand the level of decision-making and where local discretion and priority setting are possible. Focus on opportunities to influence these towards sustainability.
- A nationally specified contract stipulation may not have local flexibility.
- Understanding competing or clashing priorities can help in understanding how it is possible to find a win-win solution.

Above all, think creatively and be open to taking opportunities when they arise.

Case study: Gloucestershire

In 2022, a small group of GPs spotted an opportunity to apply for some funding from their Integrated Care Board (ICB). They were successful in applying for funding to appoint a "Green Champion" in every practice and to fund time for practices to progress in the Green Impact for Health (GIFH) toolkit. As a result of the scheme,

- 17 practices achieved GIFH awards (5 gold, 5 silver, and 7 bronze),
- the ICB achieved the best profiles for prescribing green inhalers nationally, and
- 29 practices commissioned building energy surveys.

Sustainable quality improvement. Once a clear vision has been developed, the Sustainable Quality Improvement (SusQI) methodology can be used to break into shorter-term achievable steps and SMART (Specific, Measurable, Achievable, Relevant, and Time-bound) goals.

- **Tracking progress** enables real-time understanding of what is or isn't working.
- **Perfect is the enemy of good**. There is no time to wait for a perfect plan. Getting started from the current situation is vital.
- **Some ideas will fail**. Trying – and failing but learning (or "failing forwards") – is part of the rapid small-scale cycles of Plan-Do-Study-Act that enables nimble adjustment to change ideas and scaling up those actions that are successful and adapting or abandoning those that are not.

Learning to improve care is key for primary healthcare professionals. For example, GP registrars in training are expected to be involved in Quality Improvement (QI) annually. Adopting a sustainability focus is an opportunity to support sustainable practice while ensuring good clinical outcomes for patients. Using SusQI (see Chapter 9) means considering the needs of the environment and society, and having the resources required to support health and well-being.

The journey to a more environmentally responsible primary healthcare service is not always smooth. Traction with the chief executive and executive board can be difficult if there are competing interests of financial pressures, waiting lists, and staff availability. However, for each step back, there is another step forward, and the next meeting with the chief executive or sustainability group can be positive.

Should a bottom-up or top-down approach be prioritised? Both! A combination of people doing "no regret" actions using their knowledge of which actions are most impactful and getting on with what drives them, combined with leadership structures and organisations that allow individuals and groups to make progress and not be held back by bureaucracy is likely to have the greatest impact.

A transition to a well-being economy. The transition from the current dominant consumerist capitalist model to a well-being economy is increasingly being recognised. The way forward may not always be evident and may take several "knight's moves" to reach the destination.

This means building an economy that operates within safe environmental limits and which serves the collective well-being of current and future generations first and foremost. Our economic transformation aims to fundamentally reshape our economy, delivering a just transition to a net zero, nature-positive economy based on the principles of equality, prosperity, and resilience (3).

Case study: COVID-19 and hope

COVID-19 gave the world – and healthcare specifically – an almighty jolt. Staff across healthcare committed to a kind of "war effort" for an unknown duration, as it was felt to be our duty. This jolt affected people's priorities and values. The response to COVID gave some hope and opportunity. After years of learning that change in the NHS can be painfully slow, all of a sudden, every department overnight seemed to be able to make rapid changes to how they worked. So often, the reason given for not engaging with change within the NHS is that it can involve so much work for so little action. We have many passionate, capable, resourceful people who are underrutilised, understimulated, and disenfranchised. Yet now we had this fluid organisation, powered by open minds, with levels of cooperation and cohesion previously unseen, and an incredibly heartening sense of common purpose.

If we could harness this readiness to remove barriers to change and work together like we did for COVID, we could reorganise our services to remove inefficiencies, improve care, reduce waste and unnecessary treatments, and drive wider change.

Green and healthy synergy. *To achieve population well-being, we need to move beyond the narrow confines of the NHS and work with our community and the systems that govern us.* (4). The drivers of poor population health are not going to be solved with greater medicalisation of their outcomes but by addressing the drivers of this poor health. The understanding of how environmental issues intersect with healthcare remains patchy – making pitching discussions difficult. Allying with those in the community with shared concerns and motivation can help joint working to address these challenges and to articulate to the population that sustainable lifestyles will enhance their well-being and enjoyment of their lives by keeping all healthy.

Through building on what is already there, using the principles of community development, and leading by supporting others' initiatives, moving away from a media narrative that "becoming more sustainable means giving up current lifestyles" and demonstrating moving to a well-being economy will lead to happier, more satisfied, and healthier lives. Appreciating and valuing connection to fellow human beings and the natural living world, recognising interconnectedness, and prioritising social interaction within communities are vital to collective well-being.

It is okay to keep things basic. There is a fear of being condescending or repetitive. There is a challenge to keep communication positive and fresh that can be prepared for. In such a vast subject, there is a real danger of leaving these issues to the enthusiasts and experts.

Case study

Health Connections Mendip has employed and trained Health Connectors since 2015. These are non-medical staff who are skilled in listening to patients and identifying their priority issues. These sessions can occur in the GP practice or patient home. This jointly funded (NHS and town council) project helps signpost people to the right services and support to meet their needs. These might include community groups, counselling and advocacy services, exercise and nutrition classes, home help or adult social care, or mental health services. Health Connectors also run talking cafes and goal-setting groups, organise community information events, and maintain an online directory of services. They help bridge the gap between primary care and the community.

Choosing battles wisely. A clear vision and long-term mindset can help move forwards within the complexity. Some of the choices made have immediate significant impacts on climate – for example, flying to a conference, admission for hospital treatments and operations, or prescribing ineffective medication. Other changes may seem small at an individual level but cumulatively have a large impact. Actions can change care for larger populations. For example, a single blood test may not have a large amount of harm, but preventing unnecessary repeated blood tests multiplied by the tens of thousands of patients annually has a large cumulative impact.

Health awareness campaigns have led to an improved understanding of conditions such as menopause or mental health. This hard work can be undone by pharmaceutical companies announcing medication (like semaglutide) as a potential solution to the obesity crisis and overshadows the need to redesign our obesogenic environment, facilitate more active travel, and support and encourage a diet of fresh, unprocessed food. A pill does not cure every ill.

Case study: Supporting patients with diabetes

A programme led by the Frome digital team supported by clinicians and social prescribers showed that the integration of Fitbits, structured healthy lifestyle education, and preventative apps encourages meaningful, beneficial patient engagement and better health outcomes.

- Overall, 80% of the group made improvements on one or more clinical indicators.
- Learning outcomes/understanding – 100% of the group improved their understanding of diabetes.
- Well-being – 73% of the group improved in their social and well-being factors.

Learning to be more aware of the influence of commercial interests, commodification, and the overmedicalisation of societal problems can help with independent questioning of the overmedicalisation of society (5). Focussing on what matters most to the individual and recognising them as fellow human beings – and not simply their disease cluster – can help ensure treatment is guided by human factors, as well as chronic disease guidelines.

Case study

In 2022, Dr Georgina Bell undertook a SusQI (see Chapter 9) project to review how those with moderate and severe frailty are helped to consider their priorities and plan ahead for potential changes in their health. She worked within the complex care team that cares for those who have increased frailty, are in care homes or housebound, or were recently discharged from hospital.

She worked to embed a systematic approach to inviting and calling those who didn't have a treatment escalation plan or any record of discussing one.

A practice-wide initiative to improve the recording of Rockwood Frailty scores (see Chapter 7) meant the frailest group was more completely identified through contact with different team members. For those identified as moderately or severely frail, a "planning ahead" leaflet was shared with an invitation for further discussion and followed up with a phone call.

The number who completed a *treatment escalation plan* increased from 46% to 71%. This continues and forms part of routine care in the complex care team. Prior discussion of care priorities helps ensure we focus on what matters most to patients and prevents inappropriate overinvestigation or admission when this does not align with patient wishes.

Much of the evidence on which guidelines are produced is secondary care derived or necessarily had exclusion criteria in their study design that can be challenging when extrapolation to broader primary care populations is undertaken. Discussion forums such as the RCGP overdiagnosis group and access to primary care–focused evidence can help us provide informed, unbiased information to enable shared decision-making with patients.

Case study

In Frome, through membership in the RCGP optimal testing group, the carbon impact of local phlebotomy services for patients receiving secondary care was calculated. It showed 1,700 patients travelled a total of 3,400 miles for blood tests (an average of 2 miles each). By expanding this service for secondary care testing, 200 patients who would have otherwise travelled to the local hospital 14 miles away had local tests, reducing cumulative travelling from 5,000 miles to 400 miles.

Identifying those who can't help us (yet) and ensuring we do not alienate them. Not everyone will or is able to engage with environmental sustainability. Understanding their fears, drivers, barriers (and enablers) is important. Acknowledging some feel over-whelmed by life demands or whose views are driving apathy due to despair. For example, a busy, overworked individual being asked to make changes may simply feel they do not have the energy or space to change their practice – especially if that change adds another 20 seconds to their workload. They may feel alienated or criticised for work-ing towards greater sustainability. Having a better understanding of their reasoning will help overcome this challenge and allow the rest of the team to work with them. Their difficulties and resistance can help ensure our approach is as engaging and practical as possible. Knowing who can assist and help, and who needs to be assisted and helped themselves is key.

Enable positive responses and engagement. Creating a supportive change cul-ture is important. Engaging individuals without preparation can make later attempts at change more difficult. Change may fail the first time, so perseverance can be crucial once lessons have been learned. "Failing forwards" is important so that resistance to further attempts can be overcome.

An individual tasked with completing NHS targets such as prescribing cost savings or managing practice budgets may need a different approach, and information on the financial benefits of proposals would aid their decision-making. But they may be a key ally and be able to champion the cause if time is taken to understand their position and work with them. Articulating benefits with a variety of different lenses can help to influence those who think differently. Positive impacts on finances, staff experience and morale, or patient experience and outcomes can win hearts and minds and help engage different colleagues.

Case study

Embedding sustainability into practice values and culture can bring co-benefits for recruitment. Having a reputation for sustainability and our climate conferences in Frome, together with Health Connections, Mendip, and our complex care team, have helped to raise the profile of the practice. This has increasingly been a factor for individuals choosing to come and work there, including one recent recruit joining us from New Zealand. As more like-minded staff join, the team's approach to sustain-ability strengthens further.

Building a team. Overcommitment can impede progress. Time spent building a team and sharing this vital work can help build capacity to achieve long-term goals. Working alongside others can help sustain an individual's energy and enthusiasm and help prevent burnout. Celebrating the success of others and learning from one another are as impor-tant, if not more so, than individual endeavour.

Mentorship and peer support. Reflecting on progress with a trusted friend or mentor can help keep people on track and focused. A good mentor can share their own experiences and introduce others to build a supportive network, guiding towards new opportunities and supporting goal setting and action taking.

Articulating goals can help people stay authentic to their values and maintain momentum when other competing demands are seeking attention.

Belonging matters. Trying to enable change is hard. Developing peer support is important in sustaining our efforts and can also aid

- learning alongside each other,
- sustaining enthusiasm,
- sharing frustrations and setbacks, and
- being energised by the ideas and successes of others and taking up initiatives which others have developed.

Case study

Greener Practice (6) is a network of people encouraging action on sustainability in primary care by providing information, convening groups to share learning and support and speak on the national stage.

Having started with a small group of concerned GPs meeting around a kitchen table in Sheffield, it has now become a Community Interest Company. It has over 30 local groups which have regular meetings. There are special interest groups covering clinical work, education, non-clinical carbon, trainees, QI, and working with other organisations. They have facilitated a High Quality, Low Carbon Asthma Toolkit and have regular newsletters and bulletins.

Campaigning. It is quite clear from all the evidence that not enough is being done to limit global warming to 1.5 degrees or reduce the dramatic loss of biodiversity. Neither is enough action being taken to adapt to predict events. It is important to directly campaign for net zero within healthcare organisations; it is also important that wider organisations and beyond are influenced.

Healthcare professionals are widely trusted by the public, and many argue such staff should be using this trusted status to communicate the health implications of what is happening to the natural living world. There are arguments made by some that we should be doing even more than that:

Doctors and all health professionals have a responsibility and obligation
to engage in all kinds of non-violent social protest to address the climate emergency.
That is the duty of a doctor.

Richard Horton, Editor, The Lancet 2019

Case study: Royal College of General Practitioners declares a Climate Emergency

In 2019, the South Yorkshire and North Trent Faculty of the RCGP collaborated with the North East London Faculty to propose and second a motion which was put before the RCGP council. The motion was passed:

The RCGP acknowledges the climate crisis and in line with the 2018 Lancet Commission Report the catastrophic effect on human health of not taking action decisively and urgently in climate change. The college accepts its duty to provide leadership and urgently escalates its action at local, regional and national level to decarbonise and promote environmental sustainability (7).

What can clinicians do?

- Need to make connections and inform partnerships with other organisations.
- Encourage positive partnerships and actions.
- Advocate for change.
- Choose what they do best in this arena and do it!

If you're a healthcare professional and want to get involved, I'd urge you to do it for the people you look after. That's what my work has been about: combining empathy with evidence. Thinking about the individual in front of you, asking what the risks are for the future, and why they are where they are. Asking how you can help them better understand their options and empower them to make independent decisions based on what really matters to them. Think about nature and social prescribing options. Think about what's possible; what's going to make a difference. Be refreshing, and you will both be refreshed.

Manda Brookman

Case study: Government Level – An experience of working in Scotland

My experience with civil servants and policymakers has often shown that grassroots workers can quickly dictate national policy. Often civil servants are highly capable, educated, and motivated staff, moved around from department to department. You might find someone who's worked for three months in education and then does a year in healthcare, and then suddenly, they are in charge of national policy for climate and sustainability. When that person is asked to create a policy for sustainability, they need to quickly find some safe ground to write about. This is where grassroots workers come in. Just a couple of years ago, changing which anaesthetic you gave or chose on environmental grounds would have been pretty out there, but dedicated grassroots work by anaesthetists and pharmacists led to Scotland being the first country in the world to ban the most environmentally harmful anaesthetic gas altogether: desflurane.

But it doesn't have to be huge, headline policy interventions that make the biggest impact: small projects can have significant impact on the lives of individual patients. They might spread and be adopted through word of mouth, but when documented, communicated, and published in a robust way, these projects can suddenly be the case studies which form part of national documentation, guidelines, and strategies.

How to make personal change is difficult in a system which is actively pushing back. There are many ways to take action, and everyone needs to find a way which suits them and they feel is appropriate. Actions could include the following:

- Say, "It's good for the planet and good for you" in the next consultation where the patient is advised to exercise more or alter their diets or discuss inhaler changes.
- Have a discussion with friends or colleagues.
- Sign a petition or letter. Greener Practice newsletters have "armchair activism" sections where you can take part in campaigns with minimal time and effort.
- Talk or write to your councillor or member of Parliament, explaining why you are concerned as a health professional.
- Write an article for a medical journal to explain what you are doing and why.
- Take to the streets and protest.
- Join a supportive group (see "Resources").

Case study: ULEZ, London 2023

The evidence for the Ultra-Low Emission Zone expansion in terms of improving air quality for the majority of the population was quite clear. Health professionals used their voices in many ways to help promote the scheme. They were filmed for news items, used in social media campaigns, cycled around London along the proposed boundary in a "Ride for the Lives", and wrote to and lobbied politicians in support of the scheme.

What I wish I'd known

- You don't have to be an expert to discuss the climate and ecological emergency.
- Every decision taken has a sustainability impact, so try to keep your "green goggles" on at all times.
- You are never too small or too unimportant to raise this as an issue; you just need to be brave and determined.

Pledges

Pledge – from this chapter, I will pledge to…

1.
2.
3.

References

1. https://www.bbc.com/future/article/20190513-it-only-takes-35-of-people-to-change-the-world
2. https://academic.oup.com/ije/article-abstract/14/1/32/694724
3. Wellbeing Economy Governments https://www.gov.scot/groups/wellbeing-economy-governments-wego/
4. https://www.kingsfund.org.uk/publications/community-services-assets
5. https://journals.sagepub.com/doi/full/10.1177/0141076815600908
6. https://www.greenerpractice.co.uk/
7. https://www.rcgp.org.uk/representing-you/policy-areas/sustainable-development

Resources

Green & Healthy Frome https://greenhealthyfuturefrome.org/

Sustainability at Frome Medical Practice – fromemedicalpractice.co.uk

Welcome to Health Connections Mendip – Health Connections – https://health connectionsmendip.org/

Managing eco-distress
Becki Smith-Taylor

Case study

Sara, a 30-year-old practice nurse, presents with concerns about frequent episodes of despair and worries about the climate and her and her family's future. The patients she sees have illnesses connected to changes in the climate and worsening planetary health or display their own symptoms of climate anxiety. She's thinking of stopping work, as she feels helpless. It'll be too difficult to stand by while the world continues to get hotter and patients suffer even more. In the past, she got involved in eco-activism, but now she's not involved, as there's *"no point as big business and capitalism are so powerful"*. She is eating okay and sleeping 6 hours a night, with some early morning waking.

Things to consider:

- What is eco-empathy?
- Is this more likely to be depression or anxiety?
- How common is eco-distress?
- What approaches are likely to be effective in eco-distress?

Sara's story suggests that she is experiencing eco-empathy. Eco-empathy shows the emotional connections to ecology and the natural living world, the desire to be an ethically responsible citizen, and a recognition of ecological grief at the losses across the living world. The negative aspect – eco-distress – is very common. A survey by the University of York and Global Future think tank revealed that 78% of respondents reported some level of fear about climate change, with 41% reporting high levels of fear. The survey showed that women remain significantly more anxious about climate change (45%) than men (36%) (1).

DOI: 10.1201/9781003491583-19

Eco-distress is not normally a mental health disorder but a rational response to the trouble we are in. It can be described as anxiety associated with perceptions about the negative impacts of climate change and can encompass grief, despair, hopelessness, fear, and dread (2). When faced with someone expressing these concerns, it's important to validate their feelings rather than seeking to minimise or dismiss them. If there is such severity that treatment with drugs needs to be considered, this should include a full discussion of the carbon footprint of the treatment and comparison with non-pharmacological options such as access to green and blue space.

There is a risk of medicalisation of an appropriate response (eco-empathy with linked eco-distress) as a health condition (eco-anxiety). Some writers use the words more fluidly.

Actions

There are several resources available to guide management of these difficult emotions. Most contain four core elements:

1. **Take action – doing something positive helps us not to drown in despair** (3)
   - Living and acting according to our values is empowering and energising.
   - Joining with others to work towards a shared positive vision of the future.
2. **Self-care**
   - Pacing ourselves and accepting the limits of what we, as individuals, can achieve.
   - Taking time for regeneration when we are struggling.
   - Accepting help from others and not feeling we must do everything ourselves.
   - Practising gratitude for ourselves, the people around us, and the natural world that sustains us.
3. **Nurture hope**
   - Make time to read about hope-based, solutions-focused visions of the future, not just negative information.
4. **Allow space to process distress and times to shut off from it**
   - Rather than try to avoid or dismiss difficult emotions, climate psychologists advise that we make time and space to accept and experience them without avoidance, denial, or intellectualisation. Spending time in nature can help many people.

Exploring Sara's support network and sense of agency will be important, including whether there are groups she can access to connect with like-minded people while making a difference in the living world. It may be helpful to consider talking therapies to help her express her emotions or coaching to help her choose her next actions. In addition, The Resilience Project (4) works specifically with youth activists struggling with eco-distress and burnout.

Introduction

Eco-empathy, eco-anxiety, and eco-distress are very common. This distress can be magnified for healthcare workers who are aware of the impact of climate change on health. The lack of agency to change the situation can cause moral injury.

There are many complex reasons for choosing a career. For some in healthcare, the primary motivation is to help people, to make life better for others, or to advocate for those who don't have a voice. For others it's the security of the job, the variety, the challenge.

Reflecting on this with people with eco-distress can be helpful. If the primary motivation is to make a difference, people can burn out and lose joy when they end up not being able to deliver the care they originally wanted to.

For those who are sensitive to injustice, it can be particularly hard when the system doesn't seem to move fast enough. There's a lot in the world that needs changing right now, so whether the focus is on climate change, health inequalities, or institutional racism, all these things need people who are passionate and not burnt out to champion the cause.

Many people in the healthcare system, and in the wider world, are at risk of burnout at work. They have become conditioned to ignore their basic needs and sacrifice their energy for a system that demands 110% from them all the time. They may have learnt to work for approval but then work in a system where there is no clear and supportive feedback.

They may try to perform to standards they expect of themselves even when the system has changed and standards have dropped (perfectionism). They absorb lots of information, which is complex, may be contradictory, or is difficult, which leaves them confused or paralysed.

For those experiencing burnout from work, focusing on a cause such as climate change may be appealing. However, this focus, which initially seemed like a passion project to bring variety to their work, is likely to cause burnout if pursued with the same perfectionist approach.

Signs of eco-distress or burnout

1. Overwhelm. Reading about the natural living world has moved from causing enthusiasm and energy to being overwhelming and hard work.

2. Disengagement from spending time with like-minded people. There's no longer the headspace to arrange and share ideas, as comparison with others can lead to feelings of overwhelm and failure.

3. Despair about the future. This may manifest as irritability, anger, resentment, or harsh judgement of others. Individuals may also find their sleep is poor, or they spend more time "doomscrolling" on social media.

4. Lack of joy. Things that used to bring joy don't give the same pleasure, so they are done less frequently. This can lead to a loss of sense of self.

5. Exhaustion. This may manifest as reduced resilience and new physical symptoms like migraines, nausea, and stomach cramps.

What can be done about eco-distress?

It's important to share that this is an appropriate reaction. Tell people they are not alone. Our societal and medical paradigms have created the perfect storm for people to end up here. But there are things to do. Awareness is key. Help those who have eco-distress or burnout to consider what is in their control to change.

What habits do they have which are making this harder for them? Any change of habit takes time. Start small and make it easy – e.g., for those who check emails at home and want to put in some boundaries, why not add a filter onto your phone that stops the email or messaging app from working after a certain time of night? Or stop showing messages from trigger groups on the main screen. Or delete the app from your phone! It will be uncomfortable at first, but over time, it'll become a new habit. If people are stopping something, then it's a good idea to replace it with something else, such as reading a book or listening to music.

What brings joy? Following a passion to the exclusion of all other forms of joy may cause a loss of perspective and balance. It's possible to choose to experience joy in any moment (just look at how children and animals interact with the world). It may be helpful to keep a list of things that bring joy and access this when things feel hard.

Cultivate gratitude. Feeling gratitude helps people to face difficult emotions rather than turn away. It strengthens us. Practising gratitude daily in good times means it is more available in hard times. For example, some people list three things they were grateful for on that day before going to bed.

What about needs? Make sure people are looking after their basic needs – physically, mentally, and spiritually. Managing eco-distress starts with looking after yourself.

Find "your people": the people who get it, the people who inspire and make people want to keep doing this work. Humans are hardwired for connection. It helps to feel part of something bigger and to access hope and inspiration. Volunteering, joining a group, or going to an event such as a climate café or retreat can help. Encourage people to do some things for the benefit of themselves and not as another thing to take responsibility for.

Finding a climate purpose – Which actions inspire? Help people to think about what they're passionate about *doing*. They may be passionate about climate change and health, but there are lots of things to *do* within that. One person may love giving talks to enthuse and inspire others, another person may be much more comfortable writing articles and doing research, and another being in a Samba band. To consider how each person can help with climate solutions, it's worth utilising the climate Venn diagram (Figure 19.1). It can help them find a meaningful and bespoke way to help address the climate crisis.

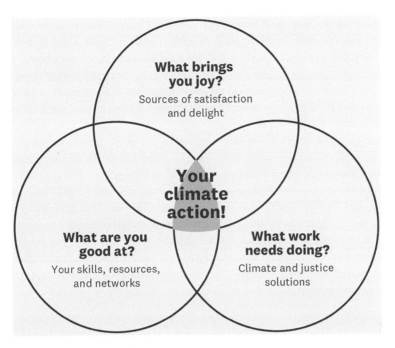

FIGURE 19.1 The climate Venn diagram (11).

Are you impatient for change?

When you look at how things are in the world today, you're certainly not alone if you think there's some room for improvement.

If you are someone who feels it all, seeing the injustice in the world right now can be really hard and it feels like things are not happening fast enough. You want a better world, for your patients, for your colleagues, for the children in your life and for the planet. I get it. If you're feeling overwhelmed, I'm not surprised.

So, if I tell you that steady does it, I know that that can feel like a hard pill to swallow but hear me out. The world needs people like you, people who can see a better world and who want to make it happen. But the world also needs you to look after yourself, to be in the best energy you can be, to maintain hope.

Steady means being steady in yourself, tapped into your inner peace and calm, experiencing joy and contentment in life so that you can stay in active hope. Unsteady looks like going all in and burning out, spreading yourself too thinly and failing to make the difference you set out to make, losing hope.

Steady looks like incremental change, step by step to a better world, tuned into the natural ebb and flow. It's feeling impatient for change but also peaceful in knowing that you can orchestrate change and you are not alone.

From one changemaker to another, I acknowledge your contribution. Can you take this as permission to go steady today? To rest, to replenish and start again tomorrow, one foot in front of the other, lighting the way to a better world in whatever way you choose.

Dr Becki Taylor Smith

Recognising feelings and emotions. Emotions are great messengers – anger can tell us when boundaries have been crossed, guilt tells us we have acted against our values and feeling vulnerable can alert us that we need to take care of ourselves.

Often, when people feel uncomfortable emotions, they push them down, keep themselves busy, turn off the news, and do something else. Sometimes it's important to put those emotional "boxes" on the shelf and carry on. Doing that all the time will eventually cause the shelf to crash down.

Bringing difficult emotions into awareness can allow people to process them and move forward in a more empowered way (5). Research shows numbing uncomfortable emotions also numbs the positive ones like joy and hope (6).

What emotion does each of us most avoid – Anger? Guilt? Fear? What would happen if we let ourselves feel that? How could we allow it in? For some, it's putting on a song or a movie that brings them to cathartic tears and release. For others, it's dancing to an angry song or doing invigorating exercise, letting the wildness take hold, just for a few minutes.

Whatever it is, it's normal and healthy to feel those emotions – we're often taught it's "embarrassing" to show emotions. The truth is allowing ourselves to feel it, then letting it pass, can set us free.

When things feel overwhelming, try this exercise from Kristen Neff (7):

Take a self-compassion break.

Bring to mind the emotion you're feeling and notice where it shows up in your body. Say the following statements to yourself.

1. This is a moment of suffering.
2. Suffering is a part of life.
3. May I be kind to myself?

You may wish to hold your hands over your heart while you send yourself love.

Managing feelings and emotions. There are several resources available to guide the management of these difficult emotions. Most contain four core elements:

1. **Take action – environmental activism is a buffer for eco-distress (4)**
    1. Living and acting according to our values is empowering and energising. A subjective sense of agency is a major factor in our well-being (5).
    2. In this strange world where people around us seem oblivious to the threat we face, being aware of the crisis can feel isolating. Joining with others to work towards a shared positive vision of the future and taking part in collective action nurtures hope, helps to validate feelings, and builds support.
2. **Self-care (8)**
    1. Pacing ourselves and accepting the limits of what we, as individuals, can achieve. Taking time for regeneration when we are struggling.

2. Accepting help from others and not feeling we must do everything ourselves.

3. Paying attention to our physical and mental well-being. Making sure we are getting enough sleep and physical activity, eating healthily, and making time to connect with the people, activities, and places that nurture and recharge us. Reconnecting with nature has been found to be particularly beneficial through nature connectedness – i.e., engagement with nature ("green prescriptions") or water ("blue prescriptions") (9).

4. Practising gratitude for ourselves, the people around us, and the natural world that sustains us.

3. **Nurture hope**

An empowerment approach known as "The Work that Reconnects" introduced the concept of active hope. It is the idea that we can become active participants in bringing about what we hope for. This doesn't require us to know that our outcome will be successful or even to be optimistic. Rather than weighing our chances and proceeding only when we feel hopeful, we focus on our intention and let it be our guide. Thus, hope becomes something we *do* rather than have (10).

1. Encourage those with eco-distress to read about hope-based, solutions-focused visions of the future.

2. Encourage them to consider what their version of active hope is.

4. **Allow space to process distress and times to shut off from it**

We often try to push away difficult feelings, but this can prevent us from processing them, and so they become disabling. Rather than try to avoid or ease these emotions, climate psychologists advise making time and space to accept and experience them without avoidance, denial, or intellectualisation. This is best done in a safe space with a supportive group of trusted people. Equally, it is important to make time to switch off and instead focus on people and activities we enjoy. Spending time in nature can help many people.

Reflections of a GP by Dr Munro Stewart

First, imagine a beautiful holiday destination or a place you'd dream of living: maybe the place you long for on seemingly never-ending working days. Have you got one? I expect that nature features for almost everyone. Even attractive cityscapes will involve parks, trees, and expanses of water. If they don't – how long will you remain happy in that place? We intuitively know that nature sustains us, but are our actions consistent with what we value?

I must have had hundreds if not thousands of conversations about mental health, and I have yet to find a patient, regardless of how desperate their plight, who wouldn't agree that time in green space or blue space (by a watercourse) makes them feel a little better.

Most people have a connection with nature, and I imagine that most people involved in healthcare started with a desire to have a positive impact on individuals and their communities. I am no different. Since long before embarking on a career in healthcare, I felt a close connection to nature, spending long summer holidays in the West Highlands of Scotland roaming free. I was lucky to have woodland at the back of my house for exploring, and I would sit on a swing up the hill near home, looking over the vast metropolis of Glasgow and ponder what was ahead of me.

I can't remember a time when I didn't care about the impact I had on the environment or didn't derive joy from having a positive impact on the people and environment around me. I feel that the flora and fauna are there to be respected, appreciated, and supported, not to be exploited. I would hope that most people feel the same, if given time and opportunity to explore their feelings and reactions when in nature.

After becoming a GP, I used my newfound freedom to explore how best to have an impact. This included volunteering for two weeks with refugees in Athens and studying international health at Copenhagen University. I was conscious that if I wanted to have an impact on health, then looking at health on a global scale could help offer perspective on how best to do that. Studying helped me "join the dots", as Dr Bansal would say. Around this time, I identified an uneasiness that had been lingering for a while under the surface: there had been clues for a long time – a discomfort in my chest and a raft of emotions which I now can identify as *ecological grief*. I experienced *flygskam* (flight shame, along with shame for eating meat, driving a car, and buying just about anything), *solastagia*, and climate anxiety when discovering news reports about the stark reality of environmental breakdown and the inadequate scale of response on all levels. It became clear to me that if I wanted to be true to my values, have an impact on the health and well-being of my community, and improve the sustainability of my environment, then I needed to look at all aspects of my life and spheres of influence, and integrate environmental considerations into all my actions and decisions. It turns out the best cure for eco-anxiety is eco-action.

Summary

- Eco-anxiety may show up as anger, irritability, grief, stress, anxiety, trouble sleeping, depression, guilt, or other emotions, but it means you are really worried about the planet.

- Your emotions make total sense. These are rational emotions in response a genuine climate emergency. Rather than pushing them away, sit with them – they show you care, and that's a good thing.

- Your eco-anxiety can help you figure out what is most important to you. They can guide you to what issues you feel most passionate about.

- Keeping difficult emotions to yourself is really tiring. Talking and connecting with others can help you feel less isolated and overwhelmed.

- Connecting with nature can feel amazing, soothing, and restorative and fire up a desire to take action.

- There is good news too – it's not all doom and gloom. Seeking out positive news can help mental health if things feel dire.
- Without eco-anxiety, there would not be any action. Feeling can energise us to take back some control – through voting, taking action, protesting, talking to others.

Conclusion

Eco-distress is common and a natural response to the reality of climate and ecological breakdown. Healthcare workers may experience distress in response to seeing the health impacts of climate change among their patients and communities. People from all backgrounds may experience eco-distress and need support to find ways forwards without becoming medicalised. It's crucial to help patients, colleagues, and healthcare workers to find meaningful work that fits with their values and unique purpose, to take care of their own well-being, and to find ways to connect with individuals or groups working towards a common goal.

There is no shame in struggling with emotions in response to the destruction of the living world. Recognising when people might be struggling, cultivating a practice of mindful awareness of emotions, and building hope will help allow a balance between times of frustration and despair and more empowering feelings like joy and hope.

We are capable of suffering with our world, and that is the true meaning of compassion.
It enables us to recognize our profound interconnectedness with all beings…
Don't apologise for the sorrow, grief, and rage you feel.
It is a measure of your humanity and your maturity.
It is a measure of your open heart, and as your heart breaks open
there will be room for the world to heal.
That is what is happening as we see people honestly confronting the sorrows of our time.

Joanna Macy

References

1. https://www.york.ac.uk/news-and-events/news/2021/research/climate-survey-cop/
2. Y. Coffey, N. Bhullar, J. Durkin, M.S. Islam, K. Usher. Understanding eco-anxiety: a systematic scoping review of current literature and identified knowledge gaps. *J. Clim. Chang. Heal.*, 3 (2021), Article 100047.
3. https://link.springer.com/article/10.1007/s12144-022-02735-6
4. https://www.theresilienceproject.org.uk/
5. https://www.climatepsychologyalliance.org/index.php/component/content/article/climate-psychology-handbook?catid=15&Itemid=101
6. The Gifts of Imperfection. *Brene Brown*. Publisher: Hazelden Information & Educational Services
7. https://self-compassion.org/exercise-2-self-compassion-break/

8. https://mentalhealth-uk.org/blog/what-is-climate-anxiety-and-what-can-we-do-about-it/
9. https://www.derby.ac.uk/blog/5-ways-closer-nature/
10. https://www.activehope.info/
11. https://www.ayanaelizabeth.com/climatevenn

Resources

https://www.activehope.info/
https://www.climatepsychologyalliance.org/
https://www.outrageandoptimism.org/
Becki Taylor-Smith – https://www.bts-coaching.co.uk/retreats
Climate Cafes – https://climatecafes.org/
The Royal College of Psychiatrists has produced a podcast (https://www.rcpsych. ac.uk/news-and-features/podcasts/detail/eco-distress-in-children-and-young-people) and fact sheets for children and young people (https://www.rcpsych. ac.uk/mental-health/parents-and-young-people/young-people/eco-distress-for-young-people) and for parents, carers, teachers and other adults who support young people.

20

Turning intentions into action
Matt Sawyer and Mike Tomson

The final chapter is ours to write.
We know what we need to do.
What happens next is up to us.

Sir David Attenborough

Dream big

If there is a vision of utopia at the outset, then a path can be formed to reach it. What would a practice delivering high-quality healthcare with little or no environmental harm look like?

With a big enough sheet of paper, money "no object", and no limit to our collective imagination, this could be achieved. Starting from scratch, with a mantra of "*start at zero, stay at zero*", in terms of emissions, might be easier but is also unrealistic with over 40,000 primary care premises currently in use across the United Kingdom alone.

Perhaps "our big dream" would have public health, illness prevention, and health creation at its heart. With plant-based diets for all, an infrastructure that enables and encourages activity and active travel, suitable warm housing, safe streets, access to green places for people, and tackling the root causes of inequality. Where healthcare is needed, it is done so from low energy premises using zero carbon electricity, goods and services supplied via a circular economy approach, and waste virtually eliminated. Clinical treatment is delivered through appropriate personalised lifestyle choices initially, then avoiding low-value testing and treatments and thoughtful, appropriate prescribing without waste.

DOI: 10.1201/9781003491583-20

There are many possible structures to any book or discussion. The following ten themes seem important as ideas that have crossed chapters or been crucial to us in seeing a future with sustainable primary care.

1. **Collaborate, don't confront**
2. **Start listening**
3. **Understand ourselves and our impacts**
4. **Engage new audiences**
5. **Identify and tackle barriers**
6. **Focus on action**
7. **Take those first steps**
8. **Community steps**
9. **Work within existing priorities**
10. **As the planet changes, so do the conditions we see**.

What sort of actions might be included in the "Guide to Doing What's Right"?

Add your own examples and suggestions from throughout the book. They could include the following.

Collaborate, don't confront

- *Hope is the most effective motivator,* so talk about real and active hope: individual shaming is likely to cause defensiveness, planning action helps.
- *People trust healthcare workers*; use this wisely.
- *Use networks*; somebody is likely to have tried it out already or have good ideas, and we can inspire each other.
- It's better to *win with a team*, even if their priority is not your biggest one, than to work alone in purity and fail.

Start listening

- **The behaviour shift thing**. It is not just about information; have a REAL conversation first. (Respect your conversation partner, Enjoy the conversation, Ask Questions, Listen) and show you've heard them. *How to Talk About Climate Change* by Rebecca Huntly gives a useful rule of thumb when discussing climate issues: use a ratio of *three parts positive* to *one part negative* when communicating environmental issues.
- **Listen and talk with staff**. Understand which areas team members want to progress and achieve in whilst recognising the areas which are biggest (such as prescribing in General Practice). Neither approach is "always right" but combine the "energy in the room" with "tackling the big hotspots".
- **Listen to and empower patients**. It can be easier (but will be less sustainable) to follow national guidance than to empower patients to choose the care they really want.

- **Talk with "the system"**. Work to positively influence, change, and improve the system in which healthcare is delivered is vital.

Understand ourselves and our impacts

- Healthcare professionals (HCP) have a high need to help,... which pushes us to suggest actions when this may be our need to feel needed rather than actually helping outcomes.
- **Be aware of our limitations**. Most of the time, clinicians overestimate the benefit of what they offer (whether tablets or operations), ... and then when people get better, we (and patients) credit ourselves/our treatment when it may well have been from chance/placebo. This is an "action bias" in our thinking.
- The world is complex. Interactions and feedback loops operate from intracellular levels to planetary health systems. Knowledge from controlled situations is useful but is not the full picture.
- **Framing makes an enormous difference** to outcomes as people make decisions based on the story they hear rather than pure logic.
- Most healthcare benefits have come from societal changes (sanitation, air quality, etc.), not from clinical care. The biggest gains in health may be similar, advocating for better nutrition, more exercise, better air quality, better connections. At the same time, each person seeking an HCP's attention deserves the most appropriate care.

Engage new audiences

- **Environmental issues are health issues**, so HCPs should talk about them! Most healthcare sustainability actions will result in better outcomes for patients.
- Identify the "great and the good" locally, using the esteem of the organisation, and the importance of the task to get people on board.

Identify and tackle barriers

- **Measure our baseline** impacts – e.g., with a GP Carbon Calculator. http://www.gpcarbon.org
- **Use the Sustainable Quality Improvement (SusQI) approach** to improve care and measure the holistic impacts.
- **Try an action** and record the outcome, whether good or bad. The 2022 and 2023 Chief Medical Officer's reports include climate and sustainability, demonstrating how grassroots work can quickly become the case studies which the leaders refer to for driving national change.
- **Changing patterns of healthcare delivery** (more nurse practitioners, physicians' associates, emergency care practitioners) are enabling the delivery of care in new ways. This may mean greater emphasis on people following guidelines

or protocols. Ensure all protocols clearly prioritise generating patient agency to prevent care being imposed on people and generating overprescribing and overtreatment.

Focus on actions

- **Start with a win**. This feels emotionally good but also builds momentum – whether emotional or financial. Success is contagious!
- **Green Impact for Health Toolkits** for General Practice and for dentistry show a range of positive actions which people and practices can take to reduce their environmental impact.
- Recognise **not all actions are the same**. Some may be complex (such as changing our pattern of overprescribing, as all parameters change so much that there is no clear path to solutions); others are complicated (changing a practice bank account is not easy and takes working out, but there are solutions).

Take those first steps

- *Understand the problem better.* There are courses on climate literacy for healthcare staff (carbonliteracy.com), sustainable healthcare (sustainablehealthcare.org.uk/), courses advertised on CPDmatch.com and e-learning for health (www.e-lfh.org.uk/), resources on asthma and other areas www.greenerpractice.co.uk/, and college sites (elearning.rcgp.org.uk/course/view.php?id=650).
- Write a *practice vision and mission* statement (see p. 000).
- Agree on a practice *Green Action Plan* (see p. 000).

Community steps

- **Build a sustainable community**. A key part of sustainability is working together, ensuring that everyone has access to what they need. Better to work with groups of people.
- **Working together** – with better health as a common goal and HCPs as trusted messengers. Health workers can help people move models from the consuming stuff approach to an awareness that connection with each other and nature and self-care through exercise is the route to happiness and health.

Work within existing priorities

- **Keep people healthy** – Prevention is better than cure.
- **Empower patients** – Healthcare is moving away from *"what works best for this disease"* to *"what works best for* this *patient".*

As the planet changes, so do the conditions we see

- Addressing the impact of the healthcare we provide on the planet is one part of planetary health. The other is retaining awareness that changes to the health of the planet changes the epidemiology of most diseases. The health conditions we will support people to manage will change because of the damaged planet.

Practices vision and mission statement (for adaptation to your needs). Planetary health can be included as a value.

At XXXXX, we aim to provide excellence in patient-centred care that is mindful of the needs of our patients, our staff, and the community. We believe that our patients and our staff have the right to a friendly, compassionate, safe, and open environment that is respectful of all beliefs and backgrounds.

As a teaching practice, we strive to stay on the cutting edge of community medicine by educating the next generation of clinicians and devoting time and resources to medical education and research. We aim to be evidence-based, contemporary, and innovative to deliver optimal quality care that is also sustainable and mindful of our resources for the benefit of our patients, staff, and community both now and in the future. Most of all, we aim to be a leader in our community and foster its growth and development through innovation, collaboration, and open lines of communication.

1. *We promote the creation of green spaces and the restoration of nature and biodiversity.*
2. *We prioritise more sustainable transport and mobility practices by prioritising pathways/ space for walking, cycling, wheeling, and public transport whilst accepting private car use might be necessary for some.*
3. *We commit to putting the protection of environmental and human health at the core of our organisation's work.*
4. *We commit to raising awareness among the population of the enormous health impact of climate change and nature loss, and the multitude of health benefits from climate and nature actions.*
5. *We will advocate with the government, relevant stakeholders, and the public for stronger, swifter climate and nature actions.*
6. *We will prioritise green procurement considerations in our organisation, working in tandem with our suppliers to facilitate this shift to strengthen supply chain resilience and support the transition to a circular economy.*
7. *We will promote the move to more sustainable diets for the benefit of human and environmental health. Encompassing a shift away from red and processed meat and ultra-processed food and drink products in favour of more whole grains, fruit, vegetables, and legumes.*

First (or next) step: write a practice Green Action Plan

A practice could work towards identifying the first three areas that the practice team wants to achieve or write a whole practice Green Action Plan. It is unrealistic and can be paralysing to aim to achieve too much too soon. So, though each of the following could be achieved in the suggested time line it is going to be better not to plan to achieve all of them immediately (Table 20.1).

TABLE 20.1 An example of what a Green Action Plan could be

THEME AREA	ACTION	WHEN	WHO	DONE?	NEXT STEP
Leadership	Sign up for Green Impact for Health scheme	This month	Deputy manager		Work towards bronze level
	Set up practice "green team"	This month	Deputy manager		Set up monthly meetings
Clinical pathways	Review purchasing and suppliers for clinical kit	End of July	Nursing/dental/optom/pharmacy team member		Bring findings to green team meeting
Digital transformation	Send travel details by text to patients for walking route to surgery and closest bus stop	In the next four weeks	Receptionist involved in booking appts and sending texts		
Travel and transport	Staff travel survey	Over next eight weeks	HCP who is a keen cyclist		Bring findings to green team meeting
	Map staff homes and see if can start shifts at same time	When runs payroll at end of the month	Practice manager		
	Explore cycle racks for patients, promote walking scheme	At next Patient Participation Group (PPG)	HCP who cycles		Involve PPG
Estates	Change electricity supplier to 100% renewable	By end of the month	Finance manager (looks after estates)	Yes	
	Check loft insulation	Next week	Deputy manager (looks after estates)		Install thicker layer of insulation
Clinical/ medicines	Electrical equipment survey and creation of responsibility plan	Within two months			
	Review SABA inhalers and acute exacerbations		Respiratory lead		

Category	Action	Timeframe	Responsible	Follow-up
	Over prescribing		Pharmacist Quality and Outcomes Framework (QoF) lead	
	Anti-cholinergic audit		Pharmacy lead	
	Overinvestigating and overdiagnosing		Pharmacist QoF lead	
	Review protocols to ensure they prioritise patient empowerment as well as being evidence based	First protocol review within three months	All clinical leads	
Procurement	Letter to accountants asking what they are doing regarding their footprint	At quarterly meeting with accountants	Senior partner and practice manager	
	Organise a paper audit to see what is used where	In the next month	Secretary	Bring findings to green team meeting
	Perform waste audit	Before end of the summer	Domestic staff	Bring findings to green team meeting
Food	Try oat, soy, and almond milk as alternatives to dairy	Next week in staff room	Receptionist to buy bottle of each with petty cash	
Adaptation	Look at risk of floods and how practice can manage in a heat wave	By autumn	Practice manager and senior partner	Draft adaptation plan as part of Business Continuity Plan

Source: Adapted from https://www.england.nhs.uk/greenernhs/wp-content/uploads/sites/51/2021/06/B0507-how-to-produce-a-green-plan-three-year-strategy-towards-net-zero-june-2021.pdf

Further reading

https://cepr.org/voxeu/columns/two-hundred-years-health-and-medical-care

https://climateoutreach.org/reports/how-to-have-a-climate-change-conversation-talking-climate/

Drop in asthma from lockdowns during Covid

https://www.theguardian.com/environment/2024/feb/09/asthma-emergency-admissions-plunged-as-lockdown-improved-air-oxford-study-finds

Appendix 20.1: Practice green action plan

AREA	WHAT WE WOULD LIKE TO DO	WHAT WE ALREADY DO	SHORT-TERM ACTIONS (THIS YEAR)	MEDIUM-TERM ACTIONS (IN THE NEXT TWO OR THREE YEARS)	LONGER TERM (OVER THE NEXT THREE TO TEN YEARS)
Clinical					
Medication					
Inhalers and respiratory care					
Non-clinical					
Energy – gas					
Energy – electric					
Travel – staff					
Travel – patients					
Procurement – goods					
Procurement – services					
Other					

A SusQI approach can be used – prevention, patient self-care, lean service delivery, and low carbon alternatives (Chapter 9)

Appendix A

List of abbreviations

ACBT	Active Cycle of Breathing Techniques
ARRS	Additional Roles Reimbursement Scheme (English scheme to improve access to healthcare)
CBT	Cognitive Behavioural Therapy
CQC	Care Quality Commission
Desflurane	An anaesthetic gas which is highly fluorinated and has a disproportionately large greenhouse gas effect.
DNACPR	Do Not Attempt Cardio-Pulmonary Resuscitation
DPI	Dry Powder Inhaler
EV	Electric Vehicles
GHG	Greenhouse Gas
GLAS toolkit	The Irish College of GP's Green toolkit (Glas = green in Gaelic)
HSE (Ireland)	The Health Service Executive provides public health and social care services to everyone living in Ireland.
ICB	Integrated Care Boards
ICE	Internal Combustion Engine
ICS	Integrated Care Systems and alternatively Inhaled CorticoSteroids
IPCC	Intergovernmental Panel for Climate Change
LABA/LAMA	Long-Acting Beta Agonist; Long-Acting Muscarinic Agonist
MART	Maintenance and Reliever Therapy (combines reliever and preventer in one inhaler)
MECC	Making Every Contact Count
MHRA	Medicines and Healthcare products Regulatory Authority
NICE	National Institute for Health and Care Excellence (English clinical guideline creator)
NNH	Number Needed to Harm
NNT	Number Needed to Treat
PCN	Primary Care Network (applies in England)

PHQ9	Patient Health Questionnaire (nine-question version)
pMDIs	pressurised Metered Dose Inhalers
PPE	Personal Protective Equipment
PPG	Patient Participation Group
PTSD	Post-Traumatic Stress Disorder
QI/SusQI	Quality Improvement/Sustainable Quality Improvement
ReSPECT form	Recommended Summary Plan for Emergency Care and Treatment.
SABA	Short-Acting Beta Agonist
SMART	Specific, Measurable, Achievable, Relevant, and Time-bound
SSRI	Specific Serotonin Receptor antagonist (commonly used group of antidepressants)
UKCCC	UK Climate Change Committee (advising the UK government)
UKHACC	United Kingdom Health Alliance on Climate Change (group includes many royal colleges and other organisations)
UN SDGs	United Nations Sustainable Development Goals https://sdgs.un.org/goals
WHO	World Health Organisation

Appendix B

Glossary

Carbon: Carbon is short for "carbon dioxide" and is a term used to refer to all human-made greenhouse gas emissions. These emissions are mainly carbon dioxide (CO_2); others are methane (CH_4), nitrous oxide (N_2O), sulphur hexafluoride (SF6), hydro-fluorocarbons (HFCs), chlorofluorocarbons (CFCs), and perfluorocarbons (PFCs).

Carbon footprint: The amount of direct and indirect greenhouse gas emissions released into the atmosphere as the result of activities by an individual, organisation, event, service, product, or place, typically expressed in tonnes of CO_2e. Bear in mind that it was an oil company that invented this to make people feel ★we★ had to change, but they didn't. And we know everyone has to change and reduce their footprint – especially fossil fuel companies. So it is a useful metric if we use it well.

Carbon offsetting: A process involving a reduction in or removal of CO_2/greenhouse gases to compensate for emissions made elsewhere. See the finance chapter. Is this giving ourselves permission to emit more carbon because someone, somewhere else is not or is planting a tree? It can be a mind trick we use on ourselves to justify not changing. Even if every offsetting action "neutered" the carbon we emit that day, we're still left with all the unwanted carbon we have already put into the atmosphere.

CO_2 equivalent (CO_2e): The many greenhouse gases can be measured together by their carbon dioxide equivalent (CO_2e). CO_2e is the amount of emitted CO_2 that would cause the same impact on climate change for a given greenhouse gas or mixture of greenhouse gases.

Greenwashing: Generally, it's sharing misleading statements about environmental performance to appear green. See the finance chapter.

Net zero: Greenhouse gas emissions are balanced by greenhouse gas removal from the atmosphere, resulting in no further net emissions and climate neutrality. However, we don't have the tech (other than plants!) to take much out. It is better to reduce carbon emissions as much as possible and not rely on the Clean-Up Fairies (see the behaviour change chapter).

Sustainable healthcare: A healthcare system that meets the present health needs of the population without compromising the health of the environment, planet, and future generations.

Appendix C

Useful organisations

Health organisations which you may want to know about that organise campaigns to influence politicians, the public, and beyond include the following:

The Centre for Sustainable Healthcare (https://sustainablehealthcare.org.uk/) runs a variety of popular courses (including one specifically for primary care), as well as competitions for clinicians such as Green Team competitions working to support the application of Sustainability in Quality Improvement https://www.susqi.org/.

The Cornwall and SW Primary Care (https://www.healthandclimateresilience.net/) health resilience network has a fabulous range of resources and links to networks.

The Green Impact for Health Toolkit (https://toolkit.sos-uk.org/greenimpact/giforhealth/login) is a Students Organising for Sustainability product supported by the RCGP. Practices complete tasks and can achieve a variety of awards.

Greener Practice (https://www.greenerpractice.co.uk/) started in Sheffield in 2017. It is a grassroots network with over 30 local groups and several national special interest groups, such as *Respiratory* and *Clinical Care* or *Education* run mainly via WhatsApp.

Health for Extinction Rebellion (https://healthforxr.com) (formerly Doctors/Pharmacists/Psychologists/etc. for Extinction Rebellion) is a collective of doctors, nurses, and other health professionals who are deeply concerned about the climate and ecological crisis. It has organised numerous disruptive protests and campaigns.

Medact (https://www.medact.org) is an organisation supporting health professionals to work together towards a world in which everyone can truly achieve and exercise their right to human health. They are involved in many campaigns, and they have a Climate and Health Group.

Our Health, Our Planet aims to make communication on the climate–health relationship more accessible to healthcare staff and patients, whilst highlighting the highest impact actions individuals can take to accelerate climate action. It has been developed solely by volunteers with support from Doctors' Association UK (https://ourhealthourplanet.co.uk).

Pharmacy Declares have had a significant impact on raising awareness of sustainability and carbon footprints in pharmacy organisations, including £17 million fossil fuel divestment, inclusion in undergrad and post-grad training, and declarations of climate emergency, resulting in the forming of a dedicated sustainability branch of the Primary Care Pharmacy Association – Greener PCPA (https://pcpa.org.uk/greener-hub.html).

SEE Sustainability (https://seesustainability.co.uk) provides carbon footprinting tools, decarbonisation guides for practices and delivering Carbon Literacy training, and supports practices, PCNs, and ICSs with Green Action Plans and consultancy.

UK Health Alliance on Climate Change (https://ukhealthalliance.org) is a membership organisation coordinating action, providing leadership, and amplifying the voices of health professionals. The BMA, RCGP, and Greener Practice are all members.

Appendix D

Further reading and resources

Global

The Lancet: Countdown on health and climate change takes stock of health and climate change. https://www.thelancet.com/journals/lancet/article/PIIS0140-6736(22)01540-9/fulltext

United Kingdom

The Health Foundation: Net zero care: what will it take? Overview of the features of low-carbon care delivery and highlight examples of where it is already happening. https://www.health.org.uk/publications/long-reads/net-zero-care-what-will-it-take

UK Health Alliance on Climate Change: Biodiversity, climate change and health includes biodiversity recommendations. https://ukhealthalliance.org/influencing-policy/biodiversity-climate-change-and-health/

Climate Change Committee: Sixth carbon budget provides ministers with advice on the volume of greenhouse gases the United Kingdom can emit during the period 2033–2037. https://www.theccc.org.uk/publication/sixth-carbon-budget/

National Audit Office sets out the United Kingdom and devolved governments' legislation, policy, strategy, governance, and monitoring arrangements relevant to achieving net-zero greenhouse gas emissions. https://www.nao.org.uk/reports/approaches-to-achieving-net-zero-across-the-uk/

Sustainability strategy support, including delivering a green plan in England, Wales, and Scotland. https://sustainablehealthcare.org.uk/green-plan-and-sustainability-strategy-support

England

NHS England via Greener NHS. *Delivering a "Net Zero" National Health Service*. Provides a detailed account of the NHS's modelling and analytics underpinning the latest NHS carbon footprint, trajectories to net zero, and the interventions required to achieve that ambition. https://www.england.nhs.uk/greenernhs/publication/delivering-a-net-zero-national-health-service

Homepage for the Greener NHS programme. https://www.england.nhs.uk/greenernhs/

Workspace on FutureNHS collaboration platform. https://future.nhs.uk/sustainabilitynetwork/grouphome

NHS England: Carbon reduction plan requirements for procurement. Details on the implementation of the requirement for all suppliers to publish a carbon reduction plan. https://www.england.nhs.uk/long-read/carbon-reduction-plan-requirements-for-the-procurement-of-nhs-goods-services-and-works/

NHS England: How to produce a green plan – a three-year strategy towards net-zero guidance for trusts and ICSs. https://www.england.nhs.uk/greenernhs/wp-content/uploads/sites/51/2021/06/B0507-how-to-produce-a-green-plan-three-year-strategy-towards-net-zero-june-2021.pdf

Wales

NHS Wales decarbonisation strategic delivery plan. https://www.gov.wales/nhs-wales-decarbonisation-strategic-delivery-plan

The Wellbeing of Future Generations (Wales) Act underpins the programme for government and continues to shape how NHS Wales works. https://www.gov.wales/sites/default/files/publications/2021-11/nhs-wales-planning-framework-2022-2025_0.pdf

Green Health Wales: A network of health-care professionals across Wales who recognise that the climate and ecological emergency is a health emergency. https://www.greenhealthwales.co.uk/

Scotland

NHS Scotland. NHS Scotland climate emergency and sustainability strategy: 2022–2026 (Internet). http://www.gov.scot/publications/nhs-scotland-climate-emergencysustainability-strategy-2022-2026/

Scottish sustainability resources. https://www.pcpd.scot.nhs.uk/Sustainability.htm

Sustainable Scotland Network: Public-sector network on sustainability and climate change. https://sustainablescotlandnetwork.org/

Mental Health

Focusing on mental health with a call to action and case studies. https://www.rcpsych.ac.uk/docs/default-source/improving-care/nccmh/net-zero-mhc/delivering-greener--more-sustainable-and-net-zero-mental-health-care---guidance-and-recommendations.pdf

Royal College of Psychiatrists advice on managing eco distress for young people. https://www.rcpsych.ac.uk/mental-health/parents-and-young-people/young-people/eco-distress---for-young-people

Royal College of Psychiatrists advice for parents and carers on eco distress. https://www.rcpsych. ac.uk/mental-health/parents-and-young-people/information-for-parents-and-carers/ eco-distress---for-parents-and-carers

Climate Psychology Alliance climate anxiety resources for young people. https://climate psychologyalliance.org/support/youngpeople/544-youth-resources

Climate Psychology Alliance climate anxiety resources for parents, teachers, and carers. https:// climatepsychologyalliance.org/support/youngpeople/545-parent-teacher-resources

Supply chain, including waste

NHS England: Carbon reduction plan and net-zero commitment requirements for the procurement of NHS goods, services, and works. https://www.england.nhs.uk/long-read/carbon-reduction-plan-requirements-for-the-procurement-of-nhs-goods-services-and-works/

NHS clinical waste strategy: The strategy aims to reduce future waste volumes. https://www. england.nhs.uk/estates/nhs-clinical-waste-strategy/

NHS Supply Chain: Waste and the circular economy guidance on the management of waste, including furniture, medical devices, and food. https://www.supplychain.nhs.uk/sustainability/ waste-and-the-circular-economy/

Buildings

NHS Net-Zero Building Standard. Provides technical guidance to support the development of sustainable, resilient, and energy-efficient buildings. https://www.england.nhs.uk/estates/ nhs-net-zero-building-standard/

Food and nutrition

Incredible Edible Network: Community example connecting people through food. https:// www.incredibleedible.org.uk/

Plant-Based Health Professionals UK provides education and advocacy on whole-food, plant-based nutrition. https://plantbasedhealthprofessionals.com/

EAT-Lancet Commission on Food, Planet, and Health. https://eatforum.org/eat-lancet-commission/

Travel

NHS England: Net-zero travel and transport strategy: Describes the interventions and modelling underpinning decarbonisation. https://www.england.nhs.uk/long-read/net-zero-travel-and-transport-strategy/

Clinical

Greener Practice: High-quality and low-carbon asthma care. A toolkit supporting quality improvement in primary care. https://www.greenerpractice.co.uk/high-quality-and-low-carbon-asthma-care/

NICE: Asthma inhalers and climate change patient decision aid intended to help discussions between patients and their health-care professionals on inhaler choice and their effect on climate change. https://www.nice.org.uk/guidance/ng80/resources/patient-decision-aid-pdf-6727144573

Good for you, good for us, good for everybody: A plan to reduce overprescribing to make patient care better and safer, support the NHS, and reduce carbon emissions. National overprescribing review report. https://www.gov.uk/government/publications/national-overprescribing-review-report

Index

Pages in *italics* refer to figures and pages in **bold** refer to tables.